# Blood Aces

# BLOOD ACES

### THE WILD RIDE OF BENNY BINION, THE TEXAS
### GANGSTER WHO CREATED VEGAS POKER

# DOUG J. SWANSON

AMBERLEY

First published 2015

Amberley Publishing
The Hill, Stroud
Gloucestershire, GL5 4EP

www.amberley-books.com

Photograph credits
Special Collections, University Libraries, University of Nevada, Las Vegas: Pages x, 92,
104, 146, 232, 242, 254, 266, 276, 306
Collections of the Texas/Dallas History and Archives Division, Dallas Public Library:
Pages 38, 48, 60, 70, 118, 134, 158, 196, 212
Courtesy of Fred Merrill Jr.: Pages 80, 186, 222
Las Vegas News Bureau: Page 298

British Library Cataloguing in Publication Data.
A catalogue record for this book is available from the British Library.

ISBN 978-1-4456-4817-0 (print)
ISBN 978-1-4456-4818-7 (ebook)

Set in Minion Pro
Designed by Daniel Lagin

Printed in the UK.

In Nevada, for a time, the lawyer, the editor, the banker, the chief desperado, the chief gambler and the saloon keeper occupied the same level in society, and it was the highest . . . To be a saloon keeper and kill a man was to be illustrious.

—Mark Twain, *Roughing It*

# Contents

# Blood Aces

Benny Binion (right) at his peak, with the actor Chill Wills (center) and an unidentified man outside the Horseshoe Club in downtown Las Vegas.

# Prologue
## THE HAPPY RACKETEER

Do your enemies before they do you.

—Benny Binion

The three men were hired killers, not ditchdiggers, and after weeks of ceaseless heat with no rain, the ground was like concrete. They labored to shovel a small hole into a dirt road that cut through Texas ranchland. A weak sliver of moon hung low, the night so dark the grunting and sweating men could hardly see their hands. It was early August 1951, and they were preparing yet another attempt to murder a gambling boss named Herbert Noble.

Eleven previous tries—bombs that didn't go off, shots that missed—had failed. But this time, the men told themselves, would be different. No more firing wildly through upstairs windows, no more harebrained schemes like packing airplane engines with explosives. This time they had patience and a plan. They also had the promise of a big payday, for the bounty on Noble had increased tenfold.

Now the hole was big enough. The men carefully nestled several sticks of dynamite next to some packs of nitroglycerin gel. They put blasting caps in, too, then covered it all with dirt. A wire ran from the blasting caps to a Delco car battery hidden in some roadside brush. Another wire extended from the battery up a small hill to a clearing behind some bushes. There they waited in the dark.

At last the sky paled, a slight breeze stirred, and birds began to sing. The sun rose—welcome at first, until it climbed higher and began its nasty beating from a cloudless sky. The men crouched in ragged shade and scanned the emptiness of the rolling landscape. There were clusters of scrub oaks scattered across the crisp, dry pastures. A barbed-wire fence, strung on cedar posts, lined the road. Minutes dragged by, hours. Finally, about eleven thirty that morning, they saw Noble's black 1950 Ford.

Noble stopped the car at the head of the driveway to his Diamond M Ranch, named for his beloved wife, Mildred, who had been blown apart by bumbling assassins two years before. As he reached for his mailbox, one of the hidden men gripped the insulated copper wire that ran from the car battery. All he had to do now was touch it to the barbed-wire fence, grounding the connection, and let the bomb do its work. Then the three could collect $50,000 in blood money—this in a state where you could have just about anybody killed for a couple of thousand.

It represented a high price for a rubout. But the man who everyone—police, criminals, even Noble himself—believed had bankrolled this particular job could easily afford it. He lived now in Las Vegas, Nevada, where he was, this very morning, putting the final touches on his greatest gambling palace ever. He was Benny Binion, one of the most feared and successful racketeers of his day.

Not that he looked it. At this stage of his life, Binion was a moonfaced, portly middle-aged casino owner in cowboy boots and a cowboy hat, with a couple of loaded handguns in his pockets and another in his boot. "A big, beefy, jovial sort of fellow," one fawning writer called him. People said he was practically illiterate, a notion he did little to dispute. Binion had thin, uncombed hair and rumpled, ill-fitting clothes. He talked with a twang that needed oil, displayed a grin that seemed fresh off the farm, and shook when he laughed. One of his sons said he looked like a happy baby with wrinkles. "You couldn't keep from liking him," said a friend and associate, R. D. Matthews.

Binion had long resembled a doughy rural-route cherub, at least until he decided he wanted somebody dead, which had happened with some frequency. Then his grin fell away and his darting blue eyes went hard. "No one in his right mind," the great poker player Doyle Brunson once said, "messed with Benny Binion."

Occasionally Binion did his own killing, as he phrased it, and other times he delegated the job to his homicidal staff. Through it all, his dim, country-cousin bit served as a convenient mask. In truth Binion combined native intelligence, shrewd calculation, and cold-blooded application. He was a rube savant who fueled his rise by manipulating, charming, intimidating, and murdering as needed, with more than a few pauses for self-mythologizing. "There's been a lot of them wanted to kill me," he once said, "but they missed."

He had started his criminal career in Texas, and soon no one there could top his power and sway. Binion ruled his Lone Star kingdom for a decade, as dollars flowed and blood ran. From his Dallas perch, he embodied the American dream, if one dreamed of an empire of vice. Then he moved to Las Vegas as the modern version of that city was being born. There he helped lead a wave of dirty money and dangerous men who transformed it from a desert watering hole to the century's great gambling capital. Binion employed timing, temperament, and access to loads of cash to be one of Las Vegas's vital new pioneers, a cowboy counterpart to the syndicates from the coasts. He brought high-stakes dice games. He created the World Series of Poker too. As much as anyone, Binion made Vegas a mecca for high rollers. Before he was done, they were putting up a statue of him and thousands were chanting his name.

The nation's history is packed with legendary outlaws. But none of them can match Binion's wild, bloody, and wholly American journey. He rubbed shoulders with some of his era's biggest celebrities and its richest men. He did business with—and counted as friends—the most notorious of mobsters. He was chased and nearly destroyed by the most powerful figures of his time, from J. Edgar Hoover to the president of the United States.

It is still said in Las Vegas that you can't understand the town without understanding Binion, that he put the gamble in Vegas, that he ignited a worldwide revolution in poker. All of it is true, but his story looms larger and wider than that.

There is simply no one who went from murderous street thug to domineering crime boss to revered businessman to civic treasure like Benny Binion. No one comes close. This is how he did it.

# PART ONE

## THE ROLL OF THE DICE
### 1904-1946

Lester Ben Binion at the age of four.

# 1

# SNIDES AND DINKS:
# AN EDUCATION

We was all grifters in those days. All we had was grift sense.

—BB

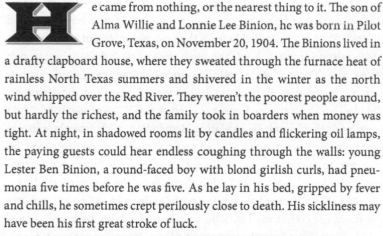e came from nothing, or the nearest thing to it. The son of Alma Willie and Lonnie Lee Binion, he was born in Pilot Grove, Texas, on November 20, 1904. The Binions lived in a drafty clapboard house, where they sweated through the furnace heat of rainless North Texas summers and shivered in the winter as the north wind whipped over the Red River. They weren't the poorest people around, but hardly the richest, and the family took in boarders when money was tight. At night, in shadowed rooms lit by candles and flickering oil lamps, the paying guests could hear endless coughing through the walls: young Lester Ben Binion, a round-faced boy with blond girlish curls, had pneumonia five times before he was five. As he lay in his bed, gripped by fever and chills, he sometimes crept perilously close to death. His sickliness may have been his first great stroke of luck.

Like dozens of small towns scattered across the rolling blackland prairie, this one was destined to vanish. Originally called Lick Skillet, it was a place of bloodshed, hard living, and ill fortune from its founding. Even after being christened with a more pastoral name, Pilot Grove scratched by as a cotton and cattle town, as close to Oklahoma as to Dallas, and a long way from anywhere. Its main street, part of an old stagecoach route, was a dirt road that gave up clouds of gray dust or bogged carriage wheels in mud, depending on the misery of the season.

Many of the town's early settlers—the Binions among them—had arrived on wagons after the Civil War, and some brought the war's vestigial agonies with them. Thick woods nearby, which had been a perfect hideout for war deserters and other fugitives, now teemed with unreconstructed Confederates nursing their bitterness. Newcomers tended to be Union sympathizers, and it made for a deadly mix. There were raids and ambushes from both sides, and gunfights in broad daylight. The town doctor treated one of the wounded rebels, an act of mercy that so enraged one of the unionists that he murdered the doctor. One frosty morning in 1871, the leader of the Union League stepped from his house to retrieve some firewood when two rebels, who had been hiding in trees all night, shot him dead.

A few good, relatively peaceful years boosted the town's population to about two hundred, then came the withering. Pilot Grove's post office was shuttered the year Ben was born. When he was four, on a May evening, a line of boiling storms rolled in from the west with a blast of wind and cascades of thunder that shook the walls. Just after dark, a lightning bolt struck Sloan's general store, and the wooden building caught fire. Flames, whipped by the gales of the storm, leaped to the barbershop, the drugstore, the blacksmith's barn, and another general store. Townspeople could do little more than watch in escalating desperation, with firelight dancing over horrified faces. Pilot Grove had no fire department, no fire wagon, no way even to spray water on the flames. At sunrise the town's commercial district lay in char and ashes, with only the hotel and one store standing.

Disaster was heaped upon catastrophe as drought and plunging prices destroyed the cotton market. Still, a farmer who had a mule and a plow could coax a living from the land around Pilot Grove, but not much of one. The Binions were not exactly noble sons of the earth, which worked to their advantage. One of Ben's grandfathers had operated a saloon. The other also owned some land, but he rented it out. One summer day, hot enough to force a retreat to a canopy of oak trees, young Ben crouched in the shade and watched as his grandfather leased acreage to a man named Kato. When their business was done, as Kato walked away, Ben's grandfather decided it was time for a lesson. "That's the best farmer I know," he said.

The boy stared. His grandfather pointed to the worn patches on the seat of the farmer's ragged overalls. "You see where his so-and-so's been sticking out there?" he asked.

"Yeah," Ben answered.

"Don't ever stick a plow in the ground."

End of lesson, and one that had apparently taken hold much earlier with Ben's father, who did not favor tending crops or any other kind of steady work. Lonnie Lee Binion listed his occupation as stockman, which meant he spent most of his time as a wandering horse trader. When he did come home, he hit the bottle. "Kind of a wild man," his son recalled. "Kind of a drunk." Such qualities did not make for a father given to soft-headed sentiment, even when considering a sick child. One day Lonnie Lee looked at the boy, turned to his wife, and said, "Well, he going to die any-how. So I'm just going to take him with me."

Off they rode on two mounts, he and his father, out of Pilot Grove and the drudgery of its cotton and sorghum fields, and into a world of rene-gades, grifters, hustlers, and highwaymen. Ben, at the age of ten, had spent little time in any classroom; after four years he was still in the second grade. This would be a different sort of school, and it gave him his life.

"There's more than one kind of education," Binion said decades later, "and maybe I prefer the one I got."

In much of America, the early 1900s marked the Progressive Era, a time of economic growth, social gains, industrial expansion, and technological leaps. But not so much in Texas. With a few notable urban exceptions, the state remained remote, parochial, and in parts lawless. Barely a generation had passed since the Indian wars had ceased. A hurricane wiped away the state's most cosmopolitan city, Galveston, in 1900. In all its great sweep, Texas had little in the way of heavy industry, and its only semblance of intellectual life was sequestered at a university or two, where it was regarded with suspicion, if not hostility. By even the most generous of estimates, Texas at the dawn of the twentieth century remained a full fifty years behind mainstream American development. Although patches of it had been conquered and settled in the previous decades, the vast land remained essentially unchanged. So, for the most part, did its people.

The roaders, as roving livestock merchants were called, had likewise failed to evolve much from the frontier days. Young Ben Binion—sometimes in the company of his father, sometimes not—became one of them. The traders with their strings of horses made their way over the rough trails and dirt roads of the Lone Star outback in clouds of dust and flies. They carried guns and lived out of wagons. In Europe, the Great War had started. The Panama Canal opened, and commercial air traffic began in this country. In the cities—even those in Texas—buildings were lit with electricity. But the roaders cooked their meals over open fires, bathed in shallow brown creeks, and moved from camp to camp, from settlement to farm to town, in search of more horseflesh deals.

Small hardscrabble farms of this time and place had little in the way of mechanization; mules or horses pulled the plows and wagons. Rare was the farmer who owned a tractor, rarer still one who had a truck or car. The horse trader, therefore, peddled an essential element of the farmer's survival. At times the stock was swapped straight up, horse for horse. Usually, though, the farmer had to throw in "boot"—food, tobacco, or occasionally cash—to make the trade.

Young Ben Binion watched and learned. He proved especially adept at gauging a horse's age by inspecting its teeth. "I was real good at it," he said decades later, talking to a historian. "All them old guys I worked for, they let me do the mouthing of the mules, and horses, and everything, you see, while they was trading and talking." When not mouthing the mules, Ben absorbed the primary lesson of this marketplace: how to deal, how to cheat, and how to avoid being cheated. The assumption was that if someone wanted to trade away a horse, that horse was defective. Everyone was out for the swindle, and he who swindled best, won.

"They had heaves in them days. They were wind-broke horses, and balkies," Binion said, referring to equine respiratory disease. "They called them snides and dinks. So you'd have to give 'em medicine to shut the heaves down." This medicine provided no cure; it merely masked the symptoms long enough to close a trade. There were other tried-and-true ways to hide infirmities. Wads of cotton, soaked in chloroform and stuffed in the nostrils of dangerously excitable horses, made them temporarily docile. Pebbles in the ear of a sluggard would transform it, for a while, into a frisky and energetic creature, prancing and shaking its head as if it were raring to go. A "sweeney" horse—one that had been so overworked that its muscles under the harness had collapsed—could be made to look instantly vibrant if the trader punctured the skin over the sagging parts and blew in air through a goose quill. "Some men were smart enough to detect it," Binion said, "and some weren't."

A ditty of the era, "The Horse Trader's Song," captured the attitude of those on the tactics' receiving end:

> It's do you know those horse traders,
> It's do you know their plan?
> Their plan is for to snide you
> And git whatever they can.

Sometimes the deception could be achieved simply through strategic staging. "Get a horse up on a kind of a high place, and get the man down on a low place, you know," Binion said. "And if he had anything wrong with him, try to keep that turned away from the guy." Not all valuable knowledge imparted to the boy had strictly to do with animals. "I learned a lot about people."

He became the man of the family, returning home now and then, a twelve-year-old grown-up. "He was an adult his whole life," his sister, Dorothy, once said. Trading balky livestock was no way to become wealthy, but it did pay for the family's groceries. When not hustling horses, he sometimes hauled fuel for an uncle's syrup mill in Pilot Grove. Then, back on the road, he found an even better way to make money.

In those years, nearly every county seat hosted monthly events known as trades days. Named for their spot on the calendar—First Monday, First Tuesday, and so on—trades days usually coincided with the arrival of the circuit-riding judge. They served as a combination of county fair, open-air market, and gathering of the rural tribes. For farmers and others in the hinterlands, they provided a monthly relief from lives of privation and isolation. The sodbusters and their families streamed in from the countryside, wagons loaded with the crops they intended to barter for dry goods and assorted services. Itinerant merchants brought everything from axle grease to snake oil. There were evangelists, buskers, blacksmiths, and rainmakers. On a typical First Monday in Dallas, the streets adjacent to the courthouse were nearly impassable with the crush of horses, wagons, and people. The air smelled of hay, manure, and sweat.

And down Houston Street, C. D. Tatum's Bar beckoned to men in overalls and felt hats. Trades days offered opportunities for recreation not available back on the farm. One might buy whiskey, smokes, or a woman, and watch dogfights, cockfights, or human fights. Into this licentious mix came the traveling gamblers, who moved from town to town, hunting suckers at trades days like predators stalking a herd. Men could be found in the alleys and side streets, or in the wagon yards at night, rolling dice on a blanket spread over the dirt, or playing cards by lanterns and firelight. Teenage Ben Binion was right there with them.

"I kind of got in with the more of a gambling type of guy, you know, the—you might say the road gamblers," he said. "And then I'd go around with them, you know, and I'd do little things for them. And they'd give me a little money, kind of kept me going . . . They was all pretty good men."

Here he served his apprenticeship. "First, I learned to play poker," Binion recalled. "And everybody had his little way of doing something to the cards, and all this, that and the other." Marking cards and crimping them were among the most popular ways to gain an advantage. "So I wasn't too long on wising up to that . . . All this time I'm kind of learning about gambling from these guys."

Soon he became a "steer man," a recruiter who wandered the trades-day towns after dark, hooking customers for the big game around the corner. "I just hustled, never did work," he said. He stayed on the lookout for someone with money to lose, but also searched for something more. Binion described his mark: "What I think makes a player is somebody with a lot of energy. Like if one of them kind of fellows come to town at night, you know, he's kind of a nervous type, and he had to have some outlet, you know, couldn't just go to bed like a ordinary person."

Even as a young man, Binion didn't gamble much. "I was never able to play anything, dice or cards or anything, myself. I was never a real good poker player," he said. Instead, he was a partner—however junior—to the game's operators. "Fact of business, from a early age, I was always kind of in, and just kind of on the top end of it." Here he received his most valuable of lessons: that hot streaks come and go, that one good roll could feed a man for weeks and a bad one could destroy him. But the properly run house always turns a profit.

The youthful Ben became known more rakishly as Benny Binion about the time he headed for El Paso, in far West Texas, around the age of eighteen. He went to El Paso because he had cousins there, but he soon discovered he had landed in a place well suited to his abilities and instincts. This was one of the country's great snake pits of smuggling.

Under Prohibition, liquor was then illegal in El Paso, as in the rest of the country. But bootleg booze—and drugs—proved far easier to obtain along the border than many other places. All the Texas importer had to do was cross the muddy, shallow Rio Grande into rollicking Ciudad Juárez, Mexico, load his wagon with whiskey, and bring it back home to sell. In the process he had to evade bands of Mexican thieves on one side of the river, and roving hijackers and American agents on the other. A fevered newspaper dispatch from El Paso described the face-off: "The brains of Texas Rangers and an army of federal customs officials and narcotic and liquor agents" were "pitted against the endless ingenuity of international smugglers in as thrilling a battle for supremacy as the romantic and adventurous days of a half century ago ever knew." The story added that "this battle of wits" makes "the plots of red-blooded fictionists seem dull and old fashioned." Trains of pack mules bearing contraband champagne had been captured. A young man "disguised as a cripple" was caught hiding cocaine in his hollowed-out crutches. Other smugglers used the chest cavities of corpses, en route to their own funerals, to transport caches of morphine and opium.

The Texas Rangers, assigned by the governor to patrol the border, routinely fired on bands of so-called rumrunners, and the runners fired back. Many of the gunfights took place on or around Cordova Island, near Juárez.

This was not an island at all, but a brushy 385-acre finger of Mexico poking into the American side of the Rio Grande, where the two sides took turns ambushing each other. A news report told of a typical encounter—a "pitched battle"—along the river: "Descending upon the rum-runners in speeding automobiles, the patrolmen mounted a fence near the Rio Grande. They were met with a fusillade of bullets from the rum-runners' rifles. The fire was returned and two of the smugglers were seen to fall to the ground."

Binion tried lawful work in El Paso, but—in this atmosphere—it didn't stick. "He had a gravel wagon and some mules, and was spreading gravel on this parking lot for Model T Fords," his son Jack recounted. "He figured out they were bootlegging out of the booth where you paid for your parking." He procured his own stock of contraband whiskey. "And he'd come down and go to work about five in the evening. Some guy would come up and say he was looking for Joe, and Benny Binion would say, 'I'll take care of you,' and sell them his own liquor."

Binion was arrested for bootlegging at least once in El Paso and put in jail. "They made him a trusty," Jack said. "One day they told him to go get judge so-and-so some liquor out of the evidence vault . . . Benny Binion went and made an imprint of the key. Sent it out and had a key made. Then he got the jailer drunk, and when the jailer went to sleep, he called up a friend with a truck, got some of the other trusties to help load it, and stole a truckload of liquor right out of the jail."

Like many Binion family stories, this one has a deceptively winking, comical aspect to it. County records are gone, and all that remains are family recollections, which tend to paint Binion as an enterprising scamp with a heart of gold. "My dad was a happy, jolly man," recalled his daughter Brenda Binion Michael. But Benny Binion roamed El Paso as a young gun in a violent place, launching a professional career of brutal strategies and heartless expediency. He once summed up this life with the declaration "I wasn't to be fucked with." When asked many years later about his El Paso days, Binion turned alternately boastful and reticent. "Hell, I didn't need a bodyguard or a chaperone or guide or nothing," he said. "I got to be known pretty fast."

Known doing what? "Well," he answered, "I'd just as soon not tell it."

Teenage Ben Binion in a family photo.

# 2

# THE BUMPER BEATER

I try to keep anybody from doing anything to me where it'll cause any trouble. But if anybody does anything to me, he's got trouble.

—BB

For reasons now lost, Binion felt a sudden urge to leave El Paso. He turned up six hundred miles away, in Dallas, at the age of nineteen. As he rolled into town, he no longer looked like a yokel who spent days on a horse, riding the range. This Benny Binion wore a dark suit, shiny cap-toed shoes, and a snap-brim fedora with a striped hatband. He stood a shade under six feet, and had a hustler's glimmer in his eye. As he was to learn soon, the city offered wondrous opportunity for a young man with a spirit of larceny underpinned by a mind for business. "Dallas," he said, "is one of the best towns that I ever seen."

It is perhaps unfair to say that the city where Binion had come to make his bones was founded by a lunatic gunslinger. The man who first settled Dallas was, when he arrived in North Texas, still a few decades away from shooting someone or going crazy. Nor is it accurate to note that the pioneers who ran Dallas knew instantly how to make money from vice. That took them at least five years to figure out.

The city was born in 1841, when Texas was still a republic. It began as a simple trading post on a low, windy bluff along the narrow, murky, and sluggish Trinity River. John Neely Bryan, a Tennessee lawyer and occasional Indian trader, made camp on the bluff with a tent, a shaggy dog named Tubby, and pipe dreams of a thriving river port. Someone—maybe Bryan, maybe a settler who trickled in behind him—decided to call it Dallas. To this day, nobody knows why.

Bryan soon married and built a log cabin for his bride. Others homesteaded too, and within a few years a town had risen, with Bryan as its first postmaster. By 1846, Dallas had impaneled its first grand jury, which promptly indicted fifty-one men for gambling at the local saloon. They had been betting on, among other things, rat and badger fights. When it came time for trial, there weren't enough unindicted citizens to fill a jury. At the courthouse—a ten-by-ten log structure—the solution was quickly engineered: After the first gambler was found guilty, he took his turn on the jury, and the juror he replaced stepped down to be tried. Next gambler, same story. Eventually all fifty-one convicted each other and fined themselves $10 apiece.

The Trinity River proved to be too full of snags and sandbars for boats to travel three hundred miles north to Dallas from the Gulf of Mexico. One paddle wheeler eventually made it all the way from Galveston, but the journey took a year and four days. So much for Bryan's vision of a port. Nonetheless, by 1850, Dallas boasted a population approaching five hundred. Within a few more years, it had a hotel, a sawmill, and a carriage factory. Soon a high school was established, and the first circus—featuring one live elephant—came to town in 1859. A city was taking shape.

The great founder Bryan did not fare so well. He suffered from the effects of cholera, heavy drinking, and an erratic disposition, and wandered away from the town he founded. After a year of prospecting for gold in California failed to yield a fortune, Bryan returned to Dallas and shot a man who insulted his wife. Poor health and mental turbulence ended a brief stretch in the Confederate army. In 1877 he was admitted to the State Lunatic Asylum in Austin. He died there seven months later, and was buried in an unmarked grave.

A few decades after Bryan's death, Dallas considered itself the commercial capital of Texas, "a city of skyscrapers, resounding with the roar of trade," in one booster's assessment. Its population exceeded 150,000 by the mid-1920s, and the twenty-nine-story Magnolia Building, the tallest in the South, had been finished downtown. Already a banking center, Dallas had a growing university, a branch of the Federal Reserve, and a major Ford plant. Conservative and insistently religious from the outset, the city presented itself as a prosperous, upright metropolis of unforgiving rectitude, the type of place where a man who stole a pearl necklace, a watch, and $21 in cash was sentenced to death. Yet for many years it also had—and openly tolerated—a place called Frogtown.

Also known as the Reservation, Frogtown looked like any other collection of hardware stores and barbershops on the edge of the central business district, but for the nearly naked young women draped in the doorways, calling to customers. Frogtown functioned as a freely accepted and legally sanctioned zone—via an ordinance by the city commission—for whorehouses. There were, by some estimates, four hundred women working there, though it was by no means the only place to find a prostitute in Dallas. One successful brothel operated out of a city-owned skating rink in Fair Park.

Police patrolled the Reservation; they simply didn't arrest prostitutes, although one chief ordered the brothels to place screens over their doors so that activities inside weren't visible from the street. The district attracted the notice of, among others, the appropriately named J. T. Upchurch, a preacher who had founded the Berachah Rescue Home for Fallen Girls, and who recorded his outrage in his periodical, the *Purity Journal*. "Some hundreds of girls are kept in this district as Slaves; Slaves to Lust, Licentiousness and Debauchery," he wrote. "They are there to gratify the unbridled passion of beastly men and to produce a few grimy, bloody dollars for the lords of the underworld." Upchurch may have been right about unbridled passion, but he misfired with his attack on the lords of the underworld. Even an outsider in town for a week could see the error in that.

In 1911 a Presbyterian minister from New York, Charles Stelzle, came to Dallas for a speaking engagement. A follower of the Social Gospel movement, which applied Christian ethics to social problems, Stelzle spent a few days wandering the city and taking notes. Then, before an audience of fifteen hundred at the Dallas downtown opera house—an ornate forum meant to replicate the great theatrical palaces of Europe—Stelzle condemned not just the fleshpots of Frogtown, but their landlords too. "What about the men who rent those houses?" Stelzle asked. "Do you know who owns them?" The crowd began to stir. "I have made investigation. Some are owned by some of your first citizens." He thundered, "I have their names!"

The audience urged him on, but Stelzle refused to divulge his list. "Not on your life," he demurred, and changed the subject. It was an open secret anyway. Chief among the brothel property owners was Dr. W. W. Samuell, a prominent physician and civic benefactor for whom a street, a park, and a high school in Dallas would come to be named.

Many people knew about this, but relatively few of them cared. After all, a Reservation landowner could easily net $50,000 a year on his investment. For Dallas, it was a matter of vigorous free enterprise trumping moral concerns. The city took much the same approach to whiskey.

July 12, 1929, was another day of hard summer heat in downtown Dallas: the midday sun like a blister in the washed blue sky, the air fouled with fumes from rattling Fords and Packards. Pedestrians cast small, hard shadows as they moved past the movie theater marquees. The Palace was showing the Marx Brothers in *The Cocoanuts*. And at the Melba—its slogan was "Always Healthfully Cool"—Dolores Costello "and a cast of 10,000" appeared in *Noah's Ark*, a forgettable love story at sea. Matinee admission, 35 cents.

Streetcar bells clanged, and the Manhattan Café on Main Street was packed at lunchtime. The clock hanging over the sidewalk at the Dallas Trust and Savings Bank showed straight-up noon. Down the block, on the steps of the county courthouse, a crowd had gathered. A celebratory air prevailed as Sheriff Hal Hood prepared to order the destruction of five thousand gallons of forbidden whiskey. Hood, the latest in a considerable line of hapless county lawmen, had been humiliated into the act.

Prohibition had long been the law of the land, even longer in Dallas, which voted to ban liquor three years before the Eighteenth Amendment took effect. The local dry forces took pride in declaring they had shuttered more than 200 saloons and 150 stills. Yet whiskey flowed freely in many parts of the city, where drinks were as easy to acquire as whores had been in Frogtown. Police conducted the occasional crackdown, and sometimes made arrests, but such actions usually served merely to generate publicity and payoffs. So lax was enforcement that *Collier's* magazine, a national publication out of New York, dispatched a writer to investigate. He found six places in a two-block stretch of downtown Dallas where he could buy liquor. "Regardless of its registered attitude in favor of strict enforcement of dry laws," he wrote, "I know of no town more bold in its violation of them."

Pretending to be outraged, Sheriff Hood immediately ordered his deputies to commence a series of raids. Like drinkers and magazine writers, his men had no trouble finding saloons. The basements of any number of downtown buildings had them—bare-bones affairs in many cases, with hand-lettered signs and hard chairs. Men drank from unlabeled amber bottles and rolled dice on the concrete floor between tiny, dark pools of tobacco spittle. Hood's deputies moved in and seized hundreds of barrels of bootleg liquor.

Now the contraband would be dumped and order restored as the city cheered. By noon, the spectators overflowed the courthouse steps. Deputies removed their coats, revealing their galluses and holstered sidearms. Ladies from the Women's Christian Temperance Union, wearing long skirts and carrying Bibles, fanned themselves, watched, and prayed. Some sang hymns and gave thanks to God for this glorious occasion.

The deputies tapped the first barrel, then another. The kegs were turned on their sides and tilted at the edge of the curb, and the whiskey gurgled out. As bystanders pitched in, even more liquor splashed into the gutter. Vapors rose in the heat, the scent of sin ascending heavenward.

This was proving to be a beautiful and triumphant moment for Sheriff Hood, at least until someone lit a match and tossed it into the gutter. First came a great *whoosh*, then an eruption of blue flames. In seconds, downtown Dallas had a river of fire rolling down Main Street. There were screams and scrambles. The fire extended for several blocks, "a long blue blaze of intense heat," in the words of one witness. The flames spread to the lot of the Fishburn Motor Company, and when at last the fire department arrived, more than twenty cars had been damaged or destroyed. Next time, vowed the embarrassed Hood, his men would pour sufficient water into the gutter along with the liquor.

Few believed there would be a next time. By the following week, the illegal saloons were back in business and as crowded as usual. Any man stepping off a streetcar in downtown Dallas could buy liquor on the corner. In fact, he could buy it from someone working for or with Benny Binion, who was just beginning the process of making himself into a racketeer.

For someone without an education, and not inclined to steady labor, bootlegging offered one of the best paths to riches. A 1925 study had shown the annual earnings of a Dallas bootlegger to be about $36,000, far surpassing that of many doctors and bank presidents. The bootlegger may have exceeded those men in prestige as well. To a legion of drinkers, who believed the government and the bluenoses had conspired against them, the whiskey man represented a blend of public servant and folk hero.

Binion, using an ever-expanding network of friends and family, quickly established himself as a middleman in the liquor trade, the modern-day equivalent of an importer-distributor. He staked out a commercial terrain between the hidden still in the country and the undercover saloon in town. Binion's crew arranged for, transported, and protected the inventory, while tacking on a sizable markup.

In this endeavor he declared himself a failure. "I never did make no money bootlegging," he said. "Every time I got ahold of any money, something'd happen, and I'd lose a bunch of whiskey or something, and just kept me poor as a church mouse, all the time."

That's not what the moonshiners believed. Most of Binion's bootlegged corn liquor came from a network of stills hidden in the hardwood bottomlands of the Trinity River near Fairfield, ninety miles southeast of Dallas. Produced by Roger Young and his family, this whiskey even had a name: Freestone County Moonshine. The Youngs' liquor was prized by drinkers for its potency and relative purity. It lacked adulterants such as lye, which caused a drinker's lips to swell in terrible pain, and lead, which brought on the partial paralysis known as jake leg.

Though an average still could produce up to sixty gallons a week, the Youngs struggled to keep up with Binion's growing business. On rare occasions when production ran ahead of demand, the Youngs wrapped gallon jugs of whiskey in burlap and buried them in a nearby cow pasture, a process they jokingly referred to as "aging." With Binion as their primary cash customer, the Youngs became one of the wealthiest families in Freestone County. "They had more money down there than anybody," a relative recalled. "They were rolling in money."

Federal revenue agents generally did not present a problem, because the moonshiners bought off the county sheriff, who tipped them to impending raids. Bad weather, however, could shut down deliveries. Heavy rain turned the dirt roads of the bottomlands into impassable bogs, so the Youngs couldn't get their liquor to the town of Corsicana, the usual rendezvous spot with Binion's driver.

When the Youngs' liquor wasn't available, Binion bought Oklahoma hooch. "But the Oklahoma whiskey didn't seem to be as good as the Freestone County whiskey," Binion remembered. Other times, he trafficked in product smuggled from a real distillery, manufactured before Prohibition. "They had bonded whiskey, which cost more money to handle, and everything, and I never did too much of that. Just once in a while, I'd fool with a little bonded whiskey. But the bootlegging, to me, was never no good."

Despite his disclaimers, Binion's reputation among the illegal distilleries was that of a man of force and will. "Binion began to muscle in on whiskey operations," a Dallas police report said, "and reportedly had gone into illegal whiskey plants and stated, 'Everything that comes in between now and midnight is mine.'"

Raids and arrests happened infrequently, but they still presented a risk to Binion's business. "Me and a guy by the name of Fat Harper, we got ahold of about $20,000 together, so we bought a lot of whiskey," Binion recalled. They decided to keep some off the market in a warehouse owned by a man named Ward. "So we stored all this whiskey up in the warehouse when the weather was good to make a killing when the weather got bad and the whiskey'd go up." But Ward fired an employee who got revenge by ratting to the police. "They came down there and arrested old man Ward and about thirteen people," Binion said. "Didn't get me and Fat, but we had to put up all the money to get them out. That whacked us out for sure."

Even with the police mustering only occasional interest, Binion himself could not avoid arrest. "I got 60 days one time, and four months another time," he said, though his record shows a $200 fine and a thirty-day sentence for violation of liquor laws.

After one collar for bootlegging, Binion faced up to five years in prison. But the judge was a friend of sorts. "I knew him and he knew me," Binion said. "And he says, 'You know, you're supposed to go to the penitentiary.' And I says, 'Your honor,' I said, 'don't sent me to the penitentiary,' something to that effect. And he says, 'Why?' 'Well,' I says, 'I'm not going to bootleg anymore.'" That wasn't true, but it kept him out of the pen.

Beyond his bootlegging problems, Binion was in and out of other trouble in Dallas, but of minor consequence. In 1924 he was charged with tire theft, but not prosecuted. Later he was no-billed after a minor gambling arrest. A 1927 arrest for burglary and felony theft went unprosecuted. And a 1929 charge of aggravated assault was also dropped. That arrest appears to have stemmed from his reaction to a traffic accident in Dallas. As one of his sons told it much later, an unarmed Binion was attacked just after the wreck by more than a dozen men and—in a gladiatorial feat—ripped the bumper from his car and used it to defeat them one and all. "They kept coming," son Ted said, "till there was fourteen of them with broken bones." But the legend doesn't quite match the facts, according to local newspaper reports, which said Binion used the damaged bumper from his car to strike just one person: the other driver, a middle-aged woman. For this, he became known to police as the Bumper Beater.

Because a large car part wasn't always available, Binion usually employed more conventional protection. Dallas police twice arrested him as a young man for carrying concealed firearms—a pistol in one case, a sawed-off shotgun in another. The pistol got him sixty days.

The jail time didn't stop him from carrying a gun. Having a piece in his pocket was an occupational necessity for a bootlegger, as Binion demonstrated on a warm, breezy October evening in 1931. He believed that another whiskey seller, a black man named Frank Bolding, had been stealing some of his liquor. The two of them met in the backyard of one of Binion's safe houses, on Pocahontas Street in South Dallas, to talk the matter over.

"Me and him was sitting down on two boxes," Binion recalled. "He was a bad bastard. So he done something I didn't like and we was talking about it, and he jumped up right quick with a knife in his hand."

The instinctive move for Binion would have been to jump up too. "Then he'd cut the shit out of me," Binion said. "But I was a little smarter than that. I just fell backward off of that box and shot the sumbitch right there."

Binion, in his later years, related other versions of the story. His son Ted told this one: "The guy hadn't pulled the knife yet, even though he did have one . . . Dad felt like he was going to stab him."

Whether or not the man brandished a blade, the result was indisputable: Bolding was shot in the throat. He fell to the ground, where he writhed and groaned. Binion stood over him and continued their discussion with, "I fooled you, didn't I, you black son a bitch." Neither Binion nor his crew sought a doctor for the wounded man, and within minutes he was dead.

Binion surrendered to authorities, claiming, "He come at me with a knife." Even if that were false, a dead black bootlegger couldn't excite much interest from the police, and it barely made the papers. Binion didn't spend so much as a night in jail for the killing. Ultimately he pleaded guilty to murder, and received a two-year suspended sentence, allowing him to walk free. He probably could have escaped completely untouched by the courts had he pressed the matter. But the suspended sentence was a better bit of backscratching.

"I'll tell you why," he later said of his benign trip through the courthouse. "Bill McCraw was the district attorney. Me and him was goddamn good friends. He was gonna run for governor as DA. It looked kind of maybe bad if he'd just turned me loose . . . But I just—we just—decided I'd take a two-year suspended sentence to kind of make him look a little better, don't you see, which we did."

Not only was he a free man, Binion had a new nickname, thanks to his quick-draw dispatch of Bolding. Now everyone called him the Cowboy.

Benny Binion,

# 3

# PANCHO AND THE KLAN

Tough times make tough people.

—BB

**D**rinkers demanded a finished product, but suckers would pay for nothing but a chance. That's why Binion considered liquor a mere stepping-stone. Soon he saw something that offered more promise than traffic in forbidden whiskey. He saw lucky numbers. "In about 1928 I opened up what they call a 'policy,'" he said. This propelled him into a wider and more adventurous criminal world. And the profits were sensational.

The policy games were nothing more than simple lotteries in which players tried to pick three lucky digits. Each operator employed a team of runners, known as policy writers, who fanned out across town with sheets of numbers printed daily in red, green, and black. Players could bet a dime for a chance to win as much as $10. Winners were selected twice a day by the turning of the policy wheels. Some of the devices were actual spinning wheels, while others were small, rotating barrels from which the winning numbers were plucked. Operators set the odds and controlled the payouts, and applied the fix as necessary. It was a common practice for them to survey the bets, determine which numbers would make the house the most money, and maneuver to select those. With no oversight, they ensured their own handsome returns.

Policy operations stayed mobile to avoid raids and robberies. Not much equipment was needed—the wheel, a mimeograph to print tickets, and an adding machine to tally the proceeds. A game might spend time under bare lightbulbs in a sweltering room of a fleabag hotel before decamping to the smoky rear parlors of a side-street tavern. If operators got a tip that a raid was coming, they could pack up and be gone in minutes.

Though Binion had entered the policy business with some apprehension, it didn't take long—about twelve hours—to see that he had strolled into a gold mine. "I started with fifty-six dollars," he recalled. "The first day I made eight hundred dollars." Even at its best, bootlegging never offered margins like that. A career was born.

Policy games operated under a strict racial structure: the owners were white and the customers were not. This represented a sizable base of potential gamblers; more than thirty thousand blacks now lived in Dallas. Some of them were descendants of the slaves brought to Texas to work the cotton fields before the Civil War. Others had fled the exhausted timberlands and spent farms of East Texas, Louisiana, and Arkansas. They generally filled the low end of the employment scale, as porters, maids, elevator operators, dishwashers, and other common laborers. They took, in other words, jobs that whites would not do.

The white citizenry of Dallas tended to view the policy business with condescension and ridicule. "The policy game is mainly supported by Negroes to whom a $10.50 return on a 10-cent investment is big money," the *Dallas Morning News* offered. The *Daily Times Herald* took it further in a front-page story that began this way: "'Cullud folks jus' gotta gamble— if'n they ain't nothin' else to bet on, they gonna bet on which way a bird fly when he leave off sittin', so there you is.' This, with a sheepish grin, constituted the most lucid answer the shambling Negro could give to a question which was asked ten of his race as they walked past city hall."

The same story allowed the head of the Dallas police vice squad to offer his own theory. "Negroes just have to bet," Captain Max Doughty said. "Their gambling instincts seem to be much more thoroughly developed than those of whites." This ignored the fact that within a one-mile radius of the police station there were at least a dozen illegal dice rooms patronized by whites.

The captain's attitude was hardly unusual. From its earliest days, Dallas had looked north in its moneyed aspirations and west in its frontier temperament. But in its race relations, it turned to the Old South. The town recorded its first lynchings in 1860, when three slaves were hanged after a raging fire destroyed most of the business district. It didn't matter that no credible evidence linked the three men to the blaze. As one member of the Dallas "vigilance committee" explained, they were probably innocent but "somebody had to hang." It could have been worse. Some of the vigilantes favored killing every black person in the county.

After the Civil War, and for the next nine decades, Dallas imposed stark segregation, with separate schools, health clinics, and parks. Municipal ordinances designated some neighborhoods white or Negro. At one point a city councilman proposed a law restricting Negro pedestrians to certain streets.

For the most part, blacks lived in the southern half of town, a squalid and—in low sections—flood-prone expanse of shanties lining unpaved roads. There were several handsome and well-tended neighborhoods of strivers and black professionals in southern Dallas, but they represented the exception. More than three-fourths of the dwellings in that part of the city were considered substandard. Most of those substandard houses had no running water. Half lacked gas or electricity. Fully one-fourth, a 1925 housing survey found, were "unfit for human habitation." Segregation did allow one loophole: a few thousand Dallas blacks were permitted to live in wealthy white neighborhoods. They were the domestics who occupied the servants' quarters of the well-to-do.

As was the case in many American cities, the Ku Klux Klan had a stranglehold on Dallas and its officials for much of the 1920s. A traveler stepping off a train at downtown's Union Station might, if he timed it right, be greeted by the Klan's fifty-member drum corps in white hoods and robes. For a time, the State Fair of Texas, which was held in Dallas, observed an annual Klan Day. Many of the most powerful men in the city, from the police commissioner to influential clergy, were KKK members or supporters, which allowed the Klan to operate as it pleased. And it pleased the Klan to terrorize black people.

In 1921, a group of Klansmen grabbed a young black man from his home, put a rope around his neck, and drove him to a secluded spot south of town. The Klansmen did not lynch him. Instead, they whipped the man—twenty-five bloody lashes across his back with a bullwhip—and burned the letters KKK into his forehead with acid. Despite a detailed account of the attack published in the *Times Herald*, with the reporter as an eyewitness, authorities refused to investigate. "As I understand the case," county sheriff Dan Harston, a Klansman, said, "the Negro was guilty of doing something which he had no right to do . . . He no doubt deserved it." The man's offense: a consensual liaison at the Adolphus Hotel with a white woman.

Nothing could incite the city's passions like blacks killing whites, as seen when Lorenzo and Frank Noel were arrested in 1925 for a series of murders and rapes. The brothers were accused of attacking white couples parked in a lovers' lane. Headlines called them the "Black Terrors." As news of the Noels' arrest spread, a crowd gathered outside the Dallas County Jail. By midnight, it had grown to a mob of five thousand. They threw bricks and rocks, and some tried to break through police lines and into the jail. Firemen blasted the rioters with water. When that didn't work, deputies fired into the crowd, fatally wounding an eighteen-year-old white bystander. The mob was repulsed, and the brothers were later able to stand trial. A jury—all white—took two minutes to find them guilty, and they were executed about six weeks later.

Someone like Binion—a poorly educated man with country roots and no great aversion to violence—might have been expected to embrace the KKK. But instead, the budding policy-wheel titan distanced himself from the Klan. "I don't believe," he explained, "in hanging my customers."

The sweet spot for Binion and his policy bagmen was Deep Ellum, a teeming black neighborhood of two- and three-story brick storefronts and narrow sidewalks east of downtown. Offering all manner of temptations, the district had inspired the song "Deep Ellum Blues," which included the lyrics "Once I knew a preacher, preached the Bible through and through / He went down in Deep Ellum, now his preaching days are through."

Deep Ellum had the Cotton Club, the Harlem movie house, and the Gypsy Tea Room. Hotel rooms went for 25 cents a night. The Wish-I-Wish Company on Central Avenue sold lucky mojo bags and mystic oils for aid in commerce or love. "Down on 'Deep Ellum' in Dallas, where Central Avenue empties into Elm Street is where Ethiopia stretches forth her hands," J. H. Owens, a columnist for the *Dallas Gazette,* wrote in the 1930s. "It is the one spot in the city that needs no daylight saving time because there is no bedtime, and working hours have no limits. The only place recorded on earth where business, religion, hoodooism, gambling and stealing goes on at the same time without friction." That was the African American version. A white writer of the day put it this way: "Under the veneer of civilization and custom there runs in Deep Ellum the undercurrent of jungle law."

Binion's operations were headquartered at the Green & White Café, 2400 Elm Street, owned by one of his lieutenants, Ivy Miller. Like Binion, Miller tended to pull his gun at the first sign of trouble. Miller, who was white, once ended a scuffle among black patrons at his café by shooting one of the fighters—a woman—in the stomach, an action for which police declined to charge him. "It's not his way," a glowing newspaper account observed, "to allow negroes to pull off scraps on his premises."

Binion's second-in-command was Harry Urban, a fellow operative from his bootlegging network. "Urban was at that time generally regarded by the local police department as a pimp, and his wife, Billie Urban, was his prostitute," a law enforcement report said. They made an odd pair—the perpetually disheveled Binion alongside the habitually dapper Urban, a cosmopolite by Dallas standards who would later in his criminal career own a pair of Cadillacs that had custom-made holsters next to the driver's seat.

The policy games bore enticing names: Hi-Noon, Grand Prize, Gold Mine, Silver Dollar. From the Green & White, Binion's captains—white men with monickers like Jelly and Fivecoat—dispatched black runners to find customers, and return with betting slips and bags bulging with coins. The bagmen also sold "dream books" to bettors. If a gambler dreamed of thunderstorms, for example, these guides would tell him which numbers to pick. A dream of zebras meant different numbers. Binion's runners collected a 25 percent commission on their sales, which was considered generous. But when one bagman tried to pocket some extra cash, Binion dealt with him—and sent a hard message to his other runners—by putting a pencil through the man's eye.

Here was the paradox that marked Benny Binion, now and for the rest of his years. He was brutal when he had to be and beneficent when the opportunity arose. He also understood that love engendered loyalty, while fear instilled discipline, but together they conveyed a singular power that could elevate and enshrine. Binion's policy operations fleeced the blacks of Dallas without mercy, and he employed mayhem as he saw fit. Yet years later, a prominent black Dallas physician, Emerson Emory, recalled his father's work as a runner for the Cowboy with deep affection. "I remember the pride that my father showed whenever he collected his small earnings, the result of miles of walking in the community," Emory said. "I remember the trucks, laden with apples and oranges that Mr. Binion had parked next to the policy shack behind the old State Theater during the Christmas season. Sometimes the fruit was the only gift the neighborhoods would receive from Santa."

Even as his policy business thrived, Binion remained a relatively small player in the hierarchy of Dallas vice. Police regarded him and his peers as little more than second tier, but he aspired to something greater. He wanted to be like Warren Diamond.

Originally a pharmacist, Diamond had matured into a felonious patrician, known as a sportsman in polite circles. Binion remembered him as "the first big dice fader I ever knew." A fader was someone who covered other dice rollers' bets.

Diamond had begun his gambling business in a wagon yard on Camp Street, near downtown Dallas. It was a primitive setup, with the wagering made among the dirt and the horses. A wooden stockade fence surrounded the yard, keeping the police out until some deputies sneaked in by hiding inside a covered wagon. They shut the operation down and arrested Diamond.

Convicted of "keeping premises for the purpose of gaming," Diamond got two years in state prison. When released, he upgraded his business, setting up shop in the St. George Hotel, a workingman's lodging—a single room with a bath was $8.75 a week—near the Dallas County courthouse.

Now he had moneyed partners, employed sufficient muscle to keep the peace, and controlled an operation that generated enough cash to make payoffs. Diamond soon owned a mansion in the town's finest neighborhood.

Binion spent much of his time hanging around the St. George operation, picking up odd jobs, parking cars, and catching a few stray pieces of the action. What he was really doing was watching and learning. "Warren Diamond was as fine a man as I ever knew," Binion said—a generous patron, always a soft touch for the down-and-out or the sick, especially the sick. "He was a big giver like that," Binion said.

Diamond also established a policy of taking any bet, no matter how big. "He opened up a Do and Don't dice game with no limit," Binion said, speaking of a common craps game. "A fellow came in there and threw an envelope on the line and said, 'Diamond, I'm going to make you look.'" But Diamond didn't flinch, and he didn't look. He just said, "Pass him the dice."

With all eyes on him, the man rolled. "He shot the dice, and caught a point and missed it," Binion said. "And they opened the envelope and there's a hundred and seventy-two one-thousand-dollar bills in it. That was the biggest shot I ever heard of. And I know it to be true because I was in the hotel lobby at the time it happened."

Binion never forgot this strategy of accepting bets of all sizes. In addition, Diamond—with his style, daring, and business acumen—presented Binion with the closest thing to a father figure he ever knew. "I guess a kid just wants to kind of pattern after some guy like that, you know," Binion said. "I admired him very much." That understated the case. "Warren Diamond was Dad's idol," said Binion's daughter Brenda.

By the early 1930s, however, Diamond often absented himself from the games at the St. George. He was fifty-five and had prostate cancer, so he spent much of his time seeking treatment at retreats and at medical clinics. When not in bed, he supervised the construction of his tomb. Diamond had seen a granite, columned mausoleum that he admired in Connecticut; he commissioned one like it for himself back home. With an interior of bronze, brass, and Italian marble, it cost $65,000, far more than most houses.

And soon he was ready for it. Diamond lay in bed at St. Paul's Sanitarium in Dallas. He had been told he had no hope of recovery, and his pain had become unbearable. He asked the nurse for his clothes and called a cab from his room. Diamond left the hospital, struggled into the taxi, and told the driver to take him home. The ride to 4224 Armstrong Parkway took no more than fifteen minutes.

His wife met him at the door. He walked past her and made a slow climb of the stairs. Then he shuffled into the second-floor bathroom, put an automatic pistol to his head, and shot himself dead.

Binion grieved the loss of his mentor, but he put his sadness away and thought of the opportunity now in front of him. "I don't miss nothing after I leave it," he said much later. "Make the best out of every situation."

Such resilience marked Binion's character throughout his life, yet there were some hard breaks from which he couldn't walk away blithely and unbent.

One of his partners in those days was another young man who had fled the fields of Pilot Grove—his younger brother, Jack. While Benny had his boisterous moments—he liked to blow off steam by stepping into the street and firing his pistol into the air—Jack took the free-spirited approach even higher. Benny liked horses, but Jack preferred motorcycles. "He'd laugh about how his little brother could whip him," Benny's daughter Brenda remembered. This didn't spring from Jack's brute strength so much as pure wildness.

Benny tended to pursue his criminal interests with at least some deliberation and planning. When Jack needed money, he grabbed it, with abandon, wherever possible. At one point he and a like-minded criminal stormed an East Dallas house in which they believed four men had a stash of bootlegging proceeds. The two failed to tie down, or shoot, one of the witnesses, who escaped and called the police. Jack and his friend robbed the occupants, ransacked the house, and fled the scene as officers arrived. Police fired a shotgun at their car, hitting Jack in the head. He lived, but he lost an eye. That was the extent of his punishment, for charges against him were later dropped. After all, the men he had robbed were black.

Months later, on a crisp winter afternoon, a single-engine Stinson Detroiter took off from Love Field with three men aboard. The Stinson banked to the southeast and headed toward White Rock Lake, the city's main reservoir. For several miles the stunting pilot kept the plane no more than twenty feet above the ground, dropping it even lower in clearings, buzzing cars and trucks, then barely clearing rooftops and power lines. A watchman at the White Rock Lake pump station stared in amazement as the plane emerged from between the trees lining the reservoir. Over the open water, it seemed almost to be skimming the sun-dappled surface. No more than a hundred feet from shore, as the pilot executed a series of sharp turns, a wing clipped the water and tore from the fuselage. The rest of the plane tumbled upside down, plunged into the shallow lake, and plowed into the muddy bottom. All three men aboard were killed. One of them was twenty-three-year-old Jack Binion.

He was buried a few days later in the family cemetery in Pilot Grove. The loss consumed his mother, and she would be dead of a stroke in seven months at the age of forty-nine. "She grieved herself to death," Binion said.

Binion, too, deeply mourned Jack's death, and then the heartbreak compounded: Jack's wife was pregnant when he died, but "she decided not to have the baby," Brenda Binion Michael said. After the abortion, "Dad never spoke to her again."

He took his brother's clothes and carefully folded them into a trunk. Binion kept them with his own possessions for the next thirty years. And when his first son was born, Binion named him for his brother.

As he returned to Dallas from his brother's funeral, Binion faced a shifting landscape. Diamond's death had created chances for expansion, and Binion's head was full of plans. He also had a pressing personal concern, and it arose from the whiskey trade. Hilliard Henderson, who ran a downtown Dallas pharmacy, operated a bootlegging business on the side. Some of his stash had been stolen, and Henderson asked Binion to track down the thieves.

Binion never found them, but he discovered something else: the bootlegging druggist had a beautiful daughter. Teddy Jane Henderson was a tiny ballerina, barely five feet tall, with long brown hair. She was only sixteen, but she and Binion fell in love and talked of marriage. If you marry Benny Binion, Teddy Jane's mother told her, you'll spend the rest of your life living in hotels above some kind of gambling game. That didn't stop her. On October 2, 1933, Teddy Jane hopped in a car with Binion and drove 110 miles north, across the Red River to Ardmore, Oklahoma, where a sixteen-year-old girl could marry a twenty-eight-year-old man with no waiting and few questions asked. Back in Dallas, they settled into an apartment on Cedar Springs Boulevard. Within four months, Teddy Jane was pregnant.

Their daughter Barbara was born on October 23, 1934, and if Binion was not an ever-present father, he proved himself sufficiently protective. Baby Barbara contracted whooping cough, and spent many sleepless nights in endless fits of coughing and crying. The upstairs neighbors complained to the landlord about the noise. When Binion learned of his neighbors' distress, he told the landlord not to worry, that he would address the problem himself. That evening Binion waited in his apartment until he heard the neighbors' footfalls upstairs. He pulled his handgun and began firing into the ceiling. When they fled to the next room, he moved under them and fired some more.

By dawn the next day the complaining neighbors had moved out.

Dallas had a population approaching three hundred thousand by the early 1930s, and was growing every year. It did especially well at attracting two types of people: the rich and the desperate. And Binion was putting himself in a position to exploit both.

Out on the empty plains of West Texas and Oklahoma, hundreds of miles from Dallas, topsoil began to dry up and blow away. It moved across the prairie like a black blizzard that buried houses, livestock, and people. Many caught in these hellish storms—a man could disappear walking from his house to his barn—believed that the end of the world had come, not with flood or fire but with dirt.

The farmers fled as the land turned against them. Thousands loaded their ragged possessions onto rickety trucks and scattered west to the paradise of California. But others came to Dallas, which had little room within its boundaries for impoverished rural outlanders. Dust Bowl refugees settled where many of the poor and dispossessed had gone before them: West Dallas. On the unincorporated, flat, and low side of the Trinity River, West Dallas was given to floods and disease. Many residents lived in tents or under trees. The lucky ones rented shanties. Sewage ran in shallow ditches and in crooked, fetid creeks. The editorialists and preachers called it the city's shame, but their railing moved few to action. Yet where some saw failure, others spotted opportunity. Like slums everywhere, the district proved a breeding ground for outlaws, and a number of Binion's most loyal and effective foot soldiers would be recruited off the unpaved streets of West Dallas.

While the Dust Bowl sent forth waves of misery, East Texas spewed riches. The Daisy Bradford No. 3 well in Rusk County started an oil boom that lasted for twenty years—millions of dollars, pouring from holes in the ground. Dallas, only 130 miles away, was the closest major city. This didn't insulate Dallas from the Depression, but it softened the blow, as dozens, then hundreds, of oil-related companies set up headquarters there. The banks filled with their deposits, and well-paid executives and oil-field workers rolled into town. "All them oil men had money," Binion said, and many of them wanted to gamble with it.

As Binion approached thirty, most of the boyishness had faded from his face. He knew the players in town—where they were the strongest and where the weakest—and he moved with growing confidence. In the spring of 1934, the Majestic Theater in downtown Dallas was showing the movie *Viva Villa!* It starred Wallace Beery and Fay Wray, and presented the highly romanticized version of Pancho Villa transforming himself from mere bandit to heralded leader of the Mexican Revolution. Binion loved the movie—the story of a petty outlaw who treasures horses, robs people, and goes on to greatness—and it remained a favorite for the rest of his life.

Like Villa, he had grander plans. The brave new underworld offered no end of possibilities.

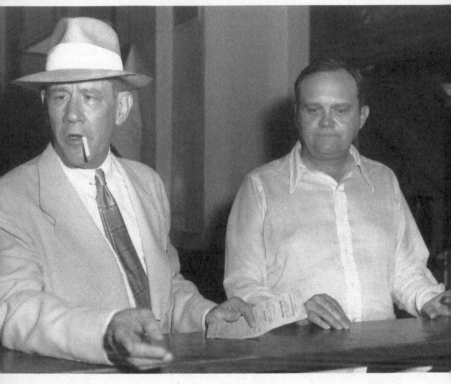

Binion (right) and Bill Decker, his best friend at the Dallas County courthouse.

# 4

# GOOD FRIENDS AND
# A DEAD RIVAL

I had a lot of high, influential friends in Texas, and it wasn't no
money thing. It was friends.

**–BB**

**B**inion often looked at a man—from an angle, with a squint—
as if he were sizing up his price per pound. He calculated
odds on nearly everyone he met. As soon as Binion saw
Fred Browning, he knew he held aces.

On a gentle North Texas afternoon, a car carrying seven girls sped past
the Arlington Downs horse track and the Baghdad Supper Club, with the
last bits of the city dropping away as they traveled west. They were bound
for the finest casino in the Southwest and one of the most elegant in the
country. Known as Top O'Hill Terrace, it was Fred Browning's place.

Soon they turned into an unmarked, paved driveway and stopped at a
massive black iron gate. A man carrying a rifle emerged from a stone,
turret-like guardhouse. He looked into the car, saw the girls, smiled, and
waved his hand. Another armed guard swung the gate open, and the car
passed into the compound. A winding road led three hundred yards uphill,
under a canopy of oak trees, until it reached the parking lot, which was full
of Cadillacs, new Pierce-Arrows, and top-dollar roadsters—two-seaters
with whitewalled tires and long, sweeping fenders, the shiny transports of

rich people. The girls could hear a band playing as they spilled from their car, ready to go to work. Mary Helen, Hazel, Joan, Gwendolyn, Mildred, Margaret, and Willetta: Ruth Laird's Texas Rockets, back for their daily dancing gig.

Set on a heavily wooded rise in Arlington, Texas—between Dallas and Fort Worth—Top O'Hill had started in the 1920s as a tearoom and bridge parlor, a place for affluent matrons to pass satisfied afternoons. Then it caught the attention of Browning, for whom the delights of the plumbing business no longer sufficed. He bought the building in 1926, and ultimately the forty-six acres surrounding it, and turned Top O'Hill into a gambling den.

Browning hid the casino in the basement of the tearoom and proceeded to dress it up. Unlike many joints of the Depression, Top O'Hill had carpeting, brass furnishings, fine china, and a studied sense of opulence. The dealers were attired in formal wear, and the Depression seemed a world away. That atmosphere, combined with the high-stakes gambling, attracted rich Texans, Howard Hughes among them. Hughes liked to wear tennis shoes with his tuxedo. "He'd say, 'My feet have got to be comfortable,'" recalled one Top O'Hill worker. Movie stars who happened to be passing through Dallas stopped by too. Mae West came, as well as Hedy Lamarr, Gene Autry, and Will Rogers. One evening oilman H. L. Hunt hired a cab at the Adolphus Hotel in downtown Dallas and rode over with a couple of his friends, Buster Keaton and W. C. Fields.

Dinners, drinks, and entertainment were comped for such customers. Top O'Hill offered one other luxury for the rich and famous: there was little chance for embarrassing arrests. Any lawmen coming in the back way would have to scale a fence, then evade armed guards and attack dogs as they climbed uphill through thick brambles, tangled vines, and assorted spiny underbrush. The only realistic entrance was the main drive, with its heavy gate. If cops managed to breach that barrier, an attendant in the guardhouse pressed a button that set off an alarm in the casino. Sliding doors opened, and gamblers fled through underground tunnels that had been dug by Chinese workers. Employees then folded the roulette, blackjack, and craps tables into hideaways in the wall, like Murphy beds. By the time the raiders made their way up the road and hit the casino, the dealers had gathered in a circle, where they held Bibles and sang hymns, a devout collection of men in black tie.

Top O'Hill had other attractions. Browning kept his thoroughbred racehorses stabled on the grounds. Next to the swimming pool he erected a boxing ring where champs such as Max Baer and Lew "Sweet Swatter from Sweetwater" Jenkins trained and sparred. And behind the casino was the brothel. The whores were gorgeous, almost as lovely as the movie stars leaning on the roulette tables. Some wore black velvet capes from Neiman Marcus. Nothing but the best at Fred Browning's place.

When it came to running a posh gambling spot and flesh palace, Browning excelled at everything except handling money, for he tended to squander his earnings at the horse track. There arose a few occasions when he needed a heavy loan or two, and that's when his friend Benny Binion—who had met Browning through gambling connections—swept in to bail him out. Binion was increasingly flush with cash from his policy games in Dallas, and he knew a promising operation when he saw one. The Cowboy not only lent Browning money in return for a share of the business, he also provided management assistance by bringing in trusted associates to help run the place—and keep an eye on Browning. Top O'Hill's revenues over a good weekend were said to exceed a quarter-million dollars, a significant portion of which went to Binion, who ultimately had a 50 percent interest. Some nights he and Browning could be found in the casino's counting room sorting through jewelry that had been won from gamblers. They set aside some of it to be melted down and reformed into silver ingots. Binion always enjoyed silver ingots.

Now it was time for the seven Texas Rockets to file into the tea garden behind the casino—a lush lawn surrounded by a low brown sandstone wall lined with rose and azalea bushes. A fountain gurgled at its center. Perhaps a hundred people, men and women, were there. Still onstage, in a boxy white suit, stood Fred Lowery, "the Blind Whistler," direct from the Early Birds radio show at WFAA in downtown Dallas, where his repertoire included the "William Tell Overture." When the whistling was done—Lowery's finale was always "Indian Love Call"—four jockeys from the nearby horse track began to wrestle a portable, roll-up, wooden dance floor.

The jockeys, wearing their brightly colored racing silks—red, blue, green, and yellow—unrolled it across the rich grass, giving the Rockets a stage. The bandleader raised his baton, and the orchestra hit its notes. The Rockets began to dance: seven girls in cowboy hats and fringed red, white, and blue uniforms, kicking and spinning. The crowd watched and drank, and encouraged the girls with warm applause.

Between numbers one of the dancers, a dark-haired beauty named Willie—short for Willetta—scanned the audience. Most of the men wore tuxedos, and the women displayed themselves in long evening gowns. One woman even sported a hat made of colorful birds' wings. Others held the long white filters of their cigarettes between fingers with polished nails. All in the garden seemed to represent the height of glamour—except for one couple. At the back of the crowd Willie spotted a man and a woman standing together but not mixing. He wore a colorless, drab suit, and she had on a dress that stood out in its plainness. The man glanced around nervously, while the woman tried to smooth wrinkles from her sleeve. "Look how ugly she is," Willie whispered to another dancer. She was talking about Bonnie Parker, next to Clyde Barrow. "Him too," Willie said. Bonnie and Clyde, Depression desperadoes, Dust Bowl Robin Hoods. At the peak of their short but notorious run of bank robberies, they were, in some circles, the most celebrated criminals of their day. But at Top O'Hill, Bonnie and Clyde were out of their league.

The band struck up "Puttin' on the Ritz," and the Rockets resumed dancing, smiles on every face. They were working-class teens forced by hard times to drop out of school and perform. Not that they resented it. This was hard but exciting work, seven days a week, two shows a day. Just children, really, but they were making their way in the world of dice-rolling grown-ups.

Binion knew that life well. He was easy to spot at Top O'Hill—one of the few men not wearing a tuxedo. Rumpled, a little sweaty, but offering the girls a fatherly glance. Willie could tell by his kindly face that he had a family of his own. When the Rockets finished their performance, Binion turned to a man next to him and said, "Pay those girls in cash, and hurry." Their total fee was $15, and a harsh world prevailed outside the gates of Top O'Hill. "They need the money," Binion told his man.

That was pure Benny: if he liked you, you couldn't have a better ally. Something like that stuck with a performing girl such as Willie. Seven decades later—her dancing days a distant memory, her oxygen coming from a tank—Willetta Stellmacher would recall him with wistful fondness. "We all liked him," she said.

Bonnie and Clyde perished on a Louisiana back road in 1934. Barrow's bullet-riddled body—he had been hit dozens of times in a lawmen's ambush—was buried at Western Heights Cemetery on the Fort Worth highway in Dallas. During the service, an airplane hired by Binion flew in low and dropped a floral wreath in the direction of Barrow's fresh grave. Though the tribute came too late to warm Clyde's heart, it made an impression with the local toughs, many of whom were attending the burial. Binion looked like the most appreciative—and grandiose—rackets man in town.

As an aspiring pasha of vice, Binion knew he needed to assemble an effective collection of associates. He was not one, given his stunted schooling and line of work, to keep paper records. But Binion cataloged people; he ranked them in his head, precisely and strategically. Even as he smiled goofily and delivered country platitudes, he studied the faces of others, their voices, the way they dressed, the way they walked. Binion could close his eyes and tell who was approaching by the sound of their footsteps. He knew who was loyal, who was cutthroat, and who could be trusted to do the dirty work and never say a word about it. Binion was also quick to see who required a payoff and who needed a beating to be kept in line.

He further realized that to rise above the ordinary scrum of thugs he would have to make a special effort to cultivate authorities. "You'd have to know somebody that is influential, that you could go and ask a favor," he said. "And I was always able to get some financial help, and political help, and this, that and the other, any time I needed it. And I never did ask nobody to do nothing out of line for me."

That's because Binion forged such powerful and intimate relationships—especially at the county courthouse—that he didn't have to ask.

The Dallas County sheriff was R. A. "Smoot" Schmid, a six-foot-six "apple-cheeked" bicycle dealer, as one newspaper described him, who had been elected in 1932 despite a complete lack of experience in police work. His previous dealings with criminals involved buying stolen merchandise from them, which he cleaned up and resold at his bicycle shop. "Because he's a big fellow and likes to eat," a local reporter noted, "the prisoners in the county jail enjoy good fare." He was, in other words, largely inconsequential if not buffoonish, and hardly worth Binion's time.

Schmid's chief deputy, James Eric "Bill" Decker, served as the heart and brains of the sheriff's office. The one-eyed Decker was a high school dropout who had begun his courthouse career as an elevator operator. He seemed to know everyone, from the most upright Baptist deacon to the lowest small-time grifter. "Every living human in Dallas knew Bill Decker even when he was a youngster," Binion remembered. "His daddy had a saloon on Griffin Street. He tended bar standing on a box." As a deputy sheriff, Decker prided himself on his professional rapport with the county's criminals. If he needed to question someone, he simply put the word on the street. Soon the suspect would be in Decker's office, talking. He was, to many, the epitome of the straight shooter, a latter-day version of the dime-novel western lawman, though one who favored a fedora over a cowboy hat.

Decker also happened to be one of Binion's closest buddies. "He liked me," Binion said. "Me and him was just goddamn good friends." Binion insisted that no money was required to cement this bond between an ambitious gangster and the county's most influential law enforcement official. "I never give him a dollar, not one dollar," Binion said. "Never bought him a hat, never give him nothing." The relationship nonetheless paid off for Binion, who went about his business with no interference whatsoever from Decker. "Bill Decker," Binion said, "had never bothered me in my operations no way, shape or form."

It wasn't enough to have connections. He also had to handle the competition. Binion's general habit was to issue a warning to those who were stealing pieces of his pie. If that caution was ignored, the guns came out.

On a Saturday afternoon in September 1936, Binion rode in his new Cadillac with an employee of his, an undercard heavy named Harlis E. "Buddy" Malone. The Caddy's engine purred as they cruised Allen Street in the Freedman's Town section of Dallas. Like the adjacent district of

Deep Ellum, Freedman's Town served as a busy mercantile and entertainment district for Dallas's black community. The streets were alive this time
of day with shoppers, errand runners, and ambling opportunists in search
of easy misdemeanors. Binion and Malone had come to check on commerce. They motored past the two-story redbrick building that housed the
Pride of Dallas Café, and saw that the café was packed. Inside, there was
music, smoke, laughter, shouts, the smell of beer. A mist of grease rose from
the griddle. People spilled out the door and onto the narrow sidewalk. The
Pride of Dallas had always been a hot spot for Binion's numbers trade, and
Saturday was the busiest day of all as the runners hunted for players who
might have a fresh week's pay folded in their pockets. Binion and Malone
took the street with a slow roll; this was their turf.

Then one of them spotted Ben Freiden's car at the curb. A black man
leaned in through the window and handed Freiden a paper bag—money
and policy slips. That was all Binion needed to see. He yelled for Malone to
stop the car. His Cadillac came to a halt inches from Freiden's Pontiac.
Binion and Malone got out. Both carried guns.

Freiden, forty-six, was by outward appearances a solid citizen with a
wife and a fourteen-year-old son, Ben Jr. He owned a nice brick house in an
affluent neighborhood and carried life insurance. He had come to Dallas
from California, and claimed to be in the produce business. If so, he had
soon realized he could make more money selling numbers than canta-
loupes, and he operated several policy wheels of his own, the Topnotch
among them. The competition was not well received in Dallas, and Binion
personally had warned him to stop. Six months earlier Freiden had been
shot in the hand by an unseen assailant as he emerged from his car in his
darkened driveway. Police made no arrests but suspected the shooter
worked for Binion.

Now, outside the Pride of Dallas, Freiden sat in the passenger seat of his
new sedan, wearing a short-sleeved shirt and slacks with $100 in his pocket.
A fan on the dashboard stirred warm air in the black car. All the windows
were down. Freiden's chauffeur, George Parker, sat behind the wheel.

Binion and Malone approached. Malone carried a .45-caliber pistol,
while Binion had a .38 and a nasty head of steam. He knew Freiden probably had a gun too, but he didn't care. Binion reached into the car and

slapped Freiden's face. "You son of a bitch," Binion yelled at him. "You're a sucker in the business."

Then the shots began, with Binion firing from the passenger's side and Malone from the driver's. The crowd on the sidewalk scattered. Freiden's terrified chauffeur pressed himself against his seat and covered his head with his arms.

Freiden never had a chance. "I hit him three times, right in the heart," Binion said later. Yet the bullets kept flying. "Buddy shot him after I done shot him," Binion said. "Old Buddy just shot the piss out of him."

With Freiden dead and pissless on the spot—he had seven bullet holes in him—Binion and Old Buddy drove away before the police arrived. Investigators who picked apart the crime scene discovered a loaded pistol in the dead man's lap. One of its bullets had been fired. On the seat next to him was the brown bag full of policy slips and cash. The chauffeur, unhurt but still in fear, gave them little information.

Binion surrendered later that afternoon, accompanied by his lawyer, Eddie Roark, attorney to some of Dallas's leading racketeers. (Roark was more than two years away from being shot dead by a gambler client who came home one day and found his attorney in bed with his wife.) Binion did not go to the city police; instead, he gave himself up to his good friend Bill Decker at the county courthouse. "Look at this," Binion said, and showed Decker a minor wound—a "bullet scratch" was the best that even the hyperbolic Roark could summon—under his right armpit. He also removed a spent bullet from inside his shirt. This allowed Binion to claim that he had shot Freiden in self-defense. "I'm lucky to be here," he insisted. When reporters pushed him for additional comment, Binion laughed and fed the press boys some country logic. "I couldn't talk when I came into this world," he said, "and I don't believe now is the time for me to do a lot of talking."

The next day, newsboys on street corners held up copies of the *Daily Times Herald* with the screaming front-page headline "One Killed in Gangland War," over a story that began, "Gangland's guns blazed on Allen Street." There followed references to a "hail of lead" and "two barking automatic pistols." The more sober *Morning News* judged that Freiden's death had been accomplished "in the style of Chicago gang executions."

Malone turned himself in the day after the shoot-out, strolling into the detectives' bureau at the Dallas Police Department and casually announcing, "Well, here I am." His arrival had been delayed, he said, because he had been "taking care of Mr. Binion's cattle." Over the next few days, police tried to piece together evidence. It was not an easy task. Many of the witnesses to the shooting—those who were on the nearby sidewalk when the gunfire began—were now claiming to have seen nothing. "Frightened Negroes," the *Morning News* explained.

Freiden was buried the following Tuesday. Before the funeral, his widow gave a brief, sobbing interview to reporters at her East Dallas home. "If talking would bring my husband back to me and my son, I would be more than willing to say anything," she said. "But as it is, what is the use?" Mrs. Freiden acknowledged that her husband had been described as a bookmaker and gambling impresario, yet, "I cannot help but feel the sympathies of the law and the public are in my husband's favor, and surely in mine." To this, one newspaper account added that "both she and her orphaned son" believed Freiden's killers would "surely be punished to the fullest measures of the law."

Perhaps in some other place and time. Binion and Malone were indeed indicted for murder, on the theory that Binion had shot himself in the arm and had planted the gun found next to Freiden. But three months later, District Attorney Robert Hurt quietly announced he had dismissed the case against them for lack of evidence.

Once again, Binion had killed a man and walked free. He was asked many years later if he had given money to the district attorney who dropped the charges. "Well, I don't know," he answered. "Maybe I had."

The Southland Hotel, downtown Dallas, headquarters for Binion's Southland Syndicate.

# 5

# THE THUG CLUB

I ain't never killed a man who didn't deserve it.

—BB

ver since Warren Diamond's death, Binion had designs on the dice business, the white man's side of gambling, where the stakes were higher and the customers richer. To run one of those operations would be a step up in racketeering class.

But Binion was blocked by Diamond's number two man, Ben Whitaker, who had seized control of the operations after Diamond's suicide. Whitaker, a businessman with a portfolio that extended far beyond dice, lived in the penthouse of the Hotel Whitmore. He had a lawn on the roof of the hotel, and invited families of his associates there to watch downtown parades. His partner, Bennie Bickers, stayed one floor below him, so that anyone wanting to kill Whitaker had to get through Bickers first, and nobody ever made it past Bickers, who was considered the best shot in Dallas.

Ultimately, Whitaker decided to divest himself of the gambling business. The word among the wagering class was that he had made too much money in thoroughbreds and the oil patch to mess with dice rooms. A confidential police report took a different view: "Whitaker foresaw the violence in these men, particularly Benny Binion, and therefore wanted no part in it."

Now Binion was poised to move in, but Bill Decker, despite their friendship, blocked it. (The Top O'Hill was in Tarrant County and therefore outside Decker's jurisdiction.) Once Whitaker yielded the turf, Decker insisted that gambler Fred Merrill control the Dallas dice business. Decker trusted the handsome and impeccably tailored Merrill to run a tight operation whose problems didn't spill into the public eye. Merrill didn't go around shooting business rivals on busy streets in broad daylight.

It represented a bitter setback for Binion, but the reproach had only temporary effect. Soon he got his greatest stroke of luck to date, and it came from a source nobody could have predicted: the proper men who controlled government and big business in the city of Dallas.

The year 1936 marked the hundredth anniversary of Texas's independence from Mexico. The state's leaders decided to celebrate its centennial in a characteristic way: big and flashy, with an exposition calculated to draw the attention, if not the envy, of the world. First they had to decide where to hold it.

The Texas legislature established a commission to award the franchise to the proper city. San Antonio made a bid; with the Alamo, it was to many a logical choice. Houston also showed strong interest, and could point to its status as the birthplace of the Texas republic, because that was where Sam Houston's revolutionaries defeated the Mexican army of General Santa Anna. And then there was Dallas, which offered no plausible historic reason to host the centennial. It had been the site of no major battles or other momentous events. But Dallas had cash, lots of it, thanks to a fund-raising campaign by R. L. Thornton, president of the Mercantile National Bank and future mayor. By pledging to spend far more than its competitors, Dallas bought the centennial.

At Fair Park, the city built a sprawling and grand exposition complex at a cost of $25 million, and it served as an instant factory of bluster. One booster promised "a world's exposition Texanic in proportions and Texanic in its revealments." Thornton, a plainspoken man born of the cotton patch, expressed an even grander assessment in fewer words. "The greatest world fair in history," he proclaimed.

The self-consciously earnest city of Dallas planned to draw crowds with an epic pageant called the Cavalcade of Texas, a sanitized historical play, heavy on the Lone Star romance. For those whose appetite for adventure remained yet unsated, the Dallas centennial featured a Hall of Religion, a Hall of Natural History, and a Hall of Horticulture. Also the Centennial Frog Farm, as well as the venue where little people lived and performed, known as Midget Village. Across the way, in the Cotton Bowl stadium, a female conjoined twin was married in front of 4,500 people, the first such nuptials in Texas history. Alas, the bride, who performed a nightclub act with her sister, filed for an annulment seven weeks later.

Frog farms and conjoined twins aside, the centennial developed a problem: it was considered a bit stuffy. Thirty-five miles west of Dallas, the rival civic leaders of Fort Worth plotted to steal the Dallas centennial's thunder, and they did it by supplementing historical pageants with some real fun. Broadway showman Billy Rose signed on to produce their Frontier Centennial Exposition. Among its spectacles was Sally Rand's Nude Ranch, which boasted an assortment of lovely cowgirls who wore hats but no shirts. Finally, something really was Texanic in its revealments. Organizers commissioned highway billboards that said "Go to Dallas for Education, Come to Fort Worth for Entertainment." The strategy seemed to work. Traffic engineers determined that more cars were in fact heading to Fort Worth than to Dallas.

When they saw that boredom was costing them money, Dallas leaders convened an off-the-record emergency meeting of the city council. Dr. J. W. Bass, the city's health director, said he was told, "We've got to open up the town. Mr. Thornton is in a hole for a lot of money and going in deeper all the time." Some of them may have regretted that they quashed early plans for a Centennial Nudist Colony.

So a desperate Dallas—despite its longing to be admired as an ascendant and sophisticated metropolis—turned to a couple of old favorites to salvage its expensive exposition: painted ladies and games of chance. The health department issued 2,400 permits to prostitutes, and police were instructed to "keep the whores as safe as possible."

And gambling, the leaders decided, would now be allowed as well. It was even permitted on the grounds of the centennial. This, a police report said, "brought in quite a substantial sum of money."

With that, the city gave Binion everything he could have wanted. Gambling was not merely tolerated, it was practically legal. No longer could police decide whom they would allow to operate. The business had been deregulated. "They just let the town go wide open," Binion said. At the age of thirty-two, with big plans and a killer's reputation, he stood on the brink of an empire.

The Southland Hotel, 1200 Main Street at Murphy in downtown Dallas, had two hundred rooms, of which seventy were air-conditioned. Rates started at $1.50 a night. When it opened in 1907, it was billed as the second hotel in the world to have rooms with "running ice water." That same year an East Texas lawman walked into the lobby, pulled his pistol, and shot out every light, just because he felt like it. By 1937 the Southland couldn't be called the best hotel in Dallas—the Adolphus held that title—but it served as suitable enough lodging for traveling salesmen and the like. Rising eight architecturally uninspiring stories, the boxy Southland had a brown-brick exterior and a lattice of fire escapes clinging to its front. Off the lobby were a coffee shop, a barbershop, and a drugstore. County deed records didn't reflect it, but police suspected that New Orleans racketeer Carlos Marcello secretly owned the building via the mobbed-up Maceo family of Galveston. The Southland's bellhops could get you a hooker if you wanted, or some dope, and there was always a dice game going. Benny Binion's dice game.

Binion wasted no time in setting up operations in the Southland once the city of Dallas ceased enforcing gambling laws. He located many of his dice rooms in downtown hotels, because downtown Dallas was a thriving, crowded place, day and night.

Movie theaters lined Elm Street: the Rialto, the Capitol, the Majestic, the Melba, and more. Every block had a greasy spoon or two, and taverns were once again—with the repeal of Prohibition—open and busy.

A gambler en route to the Southland dice room would stroll down Main Street, past the Ideal Laundry, the Oriental Café, and a fedora store called the Hatitorium, and enter through the hotel's glass doors. He would cross the lobby, maybe pausing at the cigarette stand for a pack of Old Golds—"Not a Cough in a Carload"—and a newspaper, and would climb stairs to the mezzanine. At room 226 he pressed a button next to a door marked Private. One of Binion's men slid open a speakeasy-style vent, eyed the potential entrant, and decided whether he would be allowed inside. The room was low-ceilinged and rectangular, thick with cigarette smoke. No bands played, and no Texas Rockets danced. On a normal night the place filled with perhaps fifty men in suits drinking, laughing, and throwing dice. They played with chips stamped with Binion's new trademark, a horseshoe logo. "We'd just have a big suite of rooms, have the tables in there, have a bar," said Binion, who kept an office in a side room. "We'd send out to different restaurants and get the food. Everybody knew about it."

Binion's expanding operation quickly became known as the Southland Syndicate. In addition to the Southland Hotel, he and his partners operated or controlled gambling at the Bluebonnet Hotel, the Maurice Hotel, and at least ten other spots in town. The Savoy, the Troxy, the Birdwell, and the Jefferson—all were his. Scattered across the city were dozens of others that he didn't own but that paid him a 25 percent rake, the price of peace.

Binion and Harry Urban also ran a slot machine company that serviced each of the gambling parlors. Bookies operated out of many of these same hotels, and Binion controlled them too. One of them was Schuyler Marshall Jr., and like a lot of Binion's associates, he had a past. A former sheriff of Dallas County, Marshall took up a criminal career upon leaving office. After kidnapping, robbery, and bank burglary charges against him were dropped, he decided to back away from the more violent felonies.

Many of Binion's managers were veterans of his bootlegging network, or were ex-cowboys too old and busted up to compete in rodeos anymore. The Mecca Hotel, 1001 Main Street, presented a typical setup. The Southland Syndicate owned the games, which were managed by an old liquor business crony of Binion's named Dewey Dorough. An ex-con, Dorough made his bones in 1936 when he engaged in a Dodge City–style, late-night shoot-out on a downtown Dallas corner with Ted Meyer, reputed to be a former Chicago bodyguard for Al Capone. Both men, attempting to settle a lingering dice game dispute, pulled handguns and blazed away at each other on the sidewalk. Meyer's aim was hampered by his drunkenness, and Dorough felled him with a shot to the chest.

In neighboring Fort Worth, Binion recruited George Wilderspin, a rodeo rider he had known since his horse-trading days. Wilderspin ran the East Side Club in partnership with Binion. The East Side functioned as a full-service operation; also on the grounds were a barbershop, a tourist court, a gas station, and a drugstore. Wilderspin brought along a companion from the rodeo circuit to run some of their smaller Tarrant County enterprises, a former trick rider named Louis Tindall, the sort of gent who would pistol-whip his own mother-in-law, then break her arm by beating her with a Bible.

Binion believed in the situational loyalty of these men, and trusted them to take the necessary action—without having to call the law—when matters turned rough. Such was the case when, during a game at the Southland, some of Binion's cronies found themselves in an argument with a player named Eddie Gilliland. One of them hit Gilliland in the throat, killing him on the spot. Then the crew loaded the body into a car, took it to the next county, and dumped it on the side of the road. Nobody talked about it, and few cared. "There will be," an internal police report noted, "no solution to this murder."

Some of the same high-rolling customers who frequented Top O'Hill became regulars at Binion's downtown Dallas games as well. Howard Hughes, though one of the richest men in America, kept his losses at the table relatively small. "He wasn't a high player," Binion remembered. "I didn't pay no attention to him . . . I know he never lost $10,000. Might have lost $7,500 some time. It didn't mean nothing to him." H. L. Hunt, then amassing his fortune in the East Texas oil fields, had an office within walking distance of the Southland, and would wander over at the end of the day. "When he wasn't tired, he'd probably stay there and shoot craps all night. Daylight come and he'd go home," Binion said. Actor Don Ameche—he played Alexander Graham Bell in the 1939 biographical movie—was a repeat client. "He shot the craps when he come to Dallas," Binion said. "A crap-shooting son of a bitch, he was." Local politicians showed up too. "They'd come in them places. They didn't give a shit much." At least one Dallas County district attorney was among the regulars, personally escorted to the tables by Binion.

Not all of Binion's customers were powerful officials or famous millionaires. Many came from a healthy subculture of professional gamblers. Dallas was boiling with them, their pockets stuffed with rolls of cash when they were winning, their heads full of schemes when they weren't. Some of them plotted a dual income stream: either win money at the tables or steal it in a holdup on the street, often robbing other gamblers. When not serving prison time, these people were Binion's bread and butter. One man who worked for Binion on and off for years said his boss made it a point to exclude working stiffs—naive wagering amateurs looking for that one big score—from his games. "Benny didn't want truck drivers coming up there and losing all their family's money," he said.

The practice was part empathy—Binion never forgot the hard times of his youth—and part image control. He didn't wish to be seen as someone running a fleece joint. Binion was, after all, a respectable businessman who counted among his friends the heads of some of the city's biggest banks. "There was a group of bankers there, they were the most liberal, smartest bankers in the world," he recalled. "There was never a smarter set of guys than them. They kept Dallas on top." And many of them were more than happy to quietly accept Binion's gambling proceeds in deposits. Millions of his dollars went into the Hillcrest State Bank, one of Dallas's premier financial institutions.

The bankers also served as launderers for Binion's political payoffs. Binion gave them money and they passed it to politicians, a law enforcement report said. "It is believed that all of the banks operating in the city lend them [Binion and associates] their silent support."

For a game that involves no more than rolling a pair of dice, and whose basic object is to guess whether a certain number will come up before a seven is rolled, craps is wrapped in layers of complexity. It can be baffling to the novice, maddening to the journeyman, and a bankroll destroyer even to the experts. The player who throws the dice and the gamblers betting on his roll enjoy dozens of possible bets with varying odds. Complexity aside, craps operations don't require much in the way of capital investment—felt tables, chips, and dice—or labor costs. The average house edge on each roll runs anywhere from less than 1 percent to more than 16 percent, depending on the type of bet. With such math on his side, with the breadth of his operation, and with his ancillary commercial activities, tens of thousands of dollars a week flowed into Binion's pocket. "Business was *real* good," he remembered.

In later and more quiescent years Binion liked to depict the prime days of Dallas gambling as something that might have been designed by Disney and operated by Quakers. "We all got along good together," he said of his rivals. That was true to a point; Binion had no problem getting along with dead people. As for the living, Binion showed little patience with those he believed were taking money out of his pocket.

He still had Ivy Miller helping him, along with Earl Dalton, a dice game deputy who had been around for years. Those two, an internal police report said, "played an important part in holding Binion down," which was necessary because he was "the type that wanted to kill all opposition 'so they won't bother us any more.'"

To supplement Dalton and Miller, Binion assembled a talented collection of toughs to guard his games, keep rivals under control, and mete out strategic homicides. Jim Clyde Thomas rode a reputation as a professional hit man who had murdered a West Texas doctor and his wife; the woman was beaten to death, the man shot through both eyes. Johnny "Brazil" Grisaffi was a gambler and gunman who also ran the café at the Bluebonnet Hotel. When police pulled his phone records, they found numerous long-distance calls to mobster Carlos Marcello's brother in New Orleans. Grisaffi explained that he was merely buying fish for his restaurant.

Topping the list of Binion's enforcers was Hollis DeLois Green, known as Lois. The son of a prostitute, he grew up in a Dallas brothel and began breaking the law—stealing bicycles and cars—before his teens. After a stretch in a Texas prison for auto theft, Green sought opportunity in New York City, where he emerged as a suspect in the death of a police officer. He was not convicted of that, but did time in jail there for vagrancy. It seasoned the young man, and when he returned to Dallas, Green no longer appeared the callow petty thief. Now he was dashing, in an unlettered career-criminal sort of way, and was newly convinced of the value of a diversified criminal organization. From a West Dallas hangout called the Trap, Green dispatched a gang that, by some estimates, operated in dozens of states.

Lois Green's Boys, the police called them, or the Forty Thieves, and they stole just about anything—cash, government bonds, even a load of cigars from a freight-train boxcar. "They proudly boasted that they could blow any safe in the country in thirty minutes with a sledge hammer, a drill pin and a chunk of nitroglycerine grease," a newspaper account explained, adding that grand theft was merely one division of Green's company. "They would take over prostitution in many towns of the state. They would control the flow of narcotics. They would begin large-scale safe-cracking operations all over the country. They would be killers-for-hire."

Despite his profitable network, Green personally stayed in the action, a player-coach of felonies. Home invasions were a specialty; he liked to kick in the door, tie up the terrified residents at gunpoint, and make off with the goods. His usual plunder was gold and diamond jewelry, with a pistol-whipping sometimes thrown in at the conclusion of the evening. "I'll show you how tough this Green thinks he is," a Dallas sheriff once said. "He gets on the front of the street car track, and the street car man rings his bell for him to get off . . . So Lois stopped his car right on the track, got out, pulled his gun out, and went and broke the window and said, 'If you ring that bell again, I'll blow your head off.'"

The blond, nicely tailored Green cut a hard-to-miss figure around town. He wore two-tone shoes and traveled stylishly in a late-model black Cadillac equipped with a radiotelephone, which he used to call his bail bondsman and lawyer whenever arrest appeared imminent. This ensured that his bond would be posted, or a writ filed, by the time Green reached the jailhouse. He typically spent only a few minutes behind bars. When he wasn't robbing or pimping, he enjoyed relaxing like any other local man of commerce, by playing golf.

One of the Green gang's biggest heists was a load of narcotics from a Fort Worth pharmaceutical warehouse, a job pulled by two of his henchmen, J. B. "Red" Cavanaugh and Ray Sellers. A safecracker and car thief, Sellers had recently divorced Clyde Barrow's rather fetching sister, Marie, who was on parole for beating a woman with a table leg. He was a fugitive who had escaped only weeks before from an Oklahoma penitentiary during a prison rodeo. In the warehouse caper, he and Cavanaugh stole boxes of narcotics that, with war shortages, had a street value of $250,000. Green sold some of the drugs, but he used part of the stash for his stable of prostitutes.

For these and other jobs, Binion functioned as a Stetson-crowned godfather—overseeing the action from a safe remove, sanctioning the players, and most important, extracting his percentage of the proceeds. And he was always looking to up the take. Binion didn't like the idea of splitting profits from the drug warehouse robbery with half-wit bit players like Sellers and Cavanaugh. He conveyed these misgivings to Green and Grisaffi, who took the two robbers for a ride. Sellers was next seen staggering near Northwest Highway, mortally shot in the chest. More than six years after that, a skeleton believed to be that of Cavanaugh was found in a ravine twenty miles west of Dallas, with a bullet hole in its skull.

Having long passed the point where he had to do his killing personally, Binion still occasionally found it necessary to deliver detailed instructions. "Shoot the s.o.b. in the guts and bury him alive," Binion told Green regarding one unfortunate. "It will be a tonic to any of the others who want to be hijackers." The target of this particular order was one Otto Freyer, an ex-con shortsighted enough to rob Binion's craps games. With Grisaffi as backup, Green did as told, shooting Freyer in the stomach with a shotgun next to a fresh grave. Then he rolled Freyer into the hole and, as the wounded man begged for mercy, covered him with dirt and quicklime.

All the surviving parties benefited. "Green and Grisaffi were reportedly loaned a considerable amount of money by Binion to expand their operations in the narcotics racket," an internal police memo said. And the "tonic," as described by Binion, had its intended effect. Robberies of his dice games dropped to none.

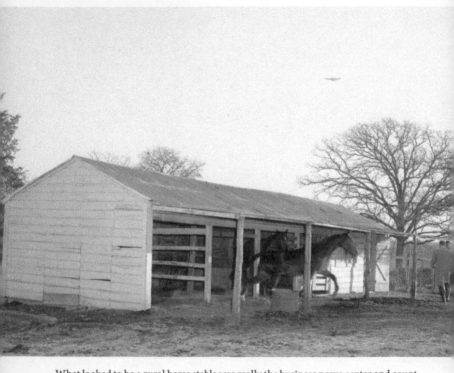

What looked to be a rural horse stable was really the business nerve center and counting-house of Binion's operations.

# 6

# SHOOT-OUTS AND PAYOFFS

You had to have political help in them days.

—BB

There were plenty of hidden homicides—private rubouts that arose from feuds, thefts, turf battles, and disputes over women. Bodies turned up in fields outside town, in the muck of the Trinity River bottoms, or in the trunks of abandoned cars. As long as the gamblers were killing only each other and the general public wasn't endangered—especially if the news didn't make the front page—authorities responded with little more than an official shrug. They couldn't do that, though, if the hoods had a shoot-out on a downtown street in midmorning. When the bullets struck the entrance of a busy ice cream parlor, and when a child was wounded, attention had to be paid. This was something Binion and Ivy Miller failed to grasp as they laid plans to take care of Sam Murray.

Dallas had grown every year—its metropolitan-area population in 1940 was about 350,000—but for the gamblers it remained a small town. An FBI report on "general crime conditions" in Dallas remarked upon this village-like atmosphere for gangsters: "In view of Dallas being a relatively small city, naturally the criminal element are acquainted with each other."

So everyone in the circle of sportsmen knew that Murray would kill some-one if he felt like it.

Murray already had a police record as a pimp and a bootlegger, and he had been charged but not convicted in 1933 for the shotgun death of a rival whiskey man at a liquor drop masquerading as a sandwich stand near Bachman Lake. Binion was a witness at the trial of Murray's accomplice. Identifying himself as a horse dealer, he helpfully testified that the lunch counter was "not a nice place." That same year, Murray spent several months in the federal prison at Leavenworth for bootlegging, and later did another stretch for violating his parole. After his release, Murray built a Dallas gambling enterprise of his own, gaining confidence all along, and eventu-ally muscling in on some of Binion's operations. Business was good enough that he had bought a ranch and owned two hundred polo ponies. In his ascendance, Murray at thirty-four was cocky and reckless, "a colorful and near-legendary figure in the annals of the local gambling and sporting fra-ternity," as one reporter described him. He had been bragging that he would kill both Binion and Miller if they did not stay out of his way.

On a warm, sunny June morning in 1940, Murray decided to make a trip to downtown Dallas. He had banking business, and his wife, Sue, wanted to do some shopping. Normally, he traveled with his bodyguard, a crimi-nally ambitious young man named Herbert Noble. But on this day, he came without protection, save for the snub-nosed .38-caliber revolver in the breast pocket of his coat.

His wife dropped him on Commerce Street, and Murray went into the Dallas National Bank. Around 10:30 a.m. he walked out of the bank's ornate lobby, stepped onto the sidewalk, and turned toward a nearby liquor store. Commerce Street was thick with cars and trucks, horns honking. Dozens of pedestrians moved along the sidewalk, and Cabell's Ice Cream and Dairy Shop had a steady stream of customers.

The roly-poly Murray was only a few steps from the bank's door when he found himself face to porcine face with a large man wearing a blue blazer, slacks, and a crisply knotted tie. It was Ivy Miller, ever the well-dressed assassin—a man, in a newspaper's description, who "had a part in maintaining some of the swankiest air-conditioned gaming rooms in

Dallas." On Miller's bulbous head rested a stylish straw boater, and in his right hand he held a .38-caliber automatic pistol.

Without a word, Miller began shooting, the automatic firing so rapidly that some witnesses thought they heard a machine gun. Pedestrians shouted and scattered. Most of the shots hit Murray, but one went wild and struck a sixteen-year-old boy in the leg, shattering his femur. The boy staggered to the curb and fell into the street between two parked cars. As Murray crumpled, he managed to pull his gun and get off one shot. It ricocheted off the marble doorframe of the ice cream shop.

Murray had been hit at least six times—four in the midsection, one in the back, one in the leg. As the wounded man lay dying on the sidewalk, Miller fled into the bank. A plainclothes police officer, gun drawn, pursued him into the lobby and shouted, "Don't move or I'll shoot." Miller turned, hesitated, then said, "I'm ready. I'm not going anywhere."

The officer cuffed Miller, escorted him from the bank, and put him in a patrol car. On the six-block ride to the police station Miller sat in the backseat, blinking hard but saying little more than "Sam threatened me and my family." Later that day Miller's lawyer, Maury Hughes, told reporters that—contrary to their wild speculations—this shoot-out did not mean a gangsters' war had erupted. The two men, Hughes explained, simply "had differences regarding livestock."

Blazing headlines followed, pushing the war news in Europe to the bottom of the front page for a day. The *Daily Times Herald* ran a large photograph of the prostrate Murray being treated by an ambulance attendant dressed all in white, hat to shoes, like the Good Humor man. Another photo showed hundreds of curiosity seekers thronging the scene. "Crowds Swarm Around Victims After Downtown Killing," the headline said. The pool of Murray's blood, covering several feet of sidewalk, drew spectators all day long. "Women and men alike gazed without show of emotion at this blood," the *Times Herald* reported, "as it thickened and darkened in the hot sun."

Authorities moved swiftly to manufacture concern. By noon the next day, witnesses to the shooting were brought before a county grand jury, which was also allowed to see Murray's bloody clothes. A quick murder indictment followed. From politicians came cries of outrage and vows of crackdowns. Yet Binion and his friends quietly continued their gambling operations uninterrupted—now with the comfort of knowing another competitor had been dispatched.

Even more than before, the money flowed. Operators of the Southland Syndicate believed they had little reason to worry, and events soon confirmed that. Six months after Murray's death, District Attorney Andrew Patton—on the last day of his term in office and with no fanfare—announced that he was dropping all charges against Miller. The reason for the dismissal, the DA explained, was lack of evidence. This for a shooting that had been witnessed by dozens of people, "in broad daylight in the heart of the city," the *Morning News* noted, "where witnesses were so plentiful they almost were breathing on the necks of the principals." As for the accidental wounding of the teenager, that matter was cleared with a $750 cash payment from Miller to the boy's family.

The Texas Centennial celebration had come and gone, but the city still failed to enforce gambling laws, as long as the proper bribes were paid. Authorities did conduct the occasional show raid. Binion described one of them: "Well, one time, I had a crap game and the sheriff and two or three deputies came and raided us. And there was eighteen or nineteen people in there, and me." But then the sheriff received a report of a murder elsewhere, and had to leave. He told Binion to take all the gamblers to his office. "So we all got in the cars, and everybody went down there," Binion recalled. "And when he [the sheriff] came in, he said, 'Well, you all got here . . . I'm going to turn you loose.'"

From time to time, an isolated city official expressed public hope that authorities would go back to enforcing the law, and these people were generally ignored. As Dallas city manager V. R. Smitham lamented, the enforcers were also customers. "The problem would be simple if only hoodlums participated," Smitham said. "But every time we make a raid on a dice game we find friends." At least as important was the matter of municipal receipts: Dallas couldn't afford to shut the dice and policy rooms down. The city government had become addicted to gambling.

This could be seen in a ritual repeated dozens of times over the course of a typical month. On one such occasion, a muggy night in August, dozens of black men and women packed a second-floor dance hall at 3115 State

Street in Freedman's Town. There was smoke and sweat, laughter and swearing, under bare lightbulbs as gamblers pressed toward the front of the room, bills clutched in their hands, to place bets on a policy wheel. Winning numbers were chalked on a blackboard behind the wheel.

From one of the windows, a lookout surveyed State Street. He watched a black Ford pull to the curb beneath a streetlight. After a moment two men got out. One was pudgy, with a hawk nose and a hat a couple of sizes too small. The other was tall and thin. Anybody who so much as glanced at them could see they were plainclothes Dallas police. And any doubt about that was removed when a newspaper photographer, loaded down with cameras, was spotted trailing behind them.

The lookout signaled someone next to the policy wheel, and all gambling came to a sudden halt. Word flashed through the crowd that a raid was coming, and gamblers dropped their tickets on the floor and scattered. Some jumped out second-floor windows. Others took the stairs down and poured onto the sidewalk.

The two cops stood and watched it all unfold before they crossed the street and entered the front door in no particular hurry. Up the stairs they went on heavy feet, and into the ballroom. Three white men waited for them there, the same as always.

The police arrested the trio and took them downtown to be charged with misdemeanors. One of the brass held a small post-bust press conference, and described the arrested men as "small fry" in the employ of Benny Binion. The raid was presented as proof that the police had finally decided to crack down—even if they didn't net the big man—on the operations of the Southland Syndicate.

Within an hour or so, a lawyer also working for Binion arrived to post bond for the three men. They walked free, and the policy game was back in business by the next day. It was simply another episode in an elaborate and regular charade. Dice games were treated the same way: the bonds would be forfeited, the money absorbed by the city and county, the paperwork lost, and the games quickly resumed.

For Binion, it was literally the price of doing business, a de facto tax on gambling. "They had a real good city administration," Binion said. "So they just come in and raid us, and wouldn't tear up nothing, or do nothing, and we'd pay big fines. And I think we paid something like, oh, $600,000 a year for fines, for a few years there." It was all worked out in advance as an unofficially budgeted supplement for a municipality that had come up a bit short. "The town got in a bad financial condition," he said. "We made a deal to pay so many fines a week, so much a week."

Binion considered it his duty. And, as usual, he depicted the matter as a bit of innocent circumstance. "There wasn't no graft," he insisted. "We helped the city out."

This setup was hardly secret. An FBI Crime Survey from the time noted, "All gambling establishments, horse books and policy establishments pay a weekly fine to the city of Dallas." After many of the raids, various politicians kept the theater going with vows to clean up the festering city. "I want everything closed down," police chief J. M. Welch declared after officers turned out the lights on Binion's Southland Hotel casino. Then Ivy Miller paid a $50 fine, and the dice were rolling again within hours.

Dallas's reputation as a sin haven reached the state capitol in Austin, where the director of the state Department of Public Safety ordered a crackdown. It didn't go well. "The Texas Rangers made approximately one raid on a gambling establishment and thereafter made no more raids," the FBI noted. That one raid had been conducted by showboating Ranger Manuel "Lone Wolf" Gonzaullas, who sometimes carried gold-plated revolvers, but who was perhaps not used to dealing with a city where the police and sheriff's departments were riddled with paid informants. By the time Gonzaullas arrived at the dice den he planned on raiding, the gamblers and all their equipment were gone, although a phone remained. When it rang, Gonzaullas answered. The caller said, "They're on their way right now." The Ranger responded, "We're already here."

Only one government entity executed any sort of effective measures against the Binion syndicate: the U.S. military. The army's Eighth Service Command headquarters was directly across the street from the Southland Hotel. Officers noted the large number of prostitutes coming and going from the place, and the resultant mini-epidemic of gonorrhea among their soldiers. After a sting operation, in which a Southland bellhop readily procured a woman for a plainclothes military policeman, the command declared the hotel off-limits to its personnel.

Other local officials remained content to look the other way. Not only was the city cleaning up on fines, but the politicians collected nice side incomes from bribes. "Gambling is presently operated in Dallas on such a large scale that the small fines do not appear to balance the tremendous scale of gambling," the local FBI office said in a report to headquarters. "Therefore, there could be and possibly is some large pay-off to high officials in the political administration of the city of Dallas." The bureau believed that Binion's lawyer, Maury Hughes, "handles all the pay-offs and collections."

Everybody was making money, the perfect arrangement for all concerned.

The next racketeer to face violent dispatch in public was Raymond James Loudermilk, a longtime lieutenant in Binion's operations who had strayed. In the Southland Syndicate, Loudermilk emerged as a valued enforcer and organizer, a man prized for both muscle and brains. His specialty was keeping the numbers runners in line, the games under control, and the money secure, and he rose as high in the syndicate as number three behind Binion and Harry Urban.

But Loudermilk began to make plans for games of his own. This did not please Binion, which in turn infuriated Loudermilk. One police report offered an additional reason for friction: "Loudermilk had developed an antagonism for Binion and felt he could operate with Binion's permission inasmuch as Binion and Loudermilk's wife were known to be cohabiting together."

However faulty the logic of that and questionable the truth—Binion generally spent far more time riding horses than chasing women—Loudermilk found himself a new wife and a new frontier. He married Sam Murray's widow, Sue, and the two left for a trip to California. When they returned to Dallas, they brought with them a scheme to set up extensive policy game operations of their own. Binion initially took the news with annoyed acceptance. What he didn't know was that Loudermilk had found a financial backer in Sam Murray's absent bodyguard, Herbert Noble. In the nearly three years since Ivy Miller ambushed Murray on Commerce Street, Noble had moved into the void left by his late employer and entered the dice-room business himself, with some success. He still had to pay 25 percent of his take to Binion, but with an eye to expansion, he bankrolled Loudermilk. When Binion learned of this, his displeasure curdled to rage. And rage within Binion usually resulted in someone shooting someone else.

On March 19, 1943, Loudermilk sat in his car on South Ervay Street, outside the Ambassador Hotel, a tired six-story rooming house south of downtown Dallas. At thirty-six, Loudermilk was not enjoying the best of times. Policy game revenues had apparently not met expectations, so he had taken a job at an aviation plant. The blissful life he once enjoyed with Sam Murray's widow had soured, probably because he had threatened to kill her. Earlier that month she had sued Loudermilk for divorce. And now, on this cool spring evening, he had to have a talk with a punk like Bob Minyard.

About 9:00 p.m., young Minyard walked through the lobby of the Ambassador—over the worn rug, past threadbare couches, and out the front doors to Ervay Street—and into the night. In the pocket of his cheap suit was a .45 pistol. Minyard, twenty-nine, lived in a furnished room at the Ambassador. For several years he had been a bit player in Binion's syndicate, an errand boy and game-room scut worker. Even his police record displayed a short list of unimpressive misdemeanors: vagrancy and disturbing the peace. But now his moment had arrived. He gripped his gun and approached Loudermilk's car.

On an upper floor of the Ambassador, from a room facing the street, an elderly woman heard shots. Mrs. M. R. Gelfan leaned out her open window and saw a man exit Loudermilk's car, step into another car that pulled alongside, and leave. Another resident of the neighborhood, out for an evening stroll half a block away, also heard gunfire. He ran to the immobile car and found a man slumped behind the steering wheel, dead. It was Loudermilk, who had been shot seven times in the chest and stomach.

Within an hour, Minyard arrived at the courthouse by taxi and surrendered to the outlaws' lawman of choice, Decker. He told the deputy sheriff only that he and Loudermilk had been "having a little trouble" and, "I shot him a few minutes ago." The next morning, while Loudermilk was being pumped full of embalming fluid at the O'Neal Funeral Home,

Minyard walked free on $10,000 bond. The high-dollar lawyer for Binion and Miller, Maury Hughes, had secured his release.

Life began to improve in quick order for Minyard. He faced no more rooming-house penury. Soon he and his wife moved into a two-story brick home—"expensively furnished," according to the *Morning News*—in Lakewood, a fine Dallas neighborhood of pricey residences and wide, tree-lined streets. Nor did Minyard remain stuck on the Southland Syndicate's lower rungs. Not long after Loudermilk's death, police considered Minyard to be Binion's right-hand man.

He led a charmed life in the county's legal system too, despite his indictment for murder. "The grand jury lost no time in indicting Minyard," District Attorney Dean Gauldin announced within two weeks of the shooting, "and we will not lose any in bringing him to trial." Gauldin sensed that citizens had tired of open-air gangland assassinations, and he sought to assure voters that the county's chief prosecutor held steadfast and vigilant. But the DA was also a friend of Binion's, and such friendships superseded hasty public posturing. The case languished, and nearly three years after Loudermilk's death, Minyard still had not faced his day in court.

The failure to prosecute his henchmen was welcome if not unexpected news for Binion. Yet the killing of Sam Murray and Loudermilk had invisible ripples. In the city at large, feelings of resentment and fear had been aroused. But there were games to be run and money to be grabbed, so no one in Binion's crowd gave much thought to these stirrings. To the gangsters, it was nothing more than smoke on the wind.

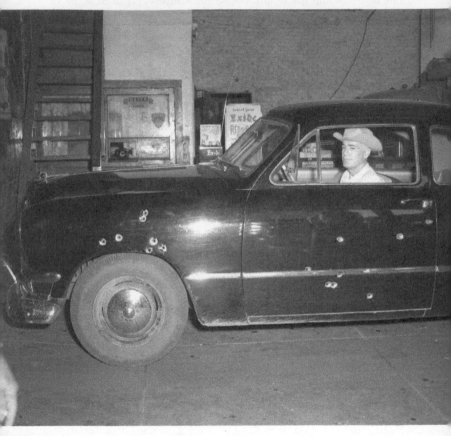

Binion nemesis Herbert Noble, after would-be killers missed him but shot up his car.

# 7

# THE MOB WAR IS JOINED

I wasn't to be fucked with. But I used to get a kick out of it.

—BB

he mid-1940s were good times for the Cowboy, with his business vibrant and his competitors dead. "Binion's interests," an FBI report later observed, "had complete control of all rackets in the Dallas area during the war years." Many of the police were his friends. Those who weren't he felt free to taunt, especially one assistant chief who had fallen from official favor and drew late-night duty at the Dallas Zoo. "Used to call him up and hoorah him 'cause he couldn't catch nobody," Binion said. "I'd call him up about four o'clock in the morning and I said, 'Monkeys go to bed yet?'"

Binion had no worry about any departmental backlash for such mockery. A prominent California criminologist hired by the city found in 1944 that the gambling business had exercised an "evil influence" over the Dallas police for many years, and that any attempts to erase it would be in vain. He proposed instead that vice enforcement be taken away entirely from the police and turned over to an independent and presumed incorruptible "Morals Chief," who would answer only to the city manager. The suggestion was ignored.

Dallas enjoyed prosperity during World War II, benefiting mightily from defense plants and nearby military training bases, and it mirrored the nation's economic upturn when the war ended. With money flowing, Binion's dice operations continued to thrive, and he was developing a reputation that extended beyond the state's borders. "A lot of people from other parts of the country, professional gamblers and bookmakers, liked to come down there," son Ted Binion told an interviewer decades later. "They came because Dad would run a high [betting] limit, and also because he was known to run honest games."

Binion also remained the undisputed king of the Dallas policy games, with an estimated 80 percent of the business countywide. He cleared hundreds of thousands of dollars a year from policy alone, and paid income taxes on a mere fraction of that. That omission caused Binion no concern, because he and his partners retained a competent and crooked accountant to cover their tracks.

The Binion syndicate controlled the local horse-racing wire too, which meant all turf betting operations in North Texas owed a piece of the action to the Southland group. And Binion still pulled his hefty percentage out of the glamorous—and impervious—Top O'Hill, which had attracted the attention of mobsters nationwide. Benjamin "Bugsy" Siegel was believed to have gone there and taken notes on how to run a swank gambling resort. Noted New York racketeer Waxey Gordon sent a team of advance goons to case Top O'Hill for a robbery. Their conclusion: such a raid was doomed to failure because the casino was too heavily fortified.

As his local operations flourished, Binion spread out. He bought property in Louisiana and Mississippi—land worth more than $1 million, by one law enforcement estimate. Another big purchase was a horse and cattle ranch in eastern Montana. He also began buying or forcing his way into far-flung criminal enterprises. He owned, or was about to own, a piece of an opulent gambling house in the booming, if gritty, West Texas oil town of Odessa. Police reports described the casino as palatial, and it was lucrative enough that Southern California mobster Mickey Cohen showed an interest. Binion also had a sizable percentage in the Log Cabin Club in Jackson Hole, Wyoming.

Binion and Teddy Jane presided over a full household of five children.

Their second daughter, Brenda, was born in 1941, and a second son, Ted, followed in 1942. Their third daughter, Becky, was born in 1944. All of them lived on a Northwest Highway spread big enough for half a dozen horses, including some Shetland ponies. Binion's ailing father, Lonnie Lee, slept in a cottage out back. Though most of the family was happy there, Teddy Jane had visions of a more stylish setting: she sat for hours chain-smoking and sketching elaborate plans for a house on seven acres the Binions owned along Turtle Creek, where many of the city's business elite lived.

Binion often made it home for the family dinner at 6:00 p.m. "He didn't work very hard," daughter Brenda recalled. The family employed a full-time cook who made his favorites, which generally meant anything with lard and salt pork. No longer the lean, hustling sharpie he had been when he first arrived in town, Binion had swelled and softened into a corpulent crime boss. He weighed well over two hundred pounds and cruised his holdings in a Cadillac driven by his chauffeur, a large man known as Gold Dollar, whom the *Morning News* referred to simply as "an enormous Negro." Gold Dollar's true name was Perry Rose, and he was an affable cowboy imported by Binion from New Mexico. He often chauffeured Binion to the Montana ranch, and was believed to be the first African American ever to set foot in the nearby town of Jordan.

For a generally disheveled man, Binion paid surprising attention to his clothes. He had his cowboy boots custom-made by Willie Lusk at Lusk's store in Lubbock, which Binion had helped finance by pulling a roll of hundreds from his pocket one day and peeling off $2,500, which he handed to Lusk with, "Pay me back when you can." His western suits came from a personal tailor on Elm Street in Dallas, although Binion's increasing girth and the .45-caliber handgun he carried in his pocket tended to mar the drape.

It can't be said that Binion ignored his Dallas syndicate, but he delegated much of its management to Ivy Miller, Harry Urban, and others. He preferred instead to spend weeks at a time in Montana, where he rode, bought, and sold horses. Now in his early forties, Binion had made himself into a wealthy ranchman who could reenact the treasured parts of his childhood on horseback. Still, it was a business. "He wouldn't put radios in the ranch trucks," daughter Brenda recalled. "He said, 'You're supposed to be thinking. You're not supposed to be listening to that garbage.'" Despite that, she remembered a happy, dedicated father. The only times he ever really got angry with his children, Brenda said, was if he believed they were mistreating a horse.

All in all, life could hardly have been better for Binion. There was, however, the nagging problem of Herbert Noble.

Like many others in the North Texas gangland, Noble had crawled out of the slums of West Dallas, but he emerged a bit more refined than most. He had some schooling, and as an adult he earned a pilot's license. Unlike Binion, who was practically born to the life, Noble embraced gambling as a simple necessity. He had tried to make a living as a truck driver, but the Depression threw him out of work. "I turned to gambling," he explained. "You had to do something to get enough to eat." His only criminal conviction on record was for auto theft in 1932, for which he received a two-year suspended sentence.

Noble had an entrepreneurial gift and a determination to excel not found in the ordinary run of car thieves. Soon he was operating his own dice games. By the mid-1940s, he was considered by police and gangsters alike to be one of the aristocrats of the local criminal class, not least because his cousin ran the vice squad. Noble's deportment contributed too. He was gentlemanly when the situation called for it, and he knew how to dress. At his ranch in Denton County, he could be found carrying a rifle in one hand and a Bible in the other. He took photographs as a hobby, and traveled to exotic climes: South America was a favorite. Relative to others in his line of work, Noble—with his groomed hair and cleft chin—had the patrician look of a worldly professional.

For all his brains and polish, Noble still operated in Binion's shadow and under his thumb. Noble's main business concern was the Airmen's Club, 1710 Live Oak Street, a gambling room in downtown Dallas. It turned a good profit, but he had to kick back 25 percent of his earnings to Binion. "I operated a little place in those days," Noble told a reporter once. "I paid the man protection money. My business grew, and he didn't like the competition."

Some police believed the real acrimony between Noble and Binion began when Binion upped his rake. Noble's games, a police internal memo said, "were making so much money that Binion's games began to suffer, and Binion, in order to force Noble out, raised his percentage from twenty-five percent to forty percent." This, the memo said, was not received well: "Noble told Binion to 'Go to hell.'" Others thought the dispute arose from Noble's constant complaint that Binion—uneducated, uncouth, and unironed—didn't respect him. Noble's financial backing of Raymond Loudermilk hadn't helped to cool matters either. Though authorities couldn't agree on a particular reason, nearly all believed that the situation was destined, sooner or later, for a deadly showdown. "Noble developed an extreme hatred for Binion," a police memo said. "The feeling between Binion and Noble became very bad."

The fuse was lit one winter afternoon in 1946 as Noble presided over operations at the Airmen's Club. He looked up from his business to see a Dallas police detective approaching—not an unusual sight, for officers regularly stopped by to collect unofficial fines. But this cop had come for something else. "We have received some complaints," the detective told Noble. The Airmen's Club, he said, would have to shut down immediately.

Noble boiled over. What, he demanded to know, about Binion? The Southland Syndicate's casinos operated full tilt, and the police barely touched them. Before the detective left, Noble made it as clear as he could that he would not go down quietly. It didn't take long—a few hours at most—for Binion to receive a full report on Noble's response. Noble knew Binion would hear about it, and he knew what that meant. "Benny had a bunch of thugs hanging around him," Noble recalled. "When Benny couldn't bluff me out, he sent those thugs after me."

No gangland arriviste himself, Noble had assembled some protection too, a police report said: he "collected a bunch of hoodlums from the West Dallas section." But his West Dallas hoods weren't with Noble on January 12, 1946, when he left the Airmen's Club around midnight. It was cold and clear as Noble started his Mercury and drove toward the Denton County town of Grapevine, about twenty-five miles to the northwest.

Glancing in his rearview mirror, Noble could see a Cadillac behind him. When he sped up, it did the same. If he slowed, his pursuers slowed with him. He made several quick turns; the Cadillac did too. What Noble didn't know was that the car carried Binion's main-attraction hired killers: Bob Minyard, Lois Green, and Johnny "Brazil" Grisaffi. Minyard was still under indictment for the murder of Loudermilk. Green retained his status as Binion's number one staff hit man. Grisaffi was enjoying a bit of free time between narcotics and robbery indictments.

Noble headed for his ranch, and the Cadillac stayed behind him even as the city lights fell away. On a dark country highway Noble gassed the Mercury until the needle on the speedometer touched 90. Only a few other cars were on the lonely road, and Noble and the Cadillac blew past them. Tires squealed as he made the curves. The more powerful Cadillac pulled closer, nearly alongside Noble now. Grisaffi leaned out the window on the Caddy's passenger side, pointed a sawed-off shotgun, and fired. Metal popped and glass shattered, but Noble kept going. Grisaffi fired again.

He steered the Mercury onto an unpaved, unlit county road, the Cadillac right behind him, the cars bouncing through the darkness. If he could reach his ranch, Noble could get to his small armory of rifles and return fire. But about a mile from home he lost control of the Mercury and slid into a ditch. Noble scrambled from the car and ran toward a farmhouse in the distance. More shots came from the Cadillac—the roar of the shotgun and the sharp report of a pistol—as Noble ran. A bullet struck him in the hip, and he staggered and fell. The shots kept coming as he crawled through the dirt, gasping for breath, with a burning pain in his lower back. He reached the farmhouse and slid under its porch. Dogs barked, lights came on, and the farmer who lived in the house opened the front door. The attackers returned to their Cadillac and fled.

Noble had been hit once; a bullet was lodged near the lower part of his spine. It was a serious wound, but not fatal. Lawmen gathered at his hospital bed and began to bombard him with questions about the shooting. But Noble gave them nothing. In the unlikely event arrests were made, he added, he would not appear as a witness against his assailants. It was the code of the gangster, but it was something else too: Noble had no need for the cops. He planned to settle the score his own way.

Back at the Southland, Binion knew that he had now started, and failed to finish, a nasty fight. He called Grisaffi into his office. "You're carrying a lot of heat on this deal," Binion told him. He instructed Grisaffi to stay at the Southland "until things cool down some." This had a dual purpose; Binion could keep an eye on Grisaffi, and use him as a bodyguard at the same time. Such a tactic made some sense until Noble, from his hospital bed, ordered his personal gunmen to attack the flank.

Two days after Noble's adventure, an Airman's Club pit boss named Slim Hays drove his own Cadillac down Gaston Avenue, through East Dallas. The sun was down, the sky had clouded over, and a cold mist descended as he passed the Lakewood Country Club, not far from White Rock Lake. Sitting in the front seat of the car with Hays was his red-haired girlfriend, a hard-bitten diner waitress who talked too much. In the backseat rode a would-be tough guy, the generally feckless Charles "Sonny" Lefors. Hays made a few turns before taking a slow roll down Avalon Street, lights off. This was a quiet, well-tended neighborhood. The curbed street was lined with smooth sidewalks that fronted handsome two-story brick houses, a world away from the unpaved roads and shotgun shacks that Hays and Lefors had known in West Dallas. Leaving the redhead, the two men got out of the car and made their way into the backyard of one of the houses. There they hid themselves in some shrubbery and waited.

Around 10:00 p.m. a set of headlights raked the yard, and a car—a new Oldsmobile—pulled into the driveway that ran along the right side of the house. The driver eased the Oldsmobile into the garage, turned the engine off, and stepped from the car. As the driver walked to the house, Hays and Lefors jumped up and began firing. One of them had a sawed-off shotgun, while the other used a .38.

Their target was Bob Minyard, Binion's newly crowned right-hand man, who fell onto the driveway with gaping, mortal wounds. Although he had been struck in the chest, he managed to pull his own gun and get off four shots, but he hit nobody, and his assailants ran to their car, with the red-haired waitress as wheelwoman. Minyard's wife grabbed the phone and called Binion's house, and when Teddy Jane answered, she screamed through her sobs that her husband had been shot.

Minutes after Minyard went down, Decker was notified at the courthouse. The deputy sheriff departed for the crime scene but made a stop en route, at a side entrance to the Southland Hotel. The car's passenger door opened and Binion got in, and the two rode together to Minyard's house. It was clear to both of them that this was not a simple robbery, for in the dead man's pockets police had found $2,400 in cash. The gang war was raging now.

A Dallas police report set the scene: "Informed underworld sources stated that Noble had Minyard killed and that Binion was more determined than ever to get Noble because if he did not, Binion would 'lose his power as boss of racket operations in Texas, and Noble would have someone kill Binion and become the new boss of gambling.'"

If he protected himself, Binion was confident that this was a war he could win. Bob Minyard's death meant little to him. Binion had more money, more firepower, and more influence in the county courthouse and at city hall than Noble could dream of possessing. But he had one critical weakness that he didn't yet understand. He couldn't control the voters.

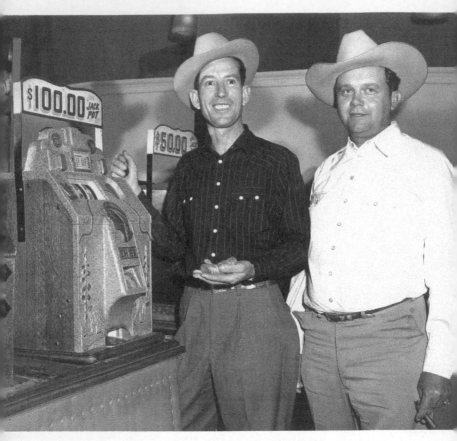

Binion (right) with his new business partner and old family friend, Fred Merrill.

# 8

# "LIT OUT RUNNING"

> Hell, you can stub your toe and fall down and kill yourself. You
> just ain't very powerful.
>
> —BB

**F**ew people paid much attention when, on a cold day in February 1946, a political neophyte named Steve Guthrie walked into the Dallas County courthouse and filed to run for sheriff. The thirty-three-year-old Guthrie, a former army sergeant and traffic cop, had never held political office and could point to no organized support. His candidacy merited but two sentences in the newspaper.

Smoot Schmid, the thirteen-year incumbent, considered Guthrie little more than a political annoyance, and couldn't be bothered to put much energy into a campaign. "I have given you law enforcement in the past," he told a crowd in a typically soporific stump speech. "I ask you to give me the opportunity to continue to give you the same service." Courthouse insiders nonetheless believed Schmid's reelection a near certainty. This was, of course, good news for Binion, who had profited handsomely from Schmid's indifference, and from chief deputy Decker's friendship.

Despite his torpor, Schmid nearly won the primary outright. In a three-man race, he collected fifteen thousand more votes than the second-place finisher, Guthrie. Now the two found themselves in a runoff.

Schmid—supremely confident and spectacularly lazy—once again refused to mount much of an effort. But the vigorous Guthrie campaigned hard, going door-to-door throughout the county, enlisting hundreds of army veterans to help, and making speeches to any group that would have him. His message: Schmid ran "the biggest political machine at the courthouse," and Dallas County was infested with organized crime. Some could have read this as a veiled threat to Binion's gambling operations. At least one person did—Herbert Noble.

Only about six months had passed since Lois Green and friends tried to gun down Noble in that wild highway chase. Noble, still gimpy from his wounds, couldn't match Binion's collection of gunslingers, but he saw in Guthrie a side door to potential advantage. Eliminate Binion's protection, Noble reasoned, and you might eliminate Binion. Noble gave Guthrie's campaign $15,000, a huge contribution for a local race. When news of this reached Binion, who was summering in Montana, tending to his ranch, the reaction came hot and fast. He ordered Buddy Malone—who had been in Montana helping with horses—back to Dallas right away. Malone's trip had only one purpose: to kill Herbert Noble.

Though he had previously proved his homicidal loyalty to Binion, most notably with his plugging of Ben Freiden, Malone was reluctant to pursue Noble's death himself. He may have feared prison, or he may have feared Noble. For whatever reason, he engaged a local gambler named Jack Darby to make the hit.

Around 3:00 a.m. on August 19, 1946, Darby called Noble and told him to come to a Dallas gambling club to pick up $12,000 he was owed. When Noble arrived, Darby pulled a snub-nosed pistol, cursed Noble, and fired several shots into the floor at Noble's feet. This may have been an attempt to force Noble to draw his own .38, so that Darby could kill him in plausible self-defense. But Noble didn't take the bait, and eventually talked Darby into putting his gun down. Then Noble picked up his $12,000 and walked out untouched. He had survived murder attempt number two.

Five days later, even worse news fell on Binion. Dallas County voters elected Guthrie sheriff by nine hundred votes. Binion's subsequent political analysis was pithy: "My sheriff just sat on his ass and pissed away the election." Now the Southland Syndicate stood at risk of losing its very foundation.

Guthrie made his intentions clear in a round of post-victory speeches to earnest civic groups and assorted clubby enclaves of Babbittry. Speaking to the East Dallas Kiwanians, he vowed, "I will wear out the Dallas County Jail" with downtown casino operators. He also promised that as soon as he took office, Bill Decker would be fired.

As bad as that sounded, Guthrie was far from Binion's only problem. Carl Hansson, the police officer whom Binion had mocked for his late-night zoo patrols, had now ascended to chief of the department. The new chief likewise made plenty of threatening speeches in which he announced a crackdown on gamblers. Beyond that, a young, ambitious lawyer named Will Wilson had been elected district attorney—replacing a DA frequently seen sporting with Binion in his casinos. A World War II veteran, Wilson was a member of the junior chamber of commerce who, at the age of thirty-four, still lived with his parents. Shortly after his election, he declared that his office would aggressively prosecute dice game operators. "The gamblers can't stand that," he said.

No one could mistake the newcomers' message: Benny Binion was a marked man.

This was nothing but good news for Herbert Noble. "Guthrie and Noble," a police memo observed, "had an extremely close personal relationship, and apparently Noble had agreed upon certain deals with Guthrie to operate gambling interests in the outskirts of the City of Dallas." Other gamblers, in the form of a rogue patrol of the Chicago syndicate, sensed an opening too. And so it happened that in 1946, Paul Roland Jones came back to town. His previous missions in Dallas hadn't gone so well, but he knew that this one would work.

A forger, jewel thief, and habitual liar, Jones had done prison time for murder in Kansas. He then bought his way into the egg dehydration business, one of a string of bad investments—a long list that ultimately included uranium mines, a shrimp brokerage, and a quack cancer clinic—that left him broke. Around 1941, he made his initial visit to Dallas, and was soon convicted of counterfeiting sugar coupons during the rationing days of World War II, for which he paid a $750 fine.

Jones claimed he had been sent to Texas the first time by Nick DeJohn, a ranking Chicago racketeer. He later told the FBI, according to an agent's memo, that DeJohn wanted him to "survey this area as to the possibility of taking over gambling, slot machines, bookees [sic] and the numbers racket." Jones determined that Binion and his gang had too tight a grip on Dallas, the FBI report said, "and that it was his opinion that they should not try to take over gambling in this area."

The slot machine and jukebox business looked to have some room to maneuver. Jones and Marcus Lipsky, an associate of what had been the Capone syndicate in Chicago, purchased a number of "music companies"—fronts for slot operations—in Louisiana and Texas. More than $500,000 in loans for these ventures, Jones later said, came from a bulwark of the Dallas commercial establishment, the Mercantile National Bank. Lipsky, a heavy-lidded thug right out of the organized-crime catalog, planned an expansion of activities: he vowed to kill Binion, Ivy Miller, and Buddy Malone, and leave their bodies outside the Dallas police station in a stolen car. Lipsky reasoned that this would announce a new power in town. Jones—realizing that such a move would only bring intense police heat on their operations—managed to talk Lipsky and the Chicago bosses out of it.

Soon more Windy City operatives were turning up in Dallas, and Deputy Sheriff Decker had seen enough. He and some deputies rounded up four of the principals, Jones among them. Decker charged them with vagrancy, jailed them briefly, drove them to the county line, and instructed them to keep going.

This ended, for a while at least, any infiltration by the Chicago machine. Ever the publicity-savvy lawman, Decker had thought to have a newspaper photographer standing by when one of his deputies loaded the four—"grimy and heavy-bearded from two days in jail," one reporter observed—into the car. The Chicago men were "topwater hoods," a Dallas columnist proclaimed, adding that "their suitcases had a lot of money." Decker told reporters the men amounted to "as hard a crew as we have ever had in the jail here."

The expulsion added to Decker's legend as a fearless frontier lawman, the type of deputy sheriff who could face down big-city toughs and order them out of town by sundown. "They were told to 'get out and stay out,'" the ever-obliging Morning News reported. Left unmentioned was its chief effect: to protect, temporarily, Binion's gambling monopoly in Dallas.

Years later, Binion was asked about outside mobsters trying to take over his operations, and in a classic example of chicken-fried dissembling, he refused to implicate his friend the deputy sheriff. "Well," Binion said of Dallas, "they just didn't come there."

"Why not?" he was asked.

"Well, I just don't know."

"The Mafia was into every other place, trying to be," his questioner said.

"Well, to tell you the honest truth about the Mafia, I think it's a overestimated thing," Binion said. "I actually never knew anything about the Mafia. I've knew people that they [police and newspapers] said was in it, knew 'em personally, but they never did tell me they's in it, so I just don't know."

But there were rumors, his questioner persisted, about the mob trying to move into Dallas and being thwarted. "I just wondered how you managed that," the researcher said.

"Well," Binion said, "I wouldn't want to go into *that*."

Paul Jones was outraged by the exodus of the Chicago crew, whom he defended as loyal "Masons and Shriners," not criminals. Complaining that he and his innocent friends had been the victims of nothing more than a political publicity stunt, Jones retreated to Mexico, where he attempted to run a mob-controlled casino. Mexican authorities quickly arrested him and turned him over to American tax agents, who shipped him back to Dallas. When the Bureau of Internal Revenue, as it was then known, determined it couldn't make a case against him, it kicked him to Decker, who brought Jones in for interrogation one late summer afternoon in 1946. At Decker's invitation, two agents from the local office of the FBI were there too.

A small man with a thin mustache, Jones, thirty-seven, dropped the innocence act and boasted that many U.S. law enforcement agencies had questioned him, and each one had accused him of being the top counterfeiter, drug dealer, and gang leader in the United States. Maybe so, but the heaviest criminal charge that Decker could lay on Jones was a theft scheme involving electric motors for vibrating "weight-reducing" machines of the sort found in beauty salons. Jones posted $2,000 bond and left for Chicago two days later on Braniff Airways. Less than two months after that, he was back in Dallas with a new criminal blueprint. He had never really lost his ambition to take over gambling in North Texas. Now, with a fresh administration about to assume office—and Decker on the way out—Jones plotted to move on a weakened Binion.

His first bit of business was to get the sheriff-elect on his side. Jones contacted Guthrie and claimed to have retained his direct connection to the current incarnation of the Capone syndicate in Chicago. What's more, he could make Guthrie rich. Although Guthrie appeared wary, he agreed to talk further with Jones. They first met on November 1, 1946, at Guthrie's house—a rather sparsely furnished place that lacked a certain homey touch—with Lieutenant George Butler of the Dallas police also present.

After talk of dogs and housing prices, Jones offered some helpful advice on covering up homicides. He told Guthrie he carried a .45-caliber Colt automatic with a clip that retained spent cartridges. That clip was important, he said, because if you ever had to kill someone on a rainy night, you didn't want to be on your hands and knees in the mud, looking for ejected shells that could be used as evidence against you.

Eventually they discussed the gambling business in Dallas. "I don't have to tell you who Benny Binion is, who Ivy Miller is," Guthrie said to Jones. "Binion takes one million flat dollars a year, one flat million. On policy alone." This was accomplished through the protection afforded by bribes. "We all know that Bill Decker is a pay-off man with Benny Binion," Guthrie said. "Everybody knows the city, the mayor, I guess, the sheriff's office—I guess they are paid off. We know they are paid off."

Jones wasn't worried. "I'll tell you how we can control Binion," he said. "We won't have to shoot nobody, and you won't have to shoot nobody." Jones proposed that the Chicago mob open a Dallas gambling club. It would be modeled, he said, on the famous Top O'Hill casino, and its likely location would be the current home of the Chicken Bar, a joint at the corner of Commerce Street and Industrial Boulevard. Local people would run the place with only one secret Chicago operative inside to watch the money.

"He looks like a preacher," Jones said. "He is not a dago, he is not a Jew . . . He protects the game." Lavish bribes would be spread through the Dallas power structure, Jones promised, and in return, the Chicago-owned casino would thrive unmolested while competitors—that is to say Binion—could be run out of business.

As for Guthrie's slice, "you should have $40,000 a month," Jones told him.

Guthrie spotted an immediate problem. "See, my salary is $7,700 a year," he said. "I could take $40,000 a month, but where in the hell would I put it?"

The Chicago boys would handle that, Jones answered. "We are going to worry about you more than you worry about yourself."

Several other conferences followed, with Jones accompanied by a couple of compatriots, among them a strong-arm named Jack Nappi. Guthrie brought the discussion back to Binion. "But here's what I really had on my mind, is the local gambling syndicate," Guthrie said. "Binion, Miller and those fellows. They make a lot of big cash, you see, and they might not want to take this lying down. They might want to fight, you see?"

Jones remained unworried by any threat Binion might pose. "We're going to cut off a lot of his stuff," he said. Later he sought to assure Guthrie that the new sheriff was dealing now with a higher class of criminal. "We are honest," Jones declared. "People can't understand that. We are very, very honest." And, he added, "we are armed."

The meetings lasted for more than ten hours total, with Jones making promises by the dozen. What he didn't know was that this home in which they were sitting wasn't really Guthrie's. It served, in essence, as a stage set for a sting: a house rented and furnished by the authorities. Guthrie and Butler, with the help of the Texas Rangers, had constructed a perfect trap for Jones. Hidden directly below them, in a dugout space under the house, Ranger Dub Naylor was hunched over a gramophone, recording everything Guthrie and Jones said. One microphone was concealed in a telephone next to Guthrie, and another in a radio. From a house across the street another Ranger filmed the mobsters as they arrived and departed from the fake Guthrie residence.

To his great surprise, Jones was cuffed, jailed, and charged. Later his lawyer tried an unusual legal defense: because Guthrie had not actually been sworn in as sheriff at the time Jones made his offer, it wasn't officially a bribe. The strategy didn't work. Jones was convicted and sentenced to three years in prison. Before he could serve that term, he had to do eight years in a federal pen for smuggling opium into Texas from Mexico.

Meanwhile, Dallas had a new crime-busting star. So compelling were the condensed transcripts of the Guthrie-Jones encounter that the Mutual radio network produced a dramatized account that was broadcast nationwide on Christmas Eve.

As 1946 drew to a close, no one in Binion's circle could quite figure Guthrie out. Was he a crusading straight arrow, as the Jones sting indicated? Or was he simply the good friend—and secretly the business partner—of Herbert Noble? Either one meant big problems for Binion and his previously cozy courthouse setup. "This arrangement," Binion recalled, "had done played out."

Still, the enormity of the situation seemed to elude Binion, at least until Decker called the gambler Fred Merrill, whom Decker had anointed years before as the king of the Dallas gambling business. Since then, Merrill had stayed on good terms with Binion. They shared some business ventures, and their children played together almost every day. Decker's message to him was blunt: Tell Binion if he doesn't get out of town, he'll either be dead or in prison.

The empire that he had built over the course of a decade had collapsed in a couple of months. Yet once again, Binion had the benefit of lucky timing. Merrill had recently hit a hot streak rolling dice at the Frontier Club in Reno, Nevada, and had walked away—after a twelve-hour session—with $188,500 in winnings. What's more, Merrill had connections in Nevada, and he could use them to help Binion buy into a Las Vegas casino.

Many years afterward, Binion summed up his professional options. "I depend on the dice to make a living," he said. "And I can go anywhere in the United States, almost, and make a living with the dice, if I had to, 'cause I could hustle up some players, and get in a room, and play with 'em. All you got to have is some square dice and a big bankroll, and some men that can deal." With Decker's dire warning and Merrill's business opportunity, Binion made his decision: relocate the dice game to a place where it was welcome and legal. He broke the news to Teddy Jane and the family that they would have to leave the house on Northwest Highway and move to Las Vegas. The decision deeply displeased his wife, but with his enemy ascendant and his life in jeopardy, Binion had no choice.

He planned to make his initial trip to Nevada, in December 1946, without his family. But there were twelve hundred miles of lonely highway between Dallas and Las Vegas, and with as much as $1 million cash in the trunk of his Cadillac, Binion needed someone to ride shotgun. He recruited two of the best: R. D. Matthews and Al Meadows.

Meadows was a squat gambler and hit man who was said to be afraid of no one but his wife. Matthews was described in an FBI report as a "burglar, armed robber, narcotics pusher, gambler, murderer," though he was never convicted of any of those crimes. As a marine in World War II, he had fought in some of the bloodiest battles of the Pacific theater. When he came home to Texas, he joined Lois Green's gang, and eventually went to work for Binion. "A strong-arm man for the collection of gambling debts," the FBI said. As such, he quickly established a reputation: screw with Matthews and you would be dead, or would wish to be. "Everybody was afraid of R.D.," said a friend of his, Mickey Bickers. "Everybody."

For this journey to Vegas, Binion had two immediate concerns. The first was the presence of agricultural inspection stations at state lines. There an overly curious trooper might search the car and find the stacks of cash, which could invite some unwelcome scrutiny. The second worry was the obvious one: hijackers who, learning of a carful of money crossing the badlands, might go after it like Wild West desperadoes robbing a stagecoach. Binion prepared for that by arming Meadows and Matthews with Thompson submachine guns.

They left Dallas in the dead of night, heading northwest on a two-lane across the prairie, and then over the Staked Plains, where only isolated cattle towns broke the emptiness. Out here a man could drive for miles and never see anyone else. They crossed the Texas Panhandle, through some of the state's great ranches, then finally into the desert. The men took turns driving and stopped only for food and gas.

For someone who had ruled his kingdom for a decade, it was an ignominious flight: the deposed emperor of dice, now one step ahead of the police and his own inferior yet triumphant rivals. But Binion had learned early on that while a man might have to make his way with fist and blood, he sometimes had no choice but to give ground. And this was one of those times.

"I just went to hollering," he explained, "and lit out running."

# DEATH AND TAXES
## 1947–1953

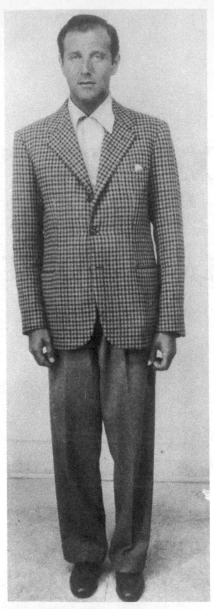

Benjamin "Bugsy" Siegel, who had the vision for a great Vegas casino, but not the requisite management skills.

# 9

# MOBBED-UP PILGRIMS

There's nothing on earth I like better than inflation and corruption.

**−BB**

e probably did not think about it in such terms, but Binion now embraced an American archetype. He had fled his past, headed west, and sought a fresh start in the wide-open spaces of the promised land. Doing so, Binion replicated the intrepid American homesteaders in covered wagons who had made the trek before him—though they had neither henchmen with tommy guns nor a cool million in the trunk. At least he wore a cowboy hat.

Less majestically, Binion had joined one of the great migrations in American organized crime history: the mob diaspora of the 1940s. They came from New York, Chicago, Cleveland, Los Angeles, Miami, and anywhere else they felt pressure from the competition or heat from the cops. And they were streaming to Nevada in their long black limos, with blond mistresses beside them and the high-dollar reek of Zizanie cologne. It was Manifest Destiny, felony division.

The great historian Frederick Jackson Turner had declared the western frontier—which he called "the meeting point between savagery and civilization" and the very expression of American individualism—closed in

1893. But Las Vegas wasn't closed even by 1946; it was, in fact opening up. This would come to represent a different sort of frontier: savagery and civilization meeting in an entirely new manner, and individualism expressed in ways not seen before. Within a mere fifteen years, U.S. attorney general Robert F. Kennedy would call Las Vegas "the bank of America's organized crime" as mobsters—their careers born anew in the Nevada desert— skimmed millions from their casino operations. And in only a few decades, the Union Plaza Hotel in downtown Las Vegas would feature a show called *Nudes on Ice,* while at the Circus Circus you might watch a dwarf boxing a kangaroo.

This magical transformation would commence as soon as the settlers staked their claims. Settlers like Benny Binion.

It was a broad desert basin of furnace heat between mostly barren mountain ranges, but it had a bit of water. Artesian springs gave the valley some grassy oases, which attracted both animals and people. Archaeological evidence indicates Native Americans lived there more than ten thousand years ago, and the Paiutes—a placid tribe that grew pumpkins and ate lizards—arrived around AD 700. Spanish explorers may have passed through the valley in the late 1700s, although no proof of that has been found.

The first non–Native American known to have set foot in the valley came seeking business opportunities. Rafael Rivera, a scout for a New Mexico trader, trotted in on horseback in late 1829. The springs came to serve as a way station on a branch of the Old Spanish Trail, the famous trade route from Santa Fe to Southern California. At some point the place was called Las Vegas, Spanish for "the meadows" or "marshy plains," depending on the translation. Army captain John Frémont and his topographical corps arrived in 1844, and he was the first to put Las Vegas on a government map. A minister, mountain man, and cannibal named Bill Williams used Las Vegas as a base for his marauding band of horse thieves in the 1840s. In 1855, some thirty Mormons were the first non-Natives who actually tried to settle. At the instruction of Brigham Young, they intended to convert the Paiute Indians to Mormonism and establish a mission. Neither effort proved successful. Drought killed most of the crops, and what little remained, the Paiutes took. Most of the Mormons were gone within a few years. As a valedictory, one of them called the valley the land the "Lord had forgotten."

But there was life in the place yet, thanks to the building of a rail line across the desert between Salt Lake City and Los Angeles. By 1905 track work was complete, and trains began passing through Las Vegas, which served as a watering and repair stop. A town took rapid shape, and within months it enjoyed its first spate of land speculation and ballooning real estate prices. Soon bars and casinos flourished, and whorehouses did heavy business in a section of town known as Block 16. The speculative fever cooled, the state outlawed gambling, and in the mid-1920s, Las Vegas hit economic hard times several years ahead of the rest of the country. It stood a good chance of becoming another wasting desert whistle-stop.

Three monumental decisions by the state and federal government saved it. In 1927 the state legalized a three-month divorce, and four years after that reduced it to six weeks, the fastest in the United States. From around the country the unhappily married—Mrs. Clark Gable among them—fled to Nevada. After residing for a mere month and a half, they could be relieved of their wedded misery. The local chamber of commerce promoted the city as the chic capital of splits—"Gable Divorce Booms Las Vegas" was the headline on one of its photomontages sent to newspapers nationwide—and some entrepreneurs opened dude ranches in the area for guests establishing their temporary residency.

The second big boost came in 1928, when President Calvin Coolidge signed the bill to dam the Colorado River at Boulder Canyon, only twenty-five miles from Las Vegas. This was one of the great public works projects of its day, and meant millions of dollars and thousands of jobs for southern Nevada. Soon workers and federal funds began pouring into the state.

Salvation number three was the great watershed moment for modern Nevada: in 1931 the state legislature made gambling legal again. Within months, casinos opened, and the timing could not have been better. The men and women—mostly men—building what would become Hoover Dam found themselves living in a federally controlled company town, Boulder City, where drinking and gambling were prohibited. They needed somewhere to spend their money and blow off steam. That place was Las Vegas.

Downtown on Fremont Street rows of bars—despite Prohibition—and casinos called to the workers and their paychecks. Large, bright neon signs of establishments such as the Boulder Club, the Golden Camel, and the Northern Club, whose display included four dice and a royal-flush poker hand, lit the desert night. This spectacle gave rise to the name Glitter Gulch. The clubs were packed nearly every night, and the whores on Block 16 once again had a rush of customers.

Then it slowed. By 1936 the dam was completed, and many of the workers departed. Las Vegas attempted to promote itself as "The City of an Assured Future," but that was hardly so, at least until it took advantage of a couple of additional breaks.

For a town in the middle of a deathly wasteland, it was blessed with a good location. With the population beginning to swell in Southern California, Las Vegas—only about three hundred miles to the northeast—was well positioned as a haven for escape. It lay far enough away to be a refuge, and conveniently over the state line, but within a day's drive. That's where Californian Guy McAfee went.

Known to everyone as the Captain, McAfee commanded the Los Angeles police vice squad. He also operated gambling houses and brothels—he was married to a Hollywood madam—and had ties to organized crime. This arrangement worked well until a new mayor pledged to clean up L.A. McAfee resigned and fled the city. By 1938 he had established himself in Las Vegas, where the business activities forbidden in L.A. were perfectly legal, or close to it. McAfee operated the Pair-O-Dice Club on Highway 91 south of town. He christened that lonely road "the Strip" in a tribute— however ironic, perverse, or prophetic—to the Sunset Strip in L.A., and the name stuck.

The first gambling hall and full resort on the Strip was developed by another Californian, a hotel man named Thomas Hull. Las Vegas legend has it that Hull's car overheated on Highway 91 en route from L.A. to Salt Lake City. Waiting for help, he noticed the number of autos with out-of-state plates passing him, and inspiration struck. A far more likely story is that he was sold on Las Vegas's future one day while having drinks with a local businessman at the Apache Hotel downtown. Whatever the provenance, by

1941 Hull built and opened his sprawling, sixty-six-acre motel complex, the El Rancho Vegas, complete with a pool, a casino, a showroom, and ample parking, all designed to entice motorists.

Another Strip resort, the Last Frontier, followed a year later. Its air-conditioned rooms, upholstered chairs, and private baths with tiled floors added a note of semi-refinement not found on Fremont Street. So unaccustomed was the town to having the furniture match the drapes that the *Las Vegas Review-Journal* remarked with wonder upon the coordination. What's more, the newspaper rhapsodized, "the color scheme in the bath harmonizes with the theme in the adjoining bedroom." The Last Frontier imported some star power too: Sophie Tucker, "the Last of the Red Hot Mamas," played its theater.

Though they were little more than dressed-up dude ranches, by Vegas norms these operations represented a great leap forward. And they marked, for the city, the dawn of middle-American mom-and-pop tourism, if mom and pop sought color-coordinated desert luxury and racy excitement. The chamber of commerce brought in out-of-town journalists who obligingly praised "tony joints" and "swank, million-dollar hotels" to which Hollywood stars flocked. In 1940, *Look* magazine called Vegas "the most sensationally cockeyed and self-consciously wicked place on earth" and an "American Gomorrah."

The 1941 movie *Las Vegas Nights* featured the uncredited screen debut of an up-and-coming young singer named Frank Sinatra, although the critic for the *New York Times* was unimpressed by the film: "There is precious little humor, little life, little anything," wrote Bosley Crowther, "save an excess of dullness in this labored musical show about a troupe of indigent entertainers adrift in the Nevada gambling town." Nonetheless, Las Vegas—and the nascent Strip in particular—had begun to attract some attention.

Most of the downtown casinos continued to flourish, but they were, in many cases, operated by relative small-timers. The joints attracted a crowd of minor-league cardsharps as well as a growing collection of junior hustlers, more of whom stepped off the train every day at Union Station. A photograph from the era of a card game at the Northern Club on Fremont shows a slickster with a pencil-thin mustache and a snap-brim fedora playing a poker hand against a gussied-up cowboy in a western tie and a neatly creased hat. It looks like Nathan Detroit squaring off against Tom Mix.

All of this received a big boost with the outbreak of World War II. The 1943 opening of a magnesium plant southeast of Las Vegas, which processed metal for bombs, provided six thousand jobs. The U.S. Army Air Corps established a gunnery school at a Las Vegas community airport, and by the end of the war, about eleven thousand servicemen were stationed there. Not a few of them wished to gamble and drink, and like the workers who built Hoover Dam, they went looking for excitement in Vegas clubs. Or, when circumstances required, the excitement came to them. The El Rancho and Last Frontier sometimes sent entertainers to the military camps for shows—public service combined with advertising—for the boys going off to war.

Las Vegas had managed to revive itself yet again, and began to enter the nation's consciousness as, in the words of one resident, "a sunny place for shady people." But these were the preliminaries. The real fun and fireworks would begin when the big boys took over.

To operate a Las Vegas casino, even a small one, was not something for the uninitiated or the inexperienced. Odds had to be calculated, dealers supervised, security maintained. Casino patrons were unlike those at most other businesses; instead of purchasing a service or product, they tried to walk away with the establishment's money, via skill, luck, or cunning larceny. There were no training grounds for people running gambling dens except the dens themselves. The universities didn't teach it, any more than they taught auto theft, and trade schools wouldn't touch it. Nor was there a collection of promising young executives being carefully groomed through the corporate hierarchy of sales divisions and branch offices. The people who knew how to operate casinos were those who had done it elsewhere, which made them outlaws.

And now they were coming to Nevada to ply their trade. "They weren't particularly Sunday school teachers or preachers or anything like that," Nevada lieutenant governor—and casino owner—Cliff Jones once acknowledged. Instead, they were crooks, killers, and impresarios of corruption.

In their own skewed way, they also served as visionaries. They found in Las Vegas—despite the effervescence of junketing newspapermen—little more than a pile of shabby buildings dropped onto a searing moonscape, with summer afternoon temperatures hitting 120 degrees. There may have been a few passably nice resorts on the Strip, most of them catering to motorists from Southern California, but much of Las Vegas remained little more than a sun-blasted watering hole.

"It was in sorry shape," said Meyer Lansky, known as organized crime's chairman of the board for his vast web of gambling and money laundering. "Living conditions were bad. No one wanted to go to Vegas to gamble. Air connections were bad. And the trip by car was bothersome. It was so hot that the wires in the cars would melt."

Yet the racketeers saw the possibilities. This was, for them, the land of opportunity: the only place in the country where gambling was legally sanctioned by the state, and only minimally regulated. They could make their own rules in this Wild West town while forever ceasing to worry about authorities attempting to shut them down.

Las Vegas didn't just tolerate the mob. The city desperately needed the mob. These gangsters brought not only expertise but access to capital as well. It might have been capital obtained by loan-sharking, prostitution, narcotics, and extortion, but it spent like any other money. Few banks of that era were willing to make loans for start-up casinos, especially in a remote town in the desert. The racketeers may not have been the first to set up in Las Vegas, but they rode in with cash and talent in amounts not seen before. Their money and their smarts were the incubators for what was to become the largest collection of legal casinos in the world.

The mobster Benjamin "Bugsy" Siegel has traditionally, and incorrectly, received most of the credit for this great transformation. That derives in no small part from Hollywood's characteristic mythmaking, most notably with the 1991 film *Bugsy*, starring Warren Beatty. The Las Vegas of that movie, when Siegel arrives, looks to be little more than a collection of shacks along a few unpaved streets. Siegel's girlfriend takes a disgusted look at one of the town's casinos and dismisses it as "this canker sore." But Beatty's Siegel has a Mojave epiphany: "I got it! I got it!" From this desolation will rise a glamorous, luxurious playground that only he can envision—the Flamingo.

That wasn't quite how it happened. A product of New York's Lower East Side, Siegel had run with Meyer Lansky as a boy. In the 1930s Lansky—who had matured into an international crime magnate—sent him to California to operate the West Coast branch of Lansky's syndicate. There Siegel worked his way into the Hollywood crowd, chumming with actors and bedding starlets. He came to Las Vegas in the early 1940s with the goal of seizing control of the race wire, which provided horse-track odds and race results to betting parlors.

Siegel did that, but he also had the sense to see that Las Vegas was attracting more and more visitors, and that the opportunity was ripe for investment, expansion, and improvement. First he tried to buy the El Rancho Vegas, but the owner, Thomas Hull, rebuffed him. "You may say for me," Hull told a local newspaper, "that the people of Las Vegas have been too good for me to repay them in that way."

The El Rancho might have been too plain for Siegel's taste anyway. He soon vowed to build "the goddamn biggest, fanciest gaming casino and hotel you bastards ever seen in your whole lives." What he really did was buy into a project already under way, that of Billy Wilkerson, a slick-talking California gambler, the founder of the *Hollywood Reporter* and the man who discovered Lana Turner. Wilkerson had begun work on the Flamingo, but had run out of money. Siegel, with mob cash from New York and Chicago, took over the project, and brought his grandiose vision: the Flamingo—the "fabulous Flamingo"—would be built with rare imported wood, the finest Italian marble, and other appointments fit for a latter-day pharaoh. It was to be an opulent gambling and entertainment showcase, a stately pleasure dome of legal sin that would deliver Hollywood glamour to the Nevada desert. Included as a bonus: a maze of underground tunnels that Siegel could use to evade any attempts on his life. Even the closets in his fourth-floor suite had escape hatches, which led to a garage with a getaway car. The Flamingo's cost overruns soon exceeded $5 million, and the mobsters on the hook for those expenses, Lansky among them, grew increasingly impatient.

But on December 26, 1946, to much fanfare and raucous celebration, the Flamingo's casino, showroom, and restaurant opened, with the hotel itself still incomplete. A few stars were flown in, though bad storms grounded most of them in L.A. Among those in attendance that night was one newly arrived Texan, Benny Binion, who gazed about in hickish amazement. "That was the biggest whoop-de-do I ever seen," he recalled. "They had Jimmy Durante, [Xavier] Cugat's band and Rosemarie, in one show." Binion somehow failed to mention Tommy Wonder and the Tune Toppers.

As impressed as he was with the Flamingo, Binion liked its front man even more. Siegel was the "most accommodating, most likable fellow, had the best personality you ever seen," in Binion's view. "If he was a bad guy, he damn sure didn't show it from the outside." This was typical of Binion, who functioned as a sort of Will Rogers of mobsters. He had a similar assessment of one "Ice Pick Willie" Alderman, a notorious killer who was said to have gained his nickname by sticking that instrument through eleven victims' ears until it penetrated their brains. Said Binion, "I don't believe all that stuff. He was the nicest, kindest-hearted man . . . I never knew a kinder-hearted man than him."

Binion did not stand alone in his generous assessment of Bugsy Siegel. Many acquaintances found him to be exquisitely charming—or, at the very least, possessed of a certain command of the room. Not long after the Flamingo's opening, the novelist Erskine Caldwell, author of *Tobacco Road* and *God's Little Acre,* visited the "resplendent" resort, as he described it. There he spotted Siegel winged by two bodyguards. "With his glowing personality, his handsome physique, and his expensively tailored dark-blue suit worn with a white-on-white monogramed shirt and black silk necktie," Caldwell wrote, "it was a magical combination that stated Bugsy's presence in unmistakable terms." At the bar, loud talk dropped to a whisper as Siegel ordered drinks. "Bugsy blew a puff of cigar smoke at one of the briefly costumed cocktail girls," Caldwell added. "She stopped as if mesmerized and stood there panting with a heaving of her breast until he motioned for her to go away."

When not causing conversation to halt and breasts to heave, Siegel could occasionally go berserk. There remains even now a substantial anecdotal collection describing how Bugsy earned the nickname—a loose synomym for crazy—that he despised. This includes the oft-repeated account of his pulling his gun on his schlubby publicity director, Abe Schiller, at the Flamingo's pool. Schiller had done something to annoy Siegel. "On your hands and knees, you son of a bitch," Siegel ordered. As Schiller crawled around the pool, Bugsy fired shots over his head and into the water.

His financial backers could tolerate the occasional outburst of violent lunacy, but they wouldn't put up with a huge and never-ending cash drain. From that first night the Flamingo hemorrhaged money, and even had to close briefly in early 1947. Siegel was many things, but an effective fiduciary was not one of them. So he was fired, mob-style. On the evening of June 20, 1947, as Siegel sat in the Beverly Hills mansion of his mistress, Virginia Hill, reading the *Los Angeles Times,* a gunman aimed a .30-caliber carbine through a window, then squeezed the trigger. Two of the rounds struck Siegel in the head, with one knocking out his left eye, and two hit his chest. He was killed instantly, and the photograph of his body—slumped in a blood-soaked tailored suit on a floral chintz sofa—ran in newspapers around the world.

Now the Las Vegas aura began to assume a life of its own. Siegel wasn't the first criminal to open a casino in Las Vegas. He wasn't even rubbed out there. But dead on his girlfriend's couch, his eyeball on the floor across the room, Siegel in halftone gave birth to an image that Las Vegas took to the bank.

The city had entered the public consciousness as a criminal wild game preserve—or, more aptly, an adult amusement park—with an unmatched collection of murderous rogues reborn as legitimate businessmen, free to roam the streets. Las Vegas offered up something that no resort in the country could match, and it would be the subtext by which the city could sell itself for decades to come. These alpha hoods came with access to capital, and they brought their expertise, but they also imported a marketable air—not too much, the right amount—of menace.

Binion alone might have been enough. But down the road from him, now helping to operate the Flamingo, was Gus Greenbaum, a bow-tied drug addict and bookmaker who had run the rackets in Arizona. "A heck of a good man," Binion said. "Oh, hell, he was the best guy."

And more: David Berman, known to colleagues as Davie the Jew, arrived from Minnesota, where he had been a top mobster. Berman owned a lively and varied criminal past. At the age of eighteen he led his personal gang of bank and post-office robbers, and later served time in Sing Sing for kidnapping. To Binion, he was "another high-class guy." Within days of Siegel's death, Berman also took a management position at the Flamingo.

Moe Dalitz, a notorious bootlegger who had grown into a syndicate heavyweight, was a Cleveland associate of Detroit's murderous Purple Gang. "Very fine man, and a terrific businessman," Binion said. With his mastery of funneling cash from questionable sources, Dalitz helped build the Desert Inn on the Strip.

Moe Sedway, a Lansky officer typically described as a "ruthless dwarf," drove over from L.A. "During periods of stress," his FBI file noted, "he wrings his hands, becomes wild eyed and resembles a small dog about to be subjected to the distasteful procedure of being bathed." On Sedway's virtues, Binion is silent. Sedway, too, assumed a post-Siegel role in running the Flamingo.

Here, then, were the founding fathers of modern Las Vegas: Benny, Bugsy, Davie, Meyer, Gus, and a couple of Moes. As far as Vegas and the world of gambling were concerned, Binion would come to outdo them all.

The Las Vegas Club on Fremont Street, Binion's first legal casino.

# 10

# TEXAS VS. VEGAS

My friends can do no wrong and my enemies can do no right.

—BB

**M**any of the newly arrived mobsters from the East, Midwest, and California aspired to be real-life versions of the heavies that actors like George Raft played in the movies, from homburgs to spats. Most were Italian or Jewish, and they tended to favor silky pin-striped suits from which they picked specks of lint with manicured nails. Cavorting with movie stars became a marker of status. Though not educated, they sought a patina of class via custom-made silk shirts and monogrammed underwear.

Then there was the Cowboy. Binion's trousers were perpetually unpressed, and the buttons of his western shirts—made from gold coins—strained at his generous paunch. His hair looked as if it had been cut by the least promising freshman at a failing barber college. With all the polish of a Piggly Wiggly clerk, he wore an up-from-the-sticks grin and delivered country bromides in a nasal twang. He sometimes greeted friends with the query "How's your mammy?"

Although mobsters like Lansky had recoiled at Las Vegas's primitive state, Binion—more accustomed to rustic conditions than the average

Flatbush Avenue hustler—believed he had been dropped into Nevada's rendition of Eden. "Well," he remembered, "wasn't but something like 18,000
people here, and the most enjoyable place that you can imagine." Sure, Las
Vegas was filling up with criminals, but they weren't the sort who would
take your bankroll at gunpoint. "Everybody was friendly," Binion said, "and
there wasn't none of this hijacking, there wasn't no stealing, wasn't nothing, just—hell you couldn't get robbed if you hollered, 'Come rob me!'" You
could, however, get taken in a card game. Shortly after Binion's arrival he
lost about $400,000 in a high-stakes poker session.

Despite that setback, Binion bought a house in Vegas on West Bonanza
Road, a couple of miles from downtown and four miles off the Strip. Even
then this was not the best neighborhood in town. The two-story structure's
stone-and-log exterior gave it the look of an overgrown cabin. It had previously served as an apartment house for women fulfilling their six-week
divorce residency, and out back was a wishing well where the soon-to-be
singles could discard their wedding rings should the mood strike. Binion
purchased the place for $68,000 cash without even setting foot inside. All
he needed to know was that it was big—seven bedrooms—and sat on
enough empty land for the family's horses. With a strong enough fence, it
would be what he wanted: half ranch, half fort. And if the doors to four of
the seven bedrooms opened to the outside—well, he would let Teddy Jane
worry about that when she got to town.

For the moment, Binion needed to concentrate on the Las Vegas Club,
a Fremont Street casino fronted by J. Kell Houssels. A businessman with no
whiff of a mob past, Houssels had his hand in all sorts of enterprises—
restaurants, cab companies, thoroughbreds, and casinos. He was a Vegas
old-timer who had come to town in 1929, and bought a one-third interest
in a poker room. This became the Las Vegas Club.

Fred Merrill, Binion's Dallas friend, was an investor. Another was Nick
"the Greek" Dandalos, who was already promoting his reputation as the
greatest gambler in the history of the world. Meyer Lansky also had a stake,
which allowed him to install two of his associates, Gus Greenbaum and
Moe Sedway, as casino managers.

Mob executives aside, this was no Flamingo. "This Las Vegas Club
wasn't the most beautiful place you ever seen," Binion recalled. "It was a

old, run-down kind of place." That description may have been charitable. Like some other joints in Glitter Gulch, it operated from a bare-bones gambling room offering table games, slots, and a bar. With banks of fluorescent lights and chrome-legged chairs, the club possessed all the ambience of a down-at-the-heels lunch counter.

Working with Houssels, Merrill, and the others, Binion did business as he had in Dallas, which brought the proprietors of other Glitter Gulch casinos to a quick boil.

These rivals were especially unhappy that Binion's betting limits in craps were higher than in nearby casinos, which meant the high rollers flocked to the Las Vegas Club. Binion recalled one dice player who was putting down $40,000 a roll, and was at one point a $300,000 winner. "The guy played so long," he said, "his feet got tired." Binion ordered his porters to wash the gambler's feet with cold beer. The dice rolling continued, and when the man was done, he had lost $470,000. "Back in them days," Binion said, "that was a whole lot of money."

Other club owners tried warning Binion that he would go broke. "And he says, 'That doesn't worry me in the least,'" recalled Robbins Cahill, a former member of the Nevada Tax Commission. "He says . . . 'I can always get a new bankroll, but I can't get new customers. But as long as they don't take my customers, and my play, why, I haven't got anything else to worry about.'"

Binion also paid his dealers more than the prevailing wage in Glitter Gulch. "I didn't pay no attention to what they was paying dealers around here or nothing," he said. This, too, enraged rival operators. "There's some old guys around here . . . that weren't too damn good in my book. They gave me a little bit of trouble on account of all this, you see . . . Some of them was a little bit on the jealous order."

As their resentment grew, his competitors plotted retribution. All they needed was an opening. Clifford Duane Helm, a former Dallas rodeo champion, gave it to them.

At forty-two, Helm had retired from the bronc-busting circuit a banged-up man: he was missing several teeth and drew whistling breaths through a crooked nose that had been broken by many falls from many horses. Other accidents claimed the tips of three fingers and all of a fourth. Helm was short, compact, and happy to settle arguments with a handgun.

He worked as Binion's bodyguard and casino security officer at the Las Vegas Club. Before Binion brought him west, Helm's one major brush with the law occurred in 1941. He had been in his Dallas home, wondering where his wife might be. The answer came to him when he looked out the window about three in the morning and saw her stepping from a taxi, arm in arm with her first husband. Helm walked outside and, in his own front yard, shot the man in the face. A Dallas County grand jury no-billed Helm on a murder charge—as expected, police records noted, "inasmuch as [the] assault [was] caused by victim's illicit association with Helm's wife."

Binion adored Helm, describing him "as honorable and honest as any man I ever had anything to do with." A good cowboy, a good blacksmith, a good cook, hunter, and fisherman. "Son of a gun could do any damn thing," Binion said. "He was a *good* guy." Helm made a different impression as he strove to maintain order at Binion and Houssel's casino. "A cold-blooded, vicious son-of-a-bitch," one Las Vegas law enforcement official called him. "He strutted around like a peacock all of the time wearing two silver forty-five caliber pistols in his holster and always dressed in black."

But a cold-blooded strutter with sidearms was what the Las Vegas Club needed. Like other Fremont Street establishments, it catered to a rough mix of crusty locals, desert rats, construction crews, and the occasional tough package who drove from L.A. They gambled, they drank, they fought, they drank some more. Helm had the perfect temperament—mean and unforgiving on his nicer days—to deal with such a crowd. Also, he was now and then called upon to handle trouble from back home.

Shortly after Binion's arrival in Las Vegas, Charles Melton "Sonny" Lefors came to town—the same Sonny Lefors who had helped kill Bob Minyard back in Texas. Jug-eared and balding, Lefors owned a West Dallas store that doubled as a fencing operation. He was at once inept, conniving, and deadly; cops and fellow thieves alike considered him completely untrustworthy. Lieutenant Butler of the Dallas police knew only one way to be certain Lefors was playing straight: "You know how you can tell when you are getting close to the truth on Sonny?" he asked. "He just shits all over himself." Butler recalled questioning Lefors about a particular gang-land killing, "and, boy, he filled his britches full."

Lefors had driven from Dallas to Las Vegas in his pickup truck and brought his wife, claiming to be looking for business opportunities. But anyone who knew about the festering feud in Dallas figured that Herbert Noble, who had given Lefors a .38 Special and $1,000 to make the trip, had sent him to case—or kill—Binion. As often happened, Lefors went about it all wrong. He had emerged from a Las Vegas casino late at night and was walking along a downtown street when a Cadillac pulled next to him and eased to a stop. Helm stepped from the car, grabbed Lefors, and forced him onto the front seat. Binion sat in the back and stared in silence. As the driver pulled away and headed for 2040 West Bonanza Road, Helm kept his gun on Lefors.

Binion's house was dark as the Cadillac, its tires crunching the desert hardpan, crept to the separate servants' quarters in the rear. Binion and Helm dragged Lefors from the car, took him inside the quarters, and searched him. "Sit down and shut up," Binion told him. Then, his manner calm and his voice quiet, he began asking questions. He asked Lefors about Dallas, about his old friends, and about Noble, especially about Noble. This continued for nearly two hours. It's not clear whether a terrified Lefors offered his usual proof of truth telling.

Through it all, Helm asked Binion again and again to let him kill Lefors. They could bury him in the desert, Helm argued, and no one would ever know what happened. Gun in hand, he begged to do it. "He almost got on his knees," Lefors said later. But Binion told Helm no, that he didn't want any unnecessary killing. Lefors's grateful response was an offer to help Binion, once back in Dallas, any way he could. For Binion, it was a satisfactory outcome. He now had a mole—a craven, stupid, double-crossing one, but a mole nonetheless—in Noble's operation. Helm, however, was deeply disappointed that he hadn't been allowed to shoot somebody. He would get another chance soon.

Johnny Beasley's real name was Frank Ferroni Jr., but he had changed it to something more cowboy-like. Beasley stumbled into Las Vegas as yet another Dallas henchman and former rodeo hand imported by Binion. He was a drug addict who had served time for second-degree murder, and even when off the dope and not killing anyone, he posed a threatening annoyance. Back in Dallas he had been given to dropping by Binion's house to cadge handouts. Binion, who had yet to bring his family to Las Vegas, didn't want his wife forced to deal with someone like that. "He was crazy," he said. "So I just loaded him up and brought him here."

For a couple of months, Binion said, Beasley was "straight as a string," working at the Las Vegas Club as a shill—a decoy player who lured real gamblers into the game. But then, as Binion described it, "he gets on that dope again." On the afternoon of March 25, 1947, Binion was home with the flu when he got a call from the club: Beasley had been caught stealing. Binion put him on the phone. "Beasley," he said, "you're going to have to leave. Where do you want to go?"

New Jersey, Beasley answered, where he might find some work with Jim Eskew's famous Wild West show and rodeo. So Binion, ever the soft touch for an old cowboy, instructed Cliff Helm to escort Beasley to the train station and buy his ticket east. During the one-block walk to the depot, Beasley hatched another plan. He told Helm to pay his bus fare to Kingman, Arizona—much cheaper than a train ride to New Jersey—and give him the balance of the cash. Helm said he needed permission to do that, and the two returned to the Las Vegas Club.

The temperature at the club was not quite right, so Helm—who, in addition to his strong-arm duties, had custodial responsibilities—went to the casino's equipment room at the rear of the building. Beasley joined him there. Once he had adjusted the air-conditioning, Helm turned to more pressing matters. He drew his Colt automatic pistol and began to beat Beasley about the head, striking him so hard that he fractured his skull in two places. Then Helm fired his gun at least twice. Somehow Beasley managed to rise from the floor and stagger out the equipment-room door. Helm pointed his pistol at the fleeing man's back. A casino employee yelled, "Don't, Cliff!" But as customers screamed and scattered, Helm resumed firing. One shot hit a bystander in the arm. Four shots struck Beasley in all: two through his arm, one through his aorta, and one in the back of the neck.

Much later, Binion summed up Helm's multiple shots as the simple diligence that a man such as Beasley required. "You've got to kill him sometime, 'cause this is the most dangerous son of a gun in the world," he said. "So he just went ahead and done a good job of it."

With the shooting finished, Binion was summoned, as was Houssels. Helm hastily wiped the blood from his hot pistol and put it back in its holster, and the gamblers returned to their tables. Within minutes, wheels were spinning and dice rolling as if nothing had happened. Never mind that Beasley's body still lay on the casino floor, blood pooling around him. The Las Vegas police finally showed, and not long after that, the phone rang at Harry Claiborne's house.

Claiborne was an angular Arkansas farm boy who had earned a law degree at a small Tennessee school. He spent some of World War II as a military policeman in Las Vegas, rousting wayward soldiers out of whorehouses and casinos. After the war, he returned to Las Vegas and joined the city police force. The Las Vegas department of 1945 was a less-than-stellar law enforcement organization—"a bunch of stupid cowboys," in the words of the Clark County district attorney. They protected the powerful and did the bidding of the moneyed. Not a few of them were on the take. The department had twenty-five officers, three cars, and a high-ranking inspector who had ordered that driving-while-intoxicated arrests were to cease "because all my goddamned friends are drunks." Thus the police department became a free taxi service, providing rides home to overserved locals.

After passing the Nevada Bar exam, Claiborne joined the district attorney's office in Las Vegas, one of two lawyers on staff, including the DA. He had been on the job less than three months when the phone call came regarding the Las Vegas Club. A detective told him, "We have a problem."

Police had gone to the club to investigate the shooting of Beasley, but Binion and Houssels refused to allow them inside. When he arrived at the casino, Claiborne found his entry blocked as well. Houssels met him at the door and advised him, "Harry, we take care of our own. That's the way it's always been and that's the way it will be."

"It may be the way it used to be," Claiborne said. "It will not be the way it is now, believe me. Times have changed."

"They can't go back," Houssels said, pointing to the detectives.

Claiborne turned to the police officers around him and told them to go to a hardware store. Buy locks and heavy chains, he said. When they returned, he ordered, they were to empty the club and padlock the doors. "You don't dare," Houssels said.

"Wait and see," Claiborne answered.

Houssels and Binion relented, and the detectives entered the club. By this time, Helm had had ample opportunity to get his story straight: he told investigators he had killed Beasley in self-defense. Beasley had tried to stab him, Helm said, and got close enough to slash Helm's tie and shirt. A dull Boy Scout knife, said to be Beasley's, was recovered from the floor of the equipment room.

Claiborne confronted Helm. "Do you have a knife, Cliff?" he asked. Helm handed his own knife to Claiborne, who dropped it into a plastic evidence bag. "I think you cut your own tie," Claiborne told him. "I think you held your tie and cut it with your own knife."

Claiborne's boss, Clark County district attorney Robert Jones, termed this a "brutal gangland killing," and immediately asked for forensic help from the FBI. One of his investigators airmailed Helm's knife and tie to the bureau's lab in Washington, DC. A few days later the special agent in charge of the FBI's Salt Lake City office, which oversaw Las Vegas, sent a telex, classified "urgent," to FBI director J. Edgar Hoover, warning that the fix was in. Binion and his pals were spending money and pulling strings in an attempt to free Helm, the telex said, and had enlisted the help of the sheriff's office and police department. Binion, a Las Vegas resident for only a few months, already had the juice, according to the agent: "District attorney Jones stated today he cannot trust certain members of Clark County SO and Las Vegas PD who may attempt to assist defense." Jones was a former FBI special agent.

At Helm's trial, two FBI lab technicians testified that microscopic fibers retrieved from the blade well of his knife matched silk fibers from his tie. No such fibers, they insisted, were recovered on the knife that was said to be Beasley's. Clearly, Helm had slashed his tie himself in an attempt to make it appear that Beasley had attacked him. He was found guilty of first-degree murder and sentenced to life.

Within hours of the verdict, the Las Vegas district attorney wrote a thank-you letter to FBI director Hoover, noting that "these two splendid agents made a remarkable impression on the jury by their straightforward, clear and convincing testimony." Two weeks later, Helm was booked into the Nevada State Prison in Carson City.

Binion suspected for decades that his friend had been railroaded. "I did everything I could for him, but the thing was stacked against him in them days here," he said. He insisted Helm wasn't the real target. "They was wanting to get rid of me, too, really. They didn't want me around here. I was a little too strong in the competition right then."

Because Binion refused to provide names to his interviewer ("They'll know who I'm talking about"), such a claim may be easy to dismiss. But some pieces of evidence, long buried, back his suspicions. First, there's a letter from Edward C. "Ted" Cupit, chief investigator for the Las Vegas district attorney's office, to Hoover four days after Beasley's death. Cupit had written to explain the physical evidence provided to the bureau. He added this: "I have given you all of this information to let you know how vital this case is to this city and to this office. There is a foreign gambling element here that we must control." Convicting Helm, the letter said, would "go a long way toward giving us the upper hand on said element."

Second, there came an unexpected crusade by the warden at the Nevada State Prison. Arthur Bernard, a former boxer, bootlegger, and mine inspector, was a famously independent warden—a hard man when necessary, but a trusting one when he could be. He presided over a prison that had no chapel but did have its own casino, operated by inmates.

Not long after Helm's arrival, Bernard put him in charge of the prison stables. "He used to take my kids riding, took my wife and her friends riding," Bernard said. "And he was honest. I would have sent him to Texas with my family and a checkbook and signed a bunch of checks, and when he came back they'd have been absolutely correct to the last nickel, and I know that nothing would have happened to my kids and my wife. He was just that good a man."

Helm talked about his case, and sufficiently intrigued Bernard that the warden read the trial transcripts. Bernard became convinced that Helm deserved a medal for killing Beasley, not a life sentence. On a trip to Las Vegas, Bernard tracked down one of the jurors, who was a friend of his. "How in the hell did you convict Helm on that murder charge?" Bernard asked him.

As the juror told it, Helm's strutting had done him no favors: "That little SOB came to court every morning in a brand new suit. A brand new Western suit, fancy cowboy boots. And he looked at us as if we were dirt, like we were dirt under his feet." But it was the forensic evidence—the fibers on Helm's knife—and the testimony of the FBI lab technicians that proved crucial. "That's what clinched it."

Some weeks later Bernard talked to the new head of the state parole board, Ted Cupit—the same man who, as the DA's investigator, had urged the FBI's help in controlling the "foreign gambling element." Bernard mentioned the Helm case and said, "There's something fishy about that." Cupit looked uncomfortable and changed the subject. Months passed, and every time Bernard mentioned Helm to Cupit, he got the same reaction. Bernard said, "Ted, you know something I should know."

Cupit struggled for an answer. "If I tell you, it's going to raise hell."

"I think you should tell me," Bernard said. "This is not something we can play with."

Cupit unloaded his story on Bernard: He had a brother-in-law on the Las Vegas police force who, during the investigation of the Helm case, furnished a house for a secret meeting of prosecutor Claiborne and police detectives. "And what they did there," Cupit said, "they took Cliff's knife and the tie from the courthouse, where it was supposed to be under lock and key. They stripped some threads out of the tie, and they put it in the knife, and they sent that to the FBI."

Bernard went straight to Cupit's brother-in-law, who confirmed the story, even providing a written and signed account. Anxious and anguished, Bernard took this new information to the chief justice of the state supreme court, who also sat on the board of pardons. "Let me think it over," the chief justice told him, "and I'll see that justice is served one way or another."

And then nothing happened. The justice sat on the evidence; each time Bernard inquired, he was told to be patient. "I'm still thinking," the justice said. "I haven't forgotten." He was apparently a slow thinker, because Helm spent more than six years in prison, until one afternoon when a guard captain came to Bernard's office and said, "Warden, there's something wrong with Cliff Helm."

He had fallen from a horse at the prison corral and had suffered a subdural hematoma. Bernard summoned the best brain surgeon in the state—he may have been the only brain surgeon in the state—to operate on Helm, but the surgery failed. Helm died a convicted murderer at forty-nine.

For Binion the Helm episode provided an early and humbling lesson in the ways of Las Vegas. In Dallas the solution to a problem with a competitor was pretty simple: control him or kill him. But Vegas had far more crosscurrents, and more plentiful and muscular operators. If he were to survive, Binion would have to learn to maneuver in this new landscape.

Nine months after Helm's conviction, Binion ran into Harry Claiborne on a sidewalk in downtown Las Vegas. It was Claiborne's last week with the district attorney's office; he had decided to enter private practice. Given his bitterness and suspicions, Binion could have shunned Claiborne, or threatened him, or plotted his destruction. Instead, he said, "I want to hire you."

Claiborne reminded Binion of his prosecution of Helm. "From all I hear," he said, "you don't like me very well."

Binion looked Claiborne in the eye and said, "Well I didn't know there was a goddamn law that said you had to fall in love with your lawyer." They laughed and shook hands.

Within days Claiborne opened his law office. It was at Binion's Las Vegas Club. He soon went to work addressing his new client's most pressing legal problems. As Binion told him, "I got some troubles coming from Texas."

The two of them became inseparable companions. "Me and Claiborne is the best friends on earth," Binion said many years afterward. "He's as honest as the day is long."

Yet Binion never shed his belief that the man who became his best pal had helped railroad Cliff Helm. "I don't doubt but what Claiborne kinda feels bad about that," he said. But a man has to do what is necessary to survive and thrive. "He had bosses," Binion reasoned.

Through all the decades of intimate friendship and close professional relationships, Binion insisted, he never asked Claiborne about the case. If he never forgot the injustice visited upon his good friend Helm, he also refused to let it interfere with his business. "I just kinda kept a-rollin'," he said. "I don't look back. Old guy told me one time, said, 'Don't never look back, or holler whoa in a bad place.'"

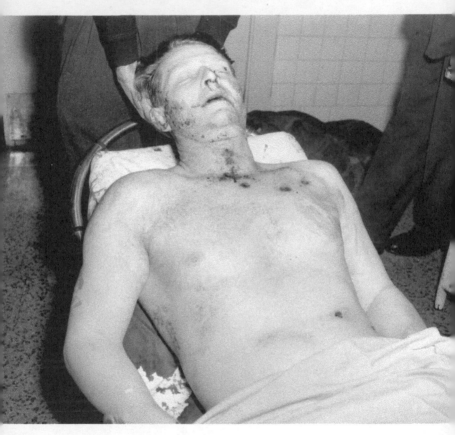

Brutal killer Lois Green finally meets his match.

# 11

# "A KILL-CRAZY MAN"

It lasts a long time when I get mad.

—BB

Binion's wife could not shake her homesickness. At the mere mention of Dallas, Teddy Jane would break into tears. Binion missed the place too, despite his stated philosophy of never looking back, and he made secret trips. "He snuck in a lot," daughter Brenda said. He sometimes brought his children on these long Cadillac rides from Nevada to Texas, with Gold Dollar at the wheel. But he had to take special precautions, especially as the car sped through backwater burgs, where he feared his kids might contract polio. "We'd drive through these little towns," Brenda said, "and he'd roll up the windows and tell us to hold our breath."

These were brief, quiet visits home, with an exit before anyone outside Binion's local band of loyalists even knew he had arrived. He realized he had too many enemies on both sides of the law to come back for good. Should he move back now, he believed, Herbert Noble would try to kill him. Noble was, at the very least, discussing ways to make it happen. One associate told him all he had to do was park a car with a bomb in it next to Binion's car.

If the killers didn't get him, the authorities would. Dallas County district attorney Will Wilson and his assistant, a bulldoggish former FBI agent named Henry Wade, nursed strong prosecutorial designs on Binion. Their strategy was to start small—putting pressure on the drones and lesser operatives—and work their way up to the top man. They began with a successful prosecution of the dice game operator at the Maurice Hotel in downtown Dallas. Binion had long controlled and profited from the game at the Maurice. Wilson proclaimed that the convictions for running a gambling hall were the first of their kind in Dallas in twenty-five years, and he promised more to come.

Binion's business was not proceeding so well in Nevada either. Kell Houssels, seeking a better real estate situation, moved the Las Vegas Club across Fremont Street, and this change required a new gambling permit—in general a routine matter. But the state tax commission, which licensed casino operators, would grant only Houssels permission to operate the new Las Vegas Club. All the additional investors—Binion, Merrill, Nick the Greek, and several others—were denied.

The decision puzzled Binion. "The Las Vegas Club was a damn good operation. We got along good there," he said. However, he didn't try to fight the state regulators. "We just cut up the bankroll there and walked off."

He found other ways to make money. Perhaps the easiest was the secret funneling of millions of dollars from prominent Dallas bankers to Las Vegas mobsters. According to confidential Texas Rangers memos, Binion arranged for $4 million in loans from Dallas banks to "Las Vegas people." Acting as a broker, he took a 5 percent cut, which gave him $200,000 for his trouble.

At least $500,000 of the $4 million went from the Republic Bank in Dallas to the Las Vegas arm of the Cleveland syndicate, principally Moe Dalitz, to help build the palatial Desert Inn on the Strip. "Big-shot racketeers," the memo noted of the Cleveland crowd. If such a stalwart Dallas institution as Republic was worried about exposure of its role in lending money to mobsters, protections were put in place. "This loan . . . was made in such a manner that it would be hard to trace back to the Bank as having been directly made to the gambling joint," the Rangers memo said. The august bank's legerdemain worked. Texas authorities took no action, and the casino bankrolling was never made public. For his efforts, Binion didn't obtain a stake in the Desert Inn, but he did secure a lifelong friend in Dalitz.

Soon Binion got a chance to invest in another relatively modest Glitter Gulch casino, the Westerner. This time, his application sailed through the tax commission, which granted him a license to operate the club in June 1949. His tenure at the Westerner was an unhappy one. Binion said he "kinda got in there with partners that was recommended by somebody, and I just didn't like it . . . And I didn't care much about it, nohow."

Among those partners was Emilio "Gambo" Georgetti, semiliterate owner of a meatpacking business and an organized crime operator of the old school. His FBI file classified him as a "Top Hoodlum" out of Northern California, and said he was the slot machine king of San Mateo County, near San Francisco. During World War II, the bureau said, Georgetti's Willow Tree club in Colma, California, was the largest gambling casino west of the Mississippi. Such bona fides aside, he and Binion failed to bond. Georgetti complained bitterly that Binion looked down on him and treated him "like a dog." For his part, Binion said his partner brought disreputable associates—meaning Georgetti's friends—to the Westerner. "They just weren't the type of people I like," Binion recalled. "I guess I've just been the boss, running these things with success so damn long, that if a guy ain't just absolutely my type of a man . . . I couldn't hardly be in partners with him."

Binion sold out and walked away from the Westerner and, potentially, from Las Vegas. "I decided I might leave," he said. He considered moving for good to his ranch in Montana, but Teddy Jane didn't like visiting there, much less settling in permanently.

Once again the family talked of returning to Dallas, and they received at least one piece of encouraging news. Their old friend Bill Decker ran for sheriff in 1948, and easily defeated the incumbent Guthrie in a campaign financed in part by Binion. "Maybe I put up something like $3,500," he said. "No strings attached to that money. I just give it to him for old times sake."

With the district attorney pursuing him, Binion still faced big legal problems in Texas. But that's what lawyers were for, and Binion had plenty of them. Perhaps more important, old rivals had to be controlled—or, failing that, eliminated. He knew the professionals to hire for that job too. They were already hard at work.

Herbert Noble still operated his gambling operation, the Airmen's Club, in downtown Dallas, and he maintained his ranch in Denton County, where he kept his airplanes. Almost two years had passed since someone had tried to shoot him. That changed on the night of May 20, 1948, as his car rumbled over the cattle guard at the entrance to his ranch. Someone—police believed it was Binion's old assassin Lois Green—fired a shotgun from the darkness. Buckshot struck Noble in the arm and wrist, but he escaped by driving to his house. That was murder attempt number three.

Next, on February 14, 1949, a friend of Noble's happened to be taking a break outside the Airmen's Club. When he saw a man crawling under Noble's car, the friend ran upstairs to make a report. Police were called, and officers found dynamite and blasting caps beneath the Mercury. Thus Noble lived through attempt number four.

And on the night of September 7, 1949, a ranch worker told Noble that a black Ford had been driving back and forth along the fence line. Noble grabbed a rifle, jumped into his own car, and found the Ford. Then came a chase, with Noble pursuing the Ford for six miles at high speed, until the Ford slid into a ditch. Several men piled out and began firing. Noble, despite being shot in the leg, fired back.

The men got away, but an investigation sorted it all out. "This attempt was made by Jack Nesbit and Jim Thomas," an internal police memo said. Thomas was the Binion hit man who had, some years earlier, murdered a doctor and his wife, and whose conviction had been reversed on appeal. Nesbit was a slow-witted gunman who worked security at Binion's Dallas dice rooms. "Information was received," the memo continued, "to the effect that Thomas and Nesbit had been hired by Binion" for the Noble attack. But as so frequently happened in these matters, the case slipped into limbo, and no charges were filed.

Noble had now survived five efforts to kill him. The deadline poets at the local papers came up with two nicknames: the Human Clay Pigeon and the Cat.

Weary of dodging bullets, Noble began to give serious thought to forsaking the casino business—and escaping Binion's enmity. He entered negotiations with a group of partners from New York to buy a decommissioned army airfield in Fort Worth. Noble's plan: turn it into a private airport, with aircraft maintenance and repair services. No gambling, no fencing, no gangsters hanging around. This was to be a lawful enterprise, or at least that was what he told others. The closing for the sale was set for November 29, 1949, in Fort Worth.

Noble's wife, Mildred, greeted this news with joy. For years she had dreaded the late-night phone call telling her that Herbert was dead; soon she wouldn't have to worry anymore. Like her husband, Mildred had risen from West Dallas poverty, but she had no active involvement in his criminal pursuits. Instead, she strove to fashion a life that modeled the city's merchant class: domestic help, ladies' luncheons, church committees, piano recitals, a house in town, and a retreat in the country. A thirty-six-year-old striking brunette, she sometimes wore a mink stole and feathered hats. The couple's teenage daughter, Frieda, attended a boarding school in Virginia.

Now, if Herbert were indeed to abandon gambling, Mildred need not change the subject when someone asked her what her husband did for a living. The couple made plans to celebrate the airfield purchase—and their freshly respectable life—with a candlelight dinner that night at home.

The morning of November 29 dawned clear and cool. Noble put on a dark double-breasted suit, set off by a crisply knotted and dimpled silk tie, and left the house at 311 Conrad Street. Because he was escorting two bankers to the signing, he took the rare step of driving his wife's Cadillac. "A nicer ride," he explained. He started the car and pulled away from his tidy home in the quiet of the morning. As he drove down Conrad Street and through the leafy neighborhood, the big news on the radio was the predawn crash of an American Airlines passenger plane at Love Field, which had killed twenty-eight. Noble proceeded on, and within an hour he had reached Fort Worth, ready to buy some real estate.

At midmorning, Mildred Noble walked out the front door of the

Conrad Street house. She planned to go to the Noble ranch and pick up their maid, who would help prepare the celebratory dinner. Mildred crossed the yard and got into her husband's black 1949 Mercury. It was parked at the curb. She pressed the Mercury's starter, which ignited the nitroglycerin gel that had been hidden behind the dashboard sometime in the night.

The explosion could be heard from eight miles. It shattered windows for blocks, and destroyed the Mercury down to its chassis. One of the car doors sailed over two rows of houses and landed in someone's backyard next to a child's sandpile. Shards of metal were driven into the doors and outside walls of houses a hundred feet away. And what was left of Mrs. Noble lay in the green grass of her front yard.

After the roar, silence. A neighbor, a woman who had known Mildred for years, ran over. She gazed at the smoking corpse, but it was so bloody, blackened, and shredded that the woman didn't recognize her friend. She returned to her house, called police, and retrieved a sheet to cover the body. Then came the sirens.

In Fort Worth, thirty-five miles to the west, Noble sat in the office of U.S. Attorney Frank Potter. He had finished signing the last of the land-transaction papers when someone said he had a phone call. He picked up the receiver, listened briefly in silence, then said, "Dead?" After a moment he put the phone down and turned to the others in the room. "The bastard killed my wife," he said.

He drove himself in a fury back to Dallas, and then to the funeral home where Mildred's remains had been taken. At the back of the mortuary, he cradled what was left of her in his arms, moaning and wailing. That afternoon a reporter went to his house and found Noble alone and bereft in his darkened living room. Noble pointed to a rusty smear on his face. "See that?" he said. "That's my wife's blood . . . I wish it had been me." To another reporter he said, "They killed an innocent woman and one of the best women who ever lived. I worshipped the ground she walked on."

Noble bought her a solid-bronze casket. It weighed two tons—too heavy to be carried by six or eight men; it had to be rolled—and was reported, at $15,000, to be the most expensive ever purchased in Dallas. "It is of a type," the *Morning News* observed, "used by the Henry Ford family." More than seven hundred mourners packed the chapel for Mildred's funeral, while four hundred others waited outside. The procession of cars to the cemetery stretched for two miles.

One day after Mildred Noble's death, Captain Will Fritz, head of the Dallas police homicide bureau, informed the public that he had questioned a "29-year-old underworld member" as a suspect. But the gangster "did not tell us anything that would help," Fritz said, adding that there was a "standing price of $5,000 on Herbert Noble's head." That was a lowball estimate. Many in Dallas gambling circles had heard someone could collect at least $20,000 for killing Noble. Others said the bounty had risen to $50,000. Everyone knew they were talking about Binion's money.

The twenty-nine-year-old to whom Fritz referred was Binion's close associate R. D. Matthews. Police believed he and Lois Green had put the dynamite in Noble's car, possibly with assistance from some roving Kansas City safecrackers who had expertise in explosives. Matthews denied any involvement, and it quickly became clear there was no hard evidence to use against him. It took police more than two years to coerce Matthews into taking a polygraph test. When he finally relented, he showed "very strong reaction," which indicated deception, to this question: "Did you use . . . rifles to cover the Noble residence the night the bomb was planted that killed Mildred Noble?" And he showed a "very good reaction," also indicating deception, to this one: "Did you ever plant a bomb in any of Noble's cars?"

From the vantage of six decades later, Matthews provided a simple rationale for his dismal performance on the polygraph, the same explanation he gave to the Dallas police officer who made him take it: "I told him those tests record if you're nervous," he said. "I told him, 'You make me nervous.'" Of Mildred Noble's death, Matthews added, "I didn't have a goddamn thing to do with it."

No one doubted that the car bomb had been meant for Noble, and now the grief and guilt consumed the man. Somehow, through all the attempts to kill him, he had assumed his family would be immune. "I have been a gambler, it is true," he said. "But my family life was decent, and my wife, daughter and I had nothing to hide."

He pledged to cooperate with the police investigation—a lie—then added, "I don't think the police can do much about it." To Noble, the problem could be easily explained: the person who wanted him dead was too powerful, and too irrationally driven to murder, for the local cops to control. "All those plans to kill me have been made by the same man—a kill-crazy man," he said. "The fellow who is behind this is 1,500 miles from Dallas right now . . . He's a mad killer."

Noble refused to name this mad killer, but that was hardly necessary. "Why in the world he continues to try to get me," he said, "is more than I can understand." He later offered one explanation for Binion's wrath: "I wouldn't bow down to him."

At a terrible personal loss, he had survived murder attempt number six. It was at this point, his friends and associates agreed, that Noble slowly began to go insane.

He bought six Chihuahuas that would yap at the sound of intruders. Then he installed floodlights around the exterior of his home, which he took to calling the "house of fear." All night long, as he paced the echoing rooms, armed with a rifle and unable to sleep, the outside was lit like a state prison yard. When morning finally came, Noble would climb into his car and head for the cemetery. He visited his wife's grave every day, and there he made a vow. Her killers might be caught by the police, he said, "and I want a front-row seat at the electrocution."

But if the police weren't up to the job—and it was soon clear they would not come close to solving this crime—Noble had backup plans.

First, Noble sent an associate to visit R. D. Matthews at home. The man told Matthews he needed a place to stay for the night, so Matthews let him. Then Matthews went to bed, but not for long. "He shot me in the head while I was sleeping," Matthews said. The man fired a .22-caliber pistol into his left eye—the bullet exiting at his temple—then ran away. Matthews staggered from bed, checked the damage in his bathroom mirror, and drove himself to the doctor. He lost the eye, but won the fight a few days later. The gunman "got killed," Matthews explained some years afterward.

Next, Noble went after Lois Green, Binion's enforcer. Not one to keep his mouth shut, Green had been overheard in a bar, laughing and bragging to some prostitutes about blowing up a woman—Mildred Noble. That was all the evidence Noble needed. Now he had to wait for a phone call from a waitress he knew at the Sky Vu Club in West Dallas. She had promised to alert him whenever Green walked in.

The Sky Vu was a cavernous dance hall and nightclub at the apex of Commerce Street and Fort Worth Avenue. It epitomized the provincial gangsters' idea of class, and the members of Green's Forty Thieves loved to take their girlfriends there, as did Green himself. The Sky Vu was owned by a friend of theirs, Joe Bonds, a former New York street hustler whose real name was Joseph Locurto. Short, bald, and plump, Bonds liked to hire underage girls and force them, in the club's back rooms, to perform what an indictment would later describe as unnatural sex acts. Bonds's wife was a former pinup girl and "singing comedienne" named Dale Belmont, a trim beauty with a thick mane. She usually starred as the Sky Vu's headliner act, backed by Johnny Cola and his five-piece band. That served as the glittering entertainment lineup on December 23, 1949, as Green motored to the Sky Vu to join his friends and their mistresses. He parked his car in an alleyway between the club and a neighboring restaurant, the Semos Drive-In, and went inside for a night of drinking and dancing.

While Dale Belmont sang and Green relaxed, two men in separate cars cruised the dark, nearby blocks. One was Herbert Noble, and the other was Sonny Lefors, who had pulled a thin rubber mask over his head. Both men carried shotguns.

By 1:00 a.m. or so Green had enjoyed his fill. He settled his customary snap-brim hat on his rather large head and left the Sky Vu alone. In the dim alley, as he opened the door to his car, someone called his name from the shadows. He turned to look. There was a boom and a flash, then another. Green fell to the ground, his throat and chest ripped by buckshot. Within minutes he was dead.

No one saw who did it. But not many hours after Green's death, Noble walked into Lefors's West Dallas grocery and slapped a morgue photo of Green on the counter. "There he is," Noble said. The black-and-white picture showed Green's corpse on a gurney, a sheet covering him from the waist down, with bloody holes in his face, neck, and torso. "There's the dirty son of a bitch."

Police rounded up dozens of hoods for questioning, and quickly determined that no small number of people, including a few members of Green's own gang, harbored reasons for wanting him dead. But no charges were filed against anyone, which might have been expected. Many officers expressed quiet gratitude that someone with a shotgun had finally managed to do what they had failed to accomplish for years: put Lois Green away for good.

If the cops were gleeful, many of the Dallas tough guys descended into grief. Three days after the Sky Vu ambush, Green's funeral attracted a standing-room-only crowd of four hundred at the chapel of the Sparkman-Brand Funeral Home in Dallas. If Binion was among them—an unlikely event—he stayed unnoticed and out of sight. All six of the pallbearers had arrest records, including one with a murder conviction, and the preacher was an ex-con. The Reverend Alfred Palmer, late of the federal prison in Seagoville, Texas, where he had served a stretch for mail fraud, delivered a restrained eulogy. "He was loved and respected by those of his world," Palmer said of the thirty-one-year-old Green. "He fought a good fight in that particular kind of world."

This gathering of the Dallas outlaw elite to pay final tribute to their "fallen chief" inspired reporter George Carter of the *Times Herald* to wax elegiac. "There were the safe burglars and narcotics thieves who had formed his board of strategy," he wrote. "There were the prostitutes dressed in fine coats and wearing dark red lipstick and mascara that had melted under their tears." And in the back rows, he noted, were those who aspired to be like Green, "satellites of an underworld they had never quite broken into—the common thieves who came in cheap clothing and looked on in awe."

Then the shiny steel casket was loaded onto a hearse. As the cortege left the funeral home, en route to the cemetery, undercover officers filmed the mourners from across the street. Many of the gangsters covered their faces with their hands as they drove away in their Cadillacs, following the black hearse. Off-duty Dallas motorcycle officers led the way, giving Green his final police escort.

Betty Green, the gangster's widow—"blond, attractive," Carter observed— had sobbed openly through the service. But to say that she remained inconsolable in her loss would be incorrect. About a week after the funeral, the police racket squad kicked in the door to the apartment of one of Green's pallbearers. There they found Mrs. Green, along with Green's former close friend and five ounces of cocaine.

With Green's death, Binion had lost one of his most hardened henchmen, and then the situation took a turn that was, for him, even worse. One day after Green's funeral, more than forty police officers and sheriff's deputies gathered in the predawn. They went over their plans, and then fanned out across the county toward a dozen different locations in unmarked cars. These were raiding parties, led by Hansson, the Dallas police chief, and Wilson, the district attorney, and they targeted Binion's North Texas operations.

Binion liked to tell people he had relinquished all his Texas interests when he fled to Las Vegas. "I left the state of Texas three years ago and left everything I had there behind me," he said. "I told the boys they could have the whole works." The raiding parties were about to prove this a lie. Four carloads of them headed in different directions. One found little more than an empty office, and another encountered a locked safe. But one of them hit pay dirt.

Right after sunrise, in silence, the raiders approached a riding stable a dozen miles northwest of Dallas. The stable itself, in a muddy field, looked unremarkable: a wood-plank exterior with peeling white paint, a rusty sheet-metal roof, and a few stalls. But when they forced open the door to the tack room, the police found a trove of evidence. Inside were seven men—all Binion cronies—with bundles of cash and policy game receipts. In the corner of the room sat an open safe that contained Binion's tax returns and stacks of records that detailed his continued hold on the local numbers racket. The papers showed a strict managerial structure: branch managers divided the city into districts, shady accountants kept the books, and Binion, the absentee landlord, took up to 66 percent of the gross. This appeared to be paying him more than $1 million a year.

For the first time, the authorities had breached Binion's inner wall. As word of this assault flashed through Dallas and out to Las Vegas, it brought a rumor too: that Herbert Noble had tipped the police to the location of the evidence. The informants in Binion's orbit could not say for certain if this was true or not, but it didn't take long—three days—for Binion's operatives to react.

---

Somehow his six patrolling Chihuahuas failed to alert him to the danger, and for one evening his level of paranoia dropped strangely to nil. On New Year's Eve 1949, Noble walked out the front door of his Dallas home about 9:00 p.m. as if he had not a care in the world. His daughter was inside the house with a friend, and Noble had decided to go to the drugstore. Now he stood only about twenty feet from where his wife had been blown up one month before. As he moved to shut the door, he was bathed in whiteness. He turned toward the street, and a car's spotlight blinded him. Next came gunfire.

The first shot missed, but not the second. A bullet from a high-powered rifle shattered Noble's left arm, ripped through his hip, and lodged near his spine. He staggered against the door, pounding with his good arm. When his daughter opened the door, he stumbled in and collapsed on the floor. The car sped away.

An ambulance rushed Noble to Methodist Hospital, where doctors initially thought he had been hit in the back with buckshot. Then they realized they were seeing the bone fragments from his arm. Noble was seriously wounded, but he would live. He had now survived murder attempt number seven.

Although he wouldn't say much to police about what had happened—as usual—Noble gave an interview to reporters from his hospital bed. "I am a gambler, and I have been, that is true," he admitted. "But I have never done anything to deserve these attacks."

Then, for reasons known only to him, Noble turned ominous. "I can't go on any longer like this. I am at the end of my road," he said. "I am afraid I am going to have to take the law into my own hands."

His remarks hit the papers in Nevada the next day. "Gambler Threatens to Make Own Law," read the headline in the *Reno Evening Gazette*. Even a Las Vegas casino owner who couldn't read very well knew what that meant.

Noble's recovery from his latest wounds proved long and arduous. More than five weeks after he was shot, he still remained in a private room at Methodist Hospital, in the Oak Cliff section of Dallas. As urban hospitals went, Methodist enjoyed something of a bucolic setting. Its brown-brick main tower rose well back from busy Colorado Boulevard, and its grounds featured several secluded courtyards framed by tall oak trees. These courtyards were dimly lit after dark, so no one noticed when, on the night of February 6, 1950, at about 11:00 p.m., a man stood in one of them and aimed his .30-caliber carbine at a fourth-floor hospital window. The window's blinds were tightly drawn, but the man with the rifle could see a shadowy silhouette behind them.

Noble, in his pajamas, was stepping from his hospital bathroom when the rifle's bullet came flying through the window glass. The bullet struck the ceiling above his bed and blew a hole in the plaster. "It sounded like a cannon," Noble said. He dropped to the floor, crawled to the wall, and unplugged a lamp, leaving the room dark. He reinjured his arm when he went down, but was otherwise unhurt.

The inept gunman at least had the sense to be long gone by the time police arrived. Police Chief Hansson took a strikingly relaxed attitude as he surveyed the scene. The chief apparently believed snipers fired through hospital windows in Dallas as a routine matter. "Criminal activity like this is cropping up all the time," he said. "This is not the first time we have had a gang shooting in Dallas." Hansson also issued a mild rebuke to the would-be assassin, as if he had done nothing more than blow his car horn in the hospital's quiet zone. This, Hansson said, was "a person with wanton disregard for people who already are sick."

District Attorney Wilson offered a more straightforward summation, one that alluded both to Lois Green's recent exit and the raid on Binion's policy game headquarters. The shooting, Wilson said, was a "straight revenge proposition."

Police said they had no plans to post an armed guard on Noble, but hospital orderlies did manage to drape a couple of dark blankets over the window. Noble climbed back into his bed and ruminated on his latest close call. "It looks like the good Lord is with me," he said, while admitting that this divine protection offered some room for improvement. "I'm getting a little gunshy," he added.

For someone who had been the repeated target of bullets, buckshot, and bombs, Noble seemed strangely surprised at the boldness of this latest attempt. "I didn't think they would try to get me in the hospital," he said. "They are watching every move I make." He vowed not to be run out of Dallas. This yielded a large headline in the next day's *Times Herald*: "Noble Determined to Stay Here Despite 'Try' on Life in Hospital." Once again the news traveled to Las Vegas: newly defiant, the Cat had survived murder attempt number eight.

He made no secret of his further intentions, going so far as to let George Butler of the Dallas police in on his plans to kill Binion. Noble said this could happen "sooner than anyone expected," Butler wrote, because he had paid $400 to someone known only as Mike, who "was supposed to have been associated with the Capone family directly." After that, Mike "went to Grand Prairie and telegraphed the money up the country." In some jurisdictions, a confession of hiring a professional murderer might result in actual law enforcement, but as so often happened in Dallas, authorities let it drop.

"This was reported to the Chief," Butler wrote, "but no further investigation was made." Perhaps Chief Hansson harbored lingering resentment over those crank calls to him at the zoo, although no proof of that existed. But the larger message was clear: anyone wishing to eliminate Binion had an unofficial endorsement from the top.

Herbert Noble, after losing a piece of his ear in a fight with a Binion ally.

# 12

# "TEARS ROLLING DOWN THE MAN'S EYES"

Courage is a fine thing, but when the shooting starts, get down on the floor.

—BB

This was getting out of hand, even by Texas's liberal standards for mayhem. The rest of the country had finally begun to notice all the gunfire and bombings in Dallas, and responded with unconcealed disgust. None other than the city of Houston, which did not enjoy a general reputation as a sanctuary of enlightenment, nosed into the act. The *Houston Press* dispatched a reporter to Big D to write about Green, Noble, and Binion. His story called Dallas a "city without shame" that was "reaping a whirlwind harvest from seeds of crime, corruption and gambling." From Colorado, the *Denver Post* sent its own metaphorically inclined wordsmith, who found Dallas to be a "hell-broth" of crime. "This devil's stew," the *Post* warned, could "boil over anytime and splatter up the nice new shirt front the 'Big D' has slipped over its past."

In Las Vegas, a town seemingly inured to embarrassment over mobsters, Binion's actual good deeds couldn't escape the taint of his recent past. Early in 1950 he gave $1,000 to the University of Nevada basketball team so it could travel to a national tournament in Kansas City. It was an act of purest goodwill on Binion's part, but when tournament officials learned of his donation, they canceled the team's invitation. The *Nevada State Journal* claimed that Binion and his soiled gift had ruined the state's reputation, such as it was. "The people of Nevada were made to look like a bunch of miscreants eager to grab an easy dollar regardless of its source," an editorial said. "University regents, heads of public and semi-public institutions must be on their guard at all times to keep from being duped by the offer of money from individuals of the Binion calibre."

Back in the hell-broth of crime, the law was working its own course toward him. Dallas DA Will Wilson wasted no time in using the material seized from Binion's back office. On January 7, 1950, a week after the raids, he charged Binion and six others, including Harry Urban and Buddy Malone, with operating an illegal policy operation. Wilson blamed at least five homicides on the policy games: Ben Freiden, the rival shot by Binion and Malone; Sam Murray, the competitor killed by Ivy Miller; Raymond Loudermilk, who was shot by Binion's henchman Bob Minyard; Minyard, gunned down in return; and Mildred Noble. "This," Wilson said of the charges, "is the beginning of the final stage of the fight."

The first thing Dallas authorities had to do was force Binion back to Texas to stand trial. Several weeks later, he was placed under arrest in Las Vegas, but only briefly before his release on personal recognizance. "I think it's a political frame," he said of the Texas charges. His lawyer, Harry Claiborne, attempted to portray Binion as a victim deserving of sympathy. "It's Noble who's doing all the hollering," he said, "but Benny is the one who had to close up and get out of Texas."

In response to Dallas prosecutors' extradition efforts, Claiborne argued that Texas officials could not prove Binion was in their state at the time of the crime. That meant he was not a fugitive and therefore not extraditable. This strategy derived from a quirk in the Nevada extradition statute that was designed to protect the state's lucrative divorce trade. As a side benefit, it allowed racketeers in Las Vegas to direct their out-of-state operations relatively free from legal care.

In private, Binion's attorneys insisted the Texas authorities didn't know what they were doing. "I don't think I ever in my life have seen as many incompetent lawyers associated with one case as was in that case," Claiborne said later. "I know that Will Wilson is highly respected, but he's a first-class dumbbell . . . God have mercy on his clients." Dumbbell or not, Wilson was making his own implacable progress in his attempts—however tortuous—to bring Binion to justice.

"Eventually," Wilson vowed, "we'll get him."

Additional pressure on Binion would soon come from an unexpected source: U.S. senator Estes Kefauver, a Democrat from Tennessee. An owlish, lanky lawyer with a fondness for Scotch and pari-mutuel wagering, not to mention the occasional hotel-room dalliance, Kefauver also harbored grand political ambitions. Though he had already attracted some notice—*Time* magazine had named him one of the nation's ten best senators—he needed a big stage and a headline-grabbing crusade. A special commission investigating the mob would fill that bill nicely. In 1950 Kefauver launched the U.S. Senate Special Committee to Investigate Crime in Interstate Commerce. To no one's surprise, it made Las Vegas one of its prime targets.

In the years since Binion's arrival, Las Vegas had enjoyed a period of strong growth, with advertising and publicity campaigns attracting waves of visitors, principally from Southern California. The Thunderbird and the Desert Inn joined the Flamingo as premier resorts on the Strip controlled by the mob. Along with some busy downtown clubs, most notably the El Cortez, they helped turn Vegas into a tax-free money machine, as skimming became a normal business practice. Millions in cash—the casinos' handle—poured through the counting rooms, and racketeers siphoned much of it off the top before it could be recorded on the balance sheets. By one account, Meyer Lansky's men skimmed $3 million for every $1 million reported. Every week bagmen left Las Vegas with bulging satchels of cash, en route to Chicago, Detroit, Miami, and other syndicate redoubts.

Some of the most lucrative diverting took place at the Flamingo, where Davie Berman now had a piece of the ownership. "Wasn't [Bugsy] Siegel or none of them guys tough like Berman," Ted Binion, Benny's son, once said. "He was a known killer." Berman's daughter, Susan, remembered him as a loving dad who taught her arithmetic with a slot machine and commissioned Liberace to perform at her birthday party. Susan Berman also witnessed skimming as a routine piece of business. "I was in the counting room," she recalled. "I saw them go, 'Three for us, one for the government, two for Meyer [Lansky].' I helped them count the bills. They cheated the government. It was a crime, all right, but in the minds of my father and his friends it wasn't a crime like having to kill people."

No one in Las Vegas, especially casino owners illegally evading taxes, wanted serious scrutiny from the feds, especially a showboating one like Senator Estes Kefauver. Binion's engaging in a cross-country, bloody front-page feud with Noble was only turning up the heat. Berman let Binion know that he and his connected friends devoutly wished for this affair to be put to rest. To broker this peace, they needed a diplomat. That's when someone—maybe Berman, maybe Binion—coughed up one Harold Shimley.

Shimley, a gambler and a con man, didn't look the part of a big-money envoy, or act it. Tall, fat, slick-haired, and always on the make, he wore sunglasses indoors and tended to jabber. One police officer who knew him well had a succinct description: "stupid and devious." On March 10, 1950, newly arrived in Dallas from Vegas, he arranged a meeting with Noble at a tourist court near Love Field to discuss the situation with Binion. "Your name and his name is the talk of the fucking country," Shimley said. Noble, sniffing a setup, persuaded a friend from the police department, the ever-present Lieutenant Butler, to hide in the next room and record the proceedings.

The summit began with some characteristic self-promotion. "I've been all over the country," Shimley said. "Now I've made up with some people out there that own the big Flamingo Hotel—this eastern outfit that owns that joint."

Noble tried to get a word in. "Well, now—"

"So now Dave Berman tells me—"

"Who?" Noble said. "Who?"

"Dave Berman," Shimley said. "Owns the Flamingo. You understand?"

"Just take it slow now," Noble said.

But Shimley poured it on: "He [Berman] says, 'Shimley,' he says. 'Do you know this fellow in Texas?' I says, 'I've known the man twenty years . . .' I says, 'I don't know what in hell this thing is all about, Dave.'" Berman explained that he was worried, Shimley said, "that this thing has gone far enough," and that Noble and Binion needed to make peace. "And he says, 'Why in the hell don't you get together and straighten this thing up?'"

Shimley also claimed he had Binion's approval for the mission. But Noble was unconvinced, and asked, "The man out yonder?"

"You ain't kiddin'," Shimley said. Binion was not only innocent of hiring the attacks on Noble, he said, but desperately wanted to catch the assailants as well. "He didn't only convince me," Shimley said, "he convinced the biggest mob in the United States." In fact, he insisted, Binion had already spent $10,000 investigating the matter himself. "The man swears by the all God, and hopes that his five kids will all die, if he knows one . . . thing about the whole proposition from start to finish."

With that, Shimley picked up the room phone, got the long-distance operator on the line, and placed a call to Binion's home in Las Vegas: "Hello, Benny. This is Shimley. Well, I'm in Dallas and I have done what I told you I thought I could do. And I think this whole thing can be straightened out 100 percent." He spent a few seconds genuflecting to Binion, then said, "Now wait a minute. I want you to talk to somebody." He offered the phone to Noble.

The Cat didn't leap to grab it. "Ask him what he wants to tell me."

"Well come on and talk to him," Shimley said. "Fuck it. Man's fifteen hundred miles away."

Noble hesitated, but took the phone, and the two bitterest of enemies finally had, after all the blood and tragedy, their man-to-man confrontation. A clash of the titans it wasn't.

"Hello, Benny. This is Herbert," Noble said. "All right, how are you? Oh, I've got a little cold." After responding to questions about his ranch—"we're out in the country, partly anyway"—he managed to address the matter at hand. "Well, I just wondered—I just wondered—I didn't know what, what the score was."

Binion apparently preferred speaking with Shimley about such matters. "Yeah, wait a minute," Noble said, "then I'll let you talk to him." Noble spent the rest of the conversation complaining about local newspaper coverage. "They done something to my wife here in the paper. I didn't like it a damn bit."

And that was that. After less than a minute on the line, he passed the phone back to Shimley, who assured Binion that the matter would soon be resolved. "You be good, and we'll see you soon," Shimley said, and hung up.

Then he went back to work on Noble, repeating his contention that Binion wanted to find the real killers. "Benny is on the square about this thing," Shimley said. "I saw tears rolling down the man's eyes, about your wife."

This sent Noble into a fit of stuttering. "I ain't got my mind right half the time," he managed to say.

The summit ended with Shimley promising Noble, "I'll get you through this, man."

That was true, but in a way that didn't become clear until a couple of days later, during Noble's second meeting with the corpulent con man. Shimley confessed that the phone conference with Binion, and all the protestations of Binion's innocence, had been a ruse. In truth, he said, Binion had offered him $25,000 and ownership of his own Dallas craps game to kill Noble.

Now, with the pressure building, Shimley decided it was time to take off for Tulsa, where he could hide. But before he left, he gave Noble a present—a map he had drawn, showing the location of Binion's house on Bonanza Road.

The Cowboy was sticking to his story. A few days after the Shimley summit, the *Dallas Morning News* ponied up some travel cash and sent its ace crime reporter, Harry McCormick, to Las Vegas to find and talk to Binion. The dapper McCormick, who customarily sported a black derby, was walking down Fremont Street, gawking at the sights, when a man "dressed in the western style so often seen on the streets of this most unusual city"— McCormick's words—approached him. It was Binion, wearing his white Stetson and alligator boots. "I heard you were looking for me," he said, adding that he had nothing to hide.

The two of them retired for a friendly chat, and Binion laid his standard charm on the reporter, depicting himself as nothing more than a rancher and businessman. Any notion that he would seek to harm poor

Herbert Noble was the handiwork of liars. "I have never laid a toothpick in Noble's way," he insisted in McCormick's newspaper rendering, which had Binion employing the syntax of an Oxford don. "I have no reason for wanting to do so."

Throughout this conversation, Binion painted a self-portrait of a peaceful and reasonable man. Of course, that was before he heard about the napalm.

In early April 1950, Lieutenant Butler paid Noble a visit at his ranch. Butler, who had known Noble for years, checked in with him every couple of weeks to supply the latest news on the investigation into Mildred Noble's death—which was to say, nothing solid. The police had dozens of leads, none of them good.

Like many others, Butler had been struck by Noble's recent downward slide. His gray hair had turned silver and he had lost so much weight he appeared to have shriveled. His heavy drinking and insomnia had left him pale, tremulous, and hollow-eyed. Haunted and hunted, he was only forty-one but looked sixty-five.

On this day Butler drove northwest out of Dallas and into the farm community of Grapevine. Soon his unmarked car was kicking up dust on the rutted dirt road that led to Noble's Diamond M Ranch. A barbed-wire fence strung on cedar posts lined the road. The rolling landscape was one of scrub oaks, pasture, and every mile or so, a farmhouse.

Butler turned off the road at Noble's mailbox, rattled over the cattle guard, and eased into the ranch. After driving about three hundred yards, Butler saw him.

Noble was stripped to the waist, working beneath the bright red wing of a Beechcraft biplane with cross-country fuel tanks—a welcome sight for Butler, because he and Noble shared an interest in aviation. As a younger man, Butler had been a pilot too, until he lost his license for the stunt of flying beneath a bridge over the Red River. Now he got out of his car and walked toward the airplane. Noble grabbed his rifle and pointed it at the policeman. The astonished Butler said, "What the hell are you doing, Herbert?" He ordered Noble to put the rifle down. The two men stared at each other until Noble dropped the gun, sank to his knees, and began to sob.

It was all Binion, Noble blubbered. He got all the breaks, he killed Mildred, he had the money, and he grabbed all the power. "I never had a chance," he said.

Butler looked at the airplane and saw that racks had been welded under the wings. Two military-surplus bombs lay on the ground near the plane, one a conventional explosive and the other filled with napalm, the jellied gasoline used for firebombing.

Noble confessed his plan: He would load the bombs onto the airplane and fly to Arizona. He would refuel at a private airstrip near Tucson owned by mobster Pete "Horse Face" Licavoli. Then he would fly to Las Vegas and, when he knew Binion and his family were at home, get his fiery vengeance by dropping his bombs on Binion's house. He would be guided by the map drawn by Harold Shimley. Noble was not arrested after this confession of a plan to murder women and children—this was, after all, Texas. But Butler did make sure the bombs were safely disposed of.

Within hours, Binion's Dallas connections had conveyed the details of Noble's plot. Binion, who generally stayed cool toward death threats, went into something that resembled a panic. He hastily loaded his wife, his five children, and their nanny in the car and sped westward, across the state line. "They had warned Daddy," said his daughter Brenda. "So we took off for California in a baby blue Cadillac." Seeking to disguise himself, Binion ditched his standard western wear and tried to look like a typical tourist sightseeing his way through Santa Monica. "He had gray slacks, a navy blue blazer, navy suede shoes and no hat," Brenda said. "The kids were cracking up." He also took a golf bag. In it, Binion concealed his 12-gauge shotgun.

Sans napalm, Noble continued to drink heavily, and the combination of liquor and pills induced a certain lack of restraint. On a warm night in June 1950 he showed up at a West Dallas beer joint, drunk again. He spotted a couple of the dimmer lights from Lois Green's gang, and he greeted one of them by clubbing him in the head with a full beer can. Two nights later, Noble was driving from Dallas to his ranch. As he turned onto the dirt road leading to his land, shotgun blasts came from a hunter's blind in an oak thicket. The buckshot blew holes in the driver's-side door and fender of his car, and punctured a tire. Noble, unhurt, ducked low and kept driving. He had survived murder attempt number nine, which only seemed to set fire to his agitation.

One night some months later he saw Jack Todd leaving Sonny Lefors's West Dallas food store. Todd had been a member of Green's gang, and knew his way around bombs. At one point he had been taken off an American Airlines plane at Love Field because he was carrying a stick of dynamite in his coat and three blasting caps in his luggage. Todd told police he was taking the explosives to New York for a fishing trip. When he heard about it, Noble offered a different theory. "That's the same stuff," he said, "that killed my wife."

Now he had the man in his sights. As Todd walked from the grocery and fencing operation, Noble grabbed his rifle, stepped from his car, and said, "If you don't tell me what you know, I'll shoot your damn brains out." He took a handgun from Todd. Then he forced him into the car and drove down Singleton Boulevard, headlights off. But they only went a couple of blocks before Noble—who had trouble steering while covering his passenger with a rifle—rolled the car into a ditch. The two men began to wrestle in the front seat, with Noble sinking his teeth into Todd's arm and Todd biting off a piece of Noble's right earlobe. Noble managed to get off one shot, but it hit the dashboard and exited through the hood. They were still fighting when sheriff's deputies arrived, opened the car doors, and pulled the men out. Back to Methodist Hospital Noble went, for fifty-plus stitches, and this time no one took a shot at him from the hospital courtyard.

Though he got the worst of the fight, Noble was arrested for his brief abduction of Todd. At his jail book-in, an officer doing the paperwork asked him the routine question that was put to all arrestees: Did he have any identifying scars? "Yeah," Noble said with a bitter laugh. "They're all over me."

Estes Kefauver's organized crime committee began holding public hearings in the summer of 1950. They were an overnight sensation, in part because the Tennessee senator turned them into a touring production, hitting fourteen cities over fifteen months. More important, they were televised, and TV was now gaining its hold on middle-class households. With a witness parade of mobsters whose testimony ranged from penitent to defiant, the hearings offered high drama in the afternoon. Viewers skipped work to sneak home and catch the broadcasts, or they slipped off to movie theaters that were showing the hearings live. Many crowded into taverns, where over beers and shots, they watched flickering black-and-white images on a Philco above the bar. "Never before," *Life* magazine wrote, "had the attention of the nation been riveted so completely on a single matter."

The hearings gave many Americans their first exposure to real mob bosses, and turned Kefauver into a celebrity crime buster who had the moxie to confront snarling racketeers. The senators sometimes got more than anticipated, especially at one closed-door grilling that was not broadcast. There Senator Charles Tobey, a self-righteous New Hampshire Republican, pressed Bugsy Siegel's former mistress, Virginia Hill, on why mobsters kept giving her piles of money. The "scorpion-tongued vixen"—one writer's description—had finally had enough of the questions. "Because," Miss Hill informed the senator, "I'm the best cocksucker in town." Later, leaving the private chambers, draped in a mink cape, she was engulfed by reporters and photographers. She kicked one in the shins and slapped another. "Get out of my fucking way!" she screamed at them. "I hope the fucking atomic bomb falls on every one of you."

In July 1950, the Kefauver committee met in room 457 of the Senate Office Building to hear from Virgil Peterson, the director of the Chicago Crime Commission. While not so provocative as Miss Hill, Peterson had an encyclopedic, if imaginative, knowledge of the mob. Or, as an FBI agent once put it, "He's got a great, big black brush that he dips in tar, and he just smears it all over." Peterson's testimony, which took two days, mentioned nearly every all-star of American organized crime: Lansky, Siegel, Lucky Luciano, Dutch Schultz, Frank Costello in New York, Tony Accardo down in Florida, and dozens of others. Peterson had their names, their records, their aliases, even their home addresses. And soon he began to tell the senators about "the king of the rackets in Dallas, Texas."

In his recitation of Binion's history, Peterson touched most of the high points—the men he killed, the rings he controlled, the long feud with Noble. He also linked Binion to Jack Dragna of Los Angeles, "one of the most notorious gangsters on the West Coast" and the "Al Capone of Los

Angeles," who was deep into gambling, robbery, and extortion. Binion and Dragna, he said, were close friends and potential business partners.

Much to his coming disadvantage, Binion had progressed over the course of thirty years from minor hustler to regional viceroy to big-league racketeer. He was rich, he was powerful, and he was now in the bull's-eye.

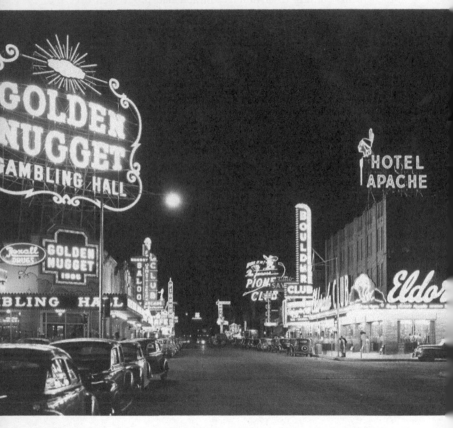

The Eldorado, lighting up Glitter Gulch, would soon become Binion's Horseshoe.

# 13

# THE BENNY BRAND
# GOES NATIONAL

The only people I don't like is the ones that try to snatch my
money away.

—BB

**D**allas County officials kept trying to force Binion's return to
Texas, but they met with no success in Nevada courts. In
August 1950 D. W. Priest, a state district judge in Las
Vegas, granted Binion's petition for a writ of habeas corpus, which in effect
blocked extradition efforts. The judge also had some advice for Dallas prosecutors: leave Las Vegas "and don't bother to come back." Even pleas for
divine intervention went unheeded. That same month, a Texas tent evan-
gelist named Bernard C. Morris held a revival in Reno and prayed for Binion to be cast out of Nevada. But the Cowboy managed to stay put.

Prosecutors settled for second best, and took Harry Urban to court.
Binion's suave lieutenant—a "mild-looking middle-aged man," in one reporter's summation, "with a faultless manicure and a Countess Mara
tie"—faced charges of operating a network of illegal policy games, the
Hi-Noon, the Tip-Top, and the Silver Dollar among them. Witnesses for
the state included an accountant who testified he had been shading the
books for Binion and Urban since 1937, and that their tax returns vastly
underreported their income. In a single year, he said, one Binion and Urban

partnership—one among many—took in more than $733,000 in policy receipts, but reported a net income of only $23,000. Prosecutors introduced stacks of checks signed by Urban in Dallas and cashed by Binion in Las Vegas. Binion hadn't even bothered to take them to the bank; he endorsed the checks at cashiers' cages at various casinos. More came from the testimony of Pete White, an investigator for the DA's office who had gone undercover to learn the inner workings of policy games. Disguised as a bum, with shabby clothes and a scraggly beard, White lived in fleabag hotels and listened to gambling deals through thin walls. He drifted from dice den to policy cave, taking notes when he could, and getting to know the precise routes of the bagmen.

On the strength of such evidence, Urban was convicted and sentenced to four years in prison. He also faced financial ruin as his home and its contents were sold to satisfy tax liens. "They didn't even leave me the trash cans and the garden hose," he lamented. His two Cadillacs—the ones with the custom-made holsters—went on the block too. Yet Binion, the bigger fish, remained free and prosperous in Las Vegas.

In the summer of 1950, District Attorney Wilson learned that Theron Lamar Caudle, the assistant attorney general in charge of the federal tax division, would be in Texas. Caudle was a large, voluble North Carolina lawyer with wavy brown hair and a grits-and-magnolia accent. He made his first stop in Tyler, in East Texas, for a bar association speech. Wilson loaded up the seized records from Binion's operations and drove a hundred miles to meet with Caudle. The two had a brief chat and agreed to talk again in Dallas. Wilson was in pursuit of a solitary goal: to persuade federal tax officials to mount a case against Binion.

One day later, Wilson and Caudle met during a party in the presidential suite of the Adolphus Hotel in downtown Dallas, a few blocks from the district attorney's office. Among the suite's winged chairs and gilt furnishings, as some sipped coffee and tea from fine china and others downed good whiskey straight up, Wilson hauled out Binion's tax documents again. Caudle, with his honeyed drawl, seemed to demonstrate a good grasp of the material, and he assured the district attorney that he would take a personal interest in the case. "This is the big one I've been waiting for," Caudle said. "We'll surely prosecute it."

Wilson left the Adolphus feeling satisfied and optimistic. If the feds could get Binion back to Texas, Wilson would take it from there. But the DA soon found he had misplaced his confidence, for despite Caudle's promises, the case languished. No one could say why, but it probably had something to do with President Harry Truman's firing of Caudle some months later, after the assistant attorney general was implicated in a shakedown scheme. There were public accusations of discounted mink coats for Caudle's wife and gifts of new cars and free trips to Europe in exchange for favorable treatment of tax scofflaws. Caudle denied much of it, but he did admit to taking a Florida fishing trip on a boat owned by a businessman under investigation for tax fraud. The name of the craft: *The Naughty Lady*. Caudle was convicted of conspiracy to defraud the government and sent to prison.

No evidence suggested that Binion's case had been part of the assorted bribery schemes, but the timing couldn't have been better for him. Nevada authorities wouldn't touch him, his lawyers had fought off all attempts to send him to Texas for state prosecution, and now a powerful man who had promised to pursue him in federal court was gone in disgrace. Once again he appeared to have given his enemies the slip. Binion's legendary luck was holding.

Throughout November 1950, Lieutenant Butler of the Dallas police often went to the Fair Park office he shared with a Texas Ranger. He would sit down at his typewriter, roll in a sheet of paper, and record the latest violent hijinks of the usual punks and miscreants. These writings served to catalog the tips that he had collected, but also provided a release for his frustration. He always knew far more than he could act upon. Mildred Noble's death, which had taken place a year ago and remained unsolved, left him especially disconsolate. "Noble has often made the statement—to lots of people—that if the Police did nothing about his wife's murder by the time of the anniversary of her death, that he was going to do something about it himself," Butler wrote one day. "No one would blame him. There are so many political ties in this mess that nothing would ever come of it if a man was arrested—which is not probable."

As for Noble, once again someone had gone after him. "It is known that

Saturday night some people went to the Noble ranch but he was not there," Butler typed. "They were reported to have gone back the next day, Sunday, and set fire to some of Noble's property. This was done to get him out of the house to fight the fire. Then they intended to kill him." Because Noble failed to appear and no shots were fired, police didn't classify it as a murder attempt.

Butler kept typing dense gray paragraphs of rumors, minutiae, and a couple of dire observations on the state of crime-fighting in the county. "The outlaws are in Dallas in droves. They seem to be having a convention in West Dallas," he observed. "It is known that [Sheriff] Decker is very uneasy about the whole thing. His hands seem to be tied. Most of the punks are armed with pistols and some are carrying shotguns."

It was, in other words, status quo in Dallas, though perhaps a bit more ominous this time. As Butler wrote, "There seems to be a killing in the air."

Las Vegas featured a number of notable performances the week of November 15, 1950. The Zany-Acks, a comedy singing trio, played spirited gigs at the Golden Nugget's lounge. The Desert Inn brought in *Minsky's Follies,* and no less than Arthur Godfrey proclaimed that the cast boasted "the most beautiful girls in the world." But the real spectacle took place a few hundred feet from Glitter Gulch as the Kefauver committee's road show made its Vegas appearance.

The brown-brick federal building at 300 Stewart Avenue contained a post office on the first floor and a cavernous courtroom on the second, where the judge's bench—lacquered oak, lined with steel—was conveniently bulletproof. Three members of the committee, including Kefauver himself, set up shop there: a rectitudinous lineup of bespectacled men in gray suits. On this morning, the hallway outside the courtroom was thick with sharply dressed casino owners and rumpled newspapermen. A small journalism riot erupted as Cliff Jones emerged from the elevator into the second-floor hallway. Jones embodied the singular Vegas perfecta: in addition to owning a piece of the Thunderbird—a Strip palace whose construction had been financed by Meyer Lansky—he served as Nevada's lieutenant governor. He therefore played the dual role of sworn witness and official in charge of welcoming the committee to town. "So many flashbulbs popped in his face," one reporter observed, "that he was partially blinded when he went in to greet the senators."

While the action played out behind the leather-upholstered doors, some of those who had been subpoenaed to appear waited on hard hallway benches, projecting studied nonchalance and forced jocularity. No one wanted to admit to fear of Kefauver and his grandstanding crew. "Privately, my father and his friends had joked that the Commission would never shut them down," recalled Susan Berman, Davie Berman's daughter. "They never had respect for politicians since they had made a career of bribing them." Yet, she said, the casino operators regarded Kefauver and his committee with understandable wariness. "Who needed this dirty laundry aired before the nation?"

Not Binion. Kefauver's lawyers had subpoenaed him, at which point he took off for his Montana ranch and stayed there, far from the reach of marshals hoping to serve papers. Further public exposure, he and his lawyers knew, could do him no good. The committee would not be hearing from the Cowboy. More than a few of Vegas's mob-connected casino operators employed the same tactic. "The top brass of the underworld suddenly remembered long-forgotten relatives in distant lands," wrote Hank Greenspun in the *Las Vegas Sun*.

One of those Nevadans who did appear, and seemed strangely happy about it, was William J. Moore, one of seven members of the state tax commission. He also owned a percentage of, and was an executive at, the Last Frontier resort and casino on the Strip, a position that paid him about $80,000 a year—ten times his state salary. He saw no inherent conflict in this setup, but did allow that such a role gave him a unique perspective on Las Vegas casino owners. He was asked if most of them were "of high integrity."

"Well," he answered, "it depends on how you describe 'high integrity.'"

After a few more questions, he acknowledged that the gambling business in Nevada might be home to "a few more shady characters" than other commercial interests elsewhere.

As if to prove Moore's point, Moe Sedway, once Bugsy Siegel's number two man and now a vice president at the Flamingo, also appeared to testify, even though he wasn't feeling so good. "I have had three major coronary thromboses," he told the committee. "And I have had diarrhea for six weeks, and I have an ulcer, hemorrhoids, and an abscess on my upper intestines. I just got out of bed and I am loaded with drugs." The senators nonetheless pushed ahead with their interrogation, and Sedway admitted that he had been in the gambling business in Las Vegas. Which, he reminded the committee, was perfectly legal, and probably not nearly as much fun or as lucrative as outsiders might imagine. "We don't get as rich as you think we do. This is hard work," Sedway testified.

Senator Tobey, the New Hampshire Republican who had elicited Virginia Hill's claim to the fellatio gold medal, compared "scum of the earth" gamblers unfavorably to the honest people who "till the soil and make $2,000" back home in the Granite State. "They have got peace of mind and can look everybody in the eye," he said of his constituents.

Sedway returned to the medical report. "Senator, you see what it got for me," he responded. "Three coronaries and ulcers."

Another witness, Wilbur Clark, developer and general manager of the Desert Inn, combined a faulty memory with a general obtuseness. This caused Tobey to blurt, in the middle of one ineffective exchange with Clark, "You have the most nebulous idea of your business I ever saw."

Clark did admit that he had taken money from Moe Dalitz and his reputed gangster friends so he could finish building the Desert Inn. (These were funds that Dalitz got from, among others, the Republic Bank of Dallas via Binion.) Tobey then asked him, "Before you got in bed with crooks . . . didn't you look into these birds at all?"

"Not too much," Clark answered.

"You didn't care where the money came from or how dirty or rotten," Tobey said, "as long as you finished the building, is that it?"

"Well," Clark said, "I wanted the building finished. I didn't hear anything bad about those fellows."

While the hearing had many such moments of bitter comedy, the committee failed to produce any kill shots. The session wrapped at day's end with nothing in the way of blockbuster revelations. But the proceedings did cause Senator Tobey to brim with disgust. "What I have seen here today leaves me with a sense of outrage and righteous indignation," he said after the session concluded. "I think it's about time somebody got damn mad and told these people where to get off."

That was possible, though unlikely. For as Tobey spoke, a block away on Fremont the colored lights glowed bright against the darkening sky. The Pioneer Club, the Nevada Club, the El Cortez: all had their beckoning signs ablaze. The Golden Nugget's street-corner diadem sparkled as always. And on the sidewalks, the evening crowd of gamblers, their pockets thick with money to lose, flowed into the casinos.

Several months after Las Vegas, Kefauver took his traveling hearings to Los Angeles. Again the committee subpoenaed Binion, and once more he escaped to Montana. The senators brought in the lawman who knew all about the Cowboy, Lieutenant Butler of the Dallas police. Butler gave the senators Binion's full criminal history, going back to his 1924 tire theft and continuing through the confrontations-by-proxy with Noble. Then Butler participated in a dramatic reading of the transcripts from Harold Shimley's meeting with Noble in Dallas, the session he had recorded. Butler performed Noble's part for the senators, while the committee's chief investigator played the role of Shimley, with the principals' many curse words deleted. And for dessert the Dallas lieutenant produced photographs of the smoking wreckage of the car in which Mildred Noble was smithereened. All in all, Butler provided the committee with a vivid portrait of Binion as a gangster of many talents, interests, and connections, and one whom the law had barely touched. This sort of exposure couldn't have pleased the city fathers or the chamber of commerce. The next day the *Dallas Morning News* displayed a blaring front-page headline: "Crime Set-Up Here Blasted into the Open."

Once the committee hearings were concluded, Kefauver—his eye on a possible run for the White House—wrote a book. He called it *Crime in America,* and it was a national best seller. Every book needs a villain, even ponderous tomes by ambitious politicians, and Kefauver had his: casinos controlled by the mob. "Hardened thugs," he wrote of those who ran such a show. "Hoodlums, racketeers and the other inevitable parasites who spring up like weeds." He wasn't talking only about outlaws backing illicit games in warehouses and on piers while police took bribes and looked the other way. Kefauver believed legalized gambling was just as bad. It constituted an "economic blight," the Tennessee senator insisted, and turned otherwise upright citizens into paupers, embezzlers, and slaves to depravity.

Las Vegas naturally emerged as this problem's hot spot. "Nevada's gambling centers have become headquarters for some of the nation's worst mobsters," he wrote. Unless something was done, he warned, "there is no weapon that can be used to keep the gamblers and their money out of politics."

Kefauver even coined a term for this most pernicious of effects, the malign influence that infected a community and wreaked horrible destruction. He called it "Binionized."

The senator's publicity campaign was followed by even more public pressure on Binion. In the spring of 1951, the Texas House of Representatives convened a special committee to study organized crime in the state, and the Cowboy dwelled on the minds of those committee members as well. Herbert Noble's presence only reinforced it. Noble testified that the price on his head had reached $50,000, and he laid that at Binion's feet. "Benny never did like me too much," he said, and repeated what he had told the papers back in Dallas: "I wouldn't bow down to him."

The house committee also subpoenaed California gangster Mickey Cohen, a short and growly ex-boxer with a florid history of bookmaking and embezzling. Several months before, he had been picked up by Texas Rangers in West Texas and strongly urged to take the next plane out. Cohen told the Rangers he was in the state looking to invest in oil exploration. "We've got nothing to hide," he said. "We're here to do business."

Now Cohen ignored the legislators' request to appear, saying he wasn't in the mood to answer "some silly questions." The committee had to settle for Warren Olney III of California's Special Crime Study Commission on Organized Crime, who journeyed to Austin to deliver dire warnings about syndicate men buying oil wells. "What will happen if the gangsters get into the oil business?" Olney asked. "What will the industry look like if the slimy ways of the corruptionist and the violence of the hoodlums becomes its day-to-day method of doing business?" This being the state legislature, no one mentioned that even without California mobsters, the Texas oil patch already came close to that.

Out in L.A., Cohen hardly talked like a rising petro-baron—although the Associated Press noted that he lived in a "radar-guarded home" in Brentwood, an exclusive neighborhood. Cohen claimed he hadn't come to Texas to testify, because he couldn't scrape together $168 for plane fare. Also, he was still under a contempt citation for failing to appear earlier, and was therefore subject to arrest as soon as he hit Austin. "I would be foolish to pay my way down there just to get pinched," he said. "Tell them to drop dead."

Cohen had other legal problems. The feds were about to charge him with tax evasion, and he faced an additional dispute concerning his car. A man who knew what it was like to be bombed and shot at, he owned a Cadillac custom-equipped with an armor-plated body and puncture-resistant tires with Seal-o-matic inner tubes. Only a bazooka could stop this rolling fortress—or a determined bureaucrat. The state of California informed Cohen that such a car needed a special permit, one exclusively reserved for law enforcement vehicles and currency-transport trucks, and it refused to grant him a personal waiver. Cohen sued the highway patrol, but a court rejected his pleadings. "It would be a fine state of affairs for people to be driving around in armored cars, promiscuously shooting at each other," superior court judge W. Turney Fox ruled. The judge added that bullets might ricochet off such cars and wound innocent bystanders.

L.A.'s top mobster now had a Cadillac built like a tank that he needed to unload. It didn't take much imagination to think of someone who could use such a vehicle. He picked up the phone and called Binion in Las Vegas, but Binion said no. Cohen—a man who knew how to work the angles— dialed Noble in Texas and offered the car to him for $12,000. But Cohen got no action there either. Recalled Noble, "I told him I didn't want any part of him or his Cadillac."

Perhaps Noble had developed a newly enhanced sense of fatalism, especially as his would-be killers grew more creative in their tactics. One day in early 1951, Noble climbed into the cabin of his single-engine Beechcraft on the dirt airstrip at his Denton County ranch. He pushed the starter switch, and the engine exploded. Pieces of hot metal sprayed in a hundred-yard radius. Noble was shaken but unhurt, because the plane's firewall kept shrapnel from penetrating the cabin. The cause of the explosion stayed a mystery for six days, until Noble's mechanic pulled the engine of another plane to see why it wouldn't start. He found that two of the cylinders had been packed with nitroglycerin gel.

Noble had survived murder attempts numbers ten and eleven.

Still, he had to wonder how long his luck could last—certainly not forever. Noble prepaid his own funeral with a Dallas mortuary. The contract included a special clause stating the undertakers would pick up his body no matter where, when, or how he was killed.

If all the attention from various investigative committees worried Binion, he didn't show it in his business affairs. In May 1951 "me and my son [Jack] went out to the Desert Inn," he said. There they bought a drab and shuttered casino operation on Fremont Street that had once been owned by Moe Sedway, Davie Berman, and Bugsy Siegel. "It was called the Eldorado. It was closed. They'd fooled around there and they'd had an $870,000 tax loss. So I bought it for $160,000."

Binion also took over the lease on the building, which included the Apache Hotel above the casino. He said the club would be remodeled top to bottom and would open soon with new management. His previous two casinos constituted mere warm-ups. This would be Binion's grandest entry into the Las Vegas market. He would call it the Horseshoe.

A few days after the purchase, Binion applied for a casino license from the state tax commission, and the agency immediately rejected it. "I was getting some pressure put on me from somewhere," he said. Like Mickey Cohen and his forbidden bulletproof Cadillac, Binion now owned a pricey asset he couldn't legally operate.

The commissioners did not explain their decision, but it was clearly related to Binion's racketeering past and his current legal problems in Texas. The glare of the Kefauver hearings had embarrassed the state, so tax commissioners adopted new policies designed to give the illusion of tough regulation. One of them prohibited licensed Nevada gamblers from owning a gambling establishment in another state, and Binion had been accused of doing that. Now, with his reputation and investment on the line in Las Vegas, Binion knew full well what had to happen next. It was time to start handing out money.

He had done it before. "I've bribed many a man in my day," he once acknowledged. The right amount of cash distributed to the right people had always made the world work in Binion's favor. He saw it as a mark of respect: "It takes a pretty good man to make you bribe him."

Near the end of his life Binion was questioned about his spreading secret money around to influential officials. "And that's always been your way?" he was asked.

"Yeah," Binion answered.

"District attorneys?"

"Yeah."

"Sheriffs?"

"Yeah."

"Governors?"

"Yeah."

"Lieutenant governors?"

"Well," Binion said, "I don't know of any lieutenant governors."

The remains of Herbert Noble's car after an ill-advised trip to the mailbox.

# 14

# THE CAT'S LAST DAYS

They said he had nine lives. Damn good thing he didn't have ten.

—BB

eighbors had seen three men in a blue pickup truck rumbling up and down the dirt roads near the Noble ranch for several days. One man wore a red cap, another a pith helmet. They came, they lingered, they went. Nobody really got a good look at them, or paid them much notice. Then they were back, at night, unseen, digging a hole in front of Noble's mailbox. There they buried nitroglycerin, dynamite, and blasting caps, and ran a wire to a new Delco car battery. When they had finished, one of them moved the truck down the road and out of sight. The other two hid in some brush sixty yards uphill from the mailbox, where they smoked cigarettes and waited for the sun to rise on August 7, 1951.

As morning came, Herbert Noble was in his sandstone ranch house less than a quarter mile away, preparing to head into town. He had been looking better lately. No longer gaunt and pale, Noble had turned ropy and tanned by working summer days around the ranch. His mental state, however, kept slipping its leash. The heavy drinking had continued, and he had, for reasons known only to him, demolished what was left of his family. His daughter, now eighteen, had gone against his wishes and married a young man from Colorado. For this, Noble drafted a new will, writing in pencil on a plain sheet of bonded paper, and cut her out of his estate. "There was nothing good enough for her at home (while Mildred and I were alive) so therefore naturally there could be nothing good enough for her here in case of my death," he wrote. His holdings were worth about $1 million—including the Airmen's Club, the eight-hundred-acre ranch, five airplanes, and 195 head of cattle—and from that he left $10 to his only child. Perhaps he had other uses for his money: police heard he had established a "revenge fund" with local toughs, money on deposit for vengeance should he actually be murdered.

Around eleven thirty that morning Noble left his house and got into his black Ford. He carried his gambler's tools with him: his rifle, his cash— about $600—and his playing cards. As he drove from the house, he passed under overhanging post oaks, which gave little respite from the beating sun. North Texas was enduring yet another brutal string of 105-degree days. The crops withered in the fields, and the cows sought any scraps of shade they could find. In the downtown offices that had no air-conditioning, workers set blocks of ice in front of large fans. The men hidden in the brush, the ones watching for Noble now, felt the heat too. But the prospect of earning $50,000 made it easier to endure.

Noble drove his car across the cattle guard and onto the dirt road that skirted his ranch, and if he noticed the freshly turned earth, he ignored it. He stopped at his mailbox. Noble liked getting the mail, one of the few happy side effects of his notoriety. The volume of letters picked up after each attempt to kill him. "I always get a lot after they try to get me," he had said. "They write from all over the country. Some just want me to send money. But most of the letter writers wish me good luck." These notes from strangers provided some small bit of solace for a man whose wife was dead and whose daughter was estranged. Maybe today's post would have another good one or two. He reached for his mailbox.

Out in Las Vegas that same week, Virginia Hill paid a visit and cut a regal swath through town on the arm of former Binion bodyguard Russian Louie Strauss. "Boisterous, buxomy Ginny Hill," the *Review-Journal* called her, "playmate of the syndicate big boys."

Binion, meanwhile, immersed himself in the final days of preparation for the opening of the Horseshoe, which was to be a big step up from the typical Fremont Street grind joint. For one thing, it wouldn't have bare floors sprinkled with sawdust. "I put the first carpet on the floor here in the Horseshoe that ever was downtown," Binion said. "Everybody said that wasn't no good, but it was." Teddy Jane helped with the design because "I don't know nothing about designing nothing." Red emerged as the dominant color, western as the prevailing theme. Texas steer horns decorated the walls. This would be a place where high and low rollers alike could be comfortable, where the moneyed clients could strut about being rich, and the lesser ranks could pretend to be.

Binion also hired some trusted dealers, bringing in many of those who had worked the tables for him with the Southland Syndicate in Dallas. But as preparations moved ahead, there remained the not inconsiderable matter of the license, which he still had not been able to secure. The Horseshoe would have to open under a ruse, and Dr. Monte Bernstein, who owned a 10 percent stake, became the beard. Bernstein had operated the Eldorado Club, and had succeeded in running it into the ground. "He was the type of man that didn't understand gambling," Binion complained. But he had a clean record—clean enough, anyway, to win a casino license from the state. Bernstein assumed the titular chairmanship of the Horseshoe, while Binion took the position of bar and restaurant manager. Bernstein assured state regulators that Binion would have nothing to do with running the casino itself, which no one in Las Vegas gaming circles believed, although most exercised enough discretion not to laugh out loud at the claim.

As far as Binion was concerned, this coupling with Bernstein constituted a temporary arrangement. While he waited for his bribes to work their magic, the planning for the big debut party was well under way. And soon he would hear good news from Dallas. The coming days were shaping up to be some of the best of Binion's life.

Noble's placement couldn't have been better, at least from his assassins' perspective. When he stopped his car, he sat directly on top of the explosives the three men had assembled and buried the night before. Now Noble leaned out the car window, his white hair in the sun, his tanned arm extended for any soothing letters he might have received. The loudest sounds were the grinding of cicadas and the low rumble of the engine of the Ford. He breathed in: the Cat's last. One of the men hidden in the bushes touched a copper wire from the battery to a barbed-wire fence, grounding the connection, and the buried bomb roared.

The blast ripped the car apart, flipping the frame on its back, and dug a crater five feet across and four feet deep. Shrapnel and body parts flew in all directions. A hunk of Noble's leg went arcing toward the killers' hide-away. If he had wanted, one of the men could have stepped from behind the brush and caught it like a football. The mailbox sailed seventy-five feet. A newspaper later said that Noble had been "rent apart by the blast," but that didn't do it justice. His body was simply gone below the shoulders.

Then it was done. As the destroyed car lay upside down next to the crater, dark and dirty smoke rose against the bleached blue sky. Dozens of twenty-dollar bills—from Noble's card-playing cache—fluttered down into the flames like high-priced autumn leaves. The killers fled, leaving a scene embellished by a couple of macabre grace notes so trite that any pulp writer who conjured them would have been laughed out of town. But there they were, two playing cards faceup on the ground, a few feet from the twisted metal, next to a charred piece of Noble's straw cowboy hat: a joker and the ace of diamonds.

His neighbors heard the blast but didn't pay much attention to it. Farms and ranches in the area set off explosives as a matter of working routine. Noble's corpse and the hot hulk of the Ford lay in the dirt road for ninety minutes before a farmer on his way home happened upon them.

This crime was big, so monumental that the top lawman in Denton County arrived to inspect the bombing scene in person, even if he couldn't see a thing. Sheriff W. O. Hodges had been blinded two years earlier when a crazed man, terrorizing the tiny town of Krum, shot him in the face with a 12-gauge. This sudden handicap impeded his investigative abilities not at all, his deputies insisted. Now the blind sheriff stood in the dirt road, run-ning his fingers over the wreckage of Noble's car. All around the sheriff, the area swarmed with investigators, including a Texas Ranger improbably outfitted in a fedora, sunglasses, and a floral Hawaiian shirt. Also joining the probe was a postal inspector, who warned that whoever killed Noble would be subject to a three-year term for damaging a mailbox. As the inspector concerned himself with this federal matter, other officers set about collecting scattered body parts.

The cops penciled sketches, took photos, drew maps, and used tape measures to add fine detail to their reports. They also made a show of searching for fingerprints, but gathered none of use. In all, it was a hot and dirty ordeal of scouring a crime scene and coming up with little more than the abandoned Delco battery, a few wires, and the vague reports of sightings of the men in the blue pickup. By the end of the day, they could have put all their clues in a suitcase and had room left over for what remained of Noble.

While the police went about their futile activities, Binion relaxed in an air-conditioned restaurant at the Last Frontier on the Las Vegas Strip, visiting with his old Dallas friend Ivy Miller. The two had plenty of good times to talk about—the policy games, the Southland Syndicate, the day Miller blew away Binion's rival Sam Murray on a crowded downtown Dallas sidewalk. Someone paged Binion. He rose from the table and took a phone call. A reporter from the *Houston Press* gave him the news that Noble had been killed. Binion paused, then said, "I'm glad he's dead."

It was not the most politic of responses, and Binion spent the rest of the day backing away. To United Press he said, "I know a lot of people think I had something to do with all those other attempts on Noble's life, and they're probably saying I had something to do with this one . . . But I had nothing to do with any of them. This is a bad thing."

And he told *the Dallas Morning News,* "I didn't have a thing to do with it. That's the graveyard truth." He wasn't all that choked up about it, though. "I don't care one way or the other," he said. "I just don't give a damn."

Nobody believed that one either.

Seven days after his rival was blown to bits, Binion presided over the grand opening of his Horseshoe Club. The debut was, fittingly, a major Vegas event, and represented a move up in class for Glitter Gulch. The city's crusty mayor, C. D. Baker, cut the ribbon, which had been lovingly draped over a shotgun. A grinning Binion circulated and greeted, wearing a cowboy hat, a billowy suit, and a patterned tie that stopped a good six inches above his belt. Nick the Greek showed too, as did a good slice of the Las Vegas gambling public. And the publicity machine had been cranked to high: "Crowds reminded us of famed Grand Central Station in N.Y.C. on a 4th of July weekend," proclaimed *Fabulous Las Vegas* magazine.

When the sun finally sank behind the mountains, the casino's signage came alive: a red-and-white "Horseshoe" in neon deco cursive atop each of two sidewalk awnings. And above the entrance loomed an electric horseshoe-shaped display, twelve feet tall and aglow in blinding white. Inside, the customers lined the tables three and four deep, the redolence of fresh paint mingling with the smell of smoke, whiskey, and perfume. The Horseshoe couldn't approach the fabulous Flamingo's luxury, but it had its charms, and the *Las Vegas Sun*, published by Binion's good friend Hank Greenspun, had played them up big. "Heralded to be one of the most lavish casinos in the downtown area, the new Horseshoe opens its doors today to expectant throngs," the *Sun*'s story gushed in advance. "Across the terrazzo entrance with its imbedded steel horseshoes, footsteps of throngs will pass, to immediately encounter deep-pile rose carpet."

That, to the *Sun*—and the throngs—was only the beginning of the Horseshoe's delights. The casino had an emerald-green ceiling, and the craps tables featured padded leather armrests and recessed drink holders. The hungry gambler was the lucky gambler, for the Horseshoe's restaurant offered "anything and everything for a gourmet's exacting taste," the *Sun* reported, and at the counter, "a waitress can dispense malted milks at any hour of the day or night." Few customers came for twenty-four-hour chocolate shakes. And they weren't looking for scantily clad chorus girls or tuxedoed lounge singers. There weren't any, and never would be, because, as Binion liked to say, he didn't want his money blowing out the end of some guy's trumpet. At the Horseshoe, all the action was in the action. From the moment the lights went on, the Horseshoe rolled as the hottest gambling spot in town. Throughout that first night it pulsed with the sound of cash changing hands—the ringing of the slots, the clatter of the roulette wheel, the soft tumble of the dice across the green felt, the cries of joy from the winners.

Too many winners, initially. "The first night," Binion said, "me and my wife went home at about four o'clock in the morning, and when we left, we was $96,000 losers." But when he returned to the casino the next afternoon, the house advantage had prevailed. "Hell, we was a hundred and some-odd thousand winners," he said. "So I ain't never been in no tight since."

Not only that, his pioneering wall-to-wall floor covering paid for itself when the company owner hit the Horseshoe tables. "The carpet cost $18,000," Binion said. "He was a player, and the first night he played, I won $18,000 exactly. So I win the carpet."

Herbert Noble's remains were buried in a concrete vault next to those of his wife, the two bombing victims now side by side at Hillcrest Memorial Park in Dallas. His feud with Binion had been so prolonged, violent, and darkly absurd that even national publications took notice of his death: *Life* magazine ran a pictorial display of the bomb scene, and *Time* weighed in with a story headlined "The Last Days of the Cat." As a continuing criminal investigation produced few hot leads, police had to console themselves with the thought that at least the Noble-Binion feud had finally run its course. Except maybe it had not. All over Dallas, people still talked of their belief that Noble had left a vengeance fund in escrow.

This notion gained new life on a Las Vegas night in late September, when Binion returned home from the Horseshoe. He rode in his Cadillac, which was driven by a bodyguard, a man named Natie Blank. Also in the car was Russian Louie Strauss. Another car pulled alongside on the dark street, and shots were fired, blowing holes in Binion's Caddy. No one was hurt, although Blank's performance may have been less than sterling. He soon found himself discharged from Binion's staff.

Binion and his friends among the local authorities managed to suppress news of the incident for a while. "The law enforcing here has always been honest and tops," Binion once explained. "Of course, they've let little old things go, which I was in favor of." But several weeks after the shooting, United Press broke the story, calling the incident a possible "underworld assassination attempt." Police said they had no clues and no leads, and that "officers were unable to trace down any secret repair job on Binion's auto." The story added this description of his home: "The Binion yard is patrolled by two vicious Great Dane dogs, and visitors must be escorted personally to the house for protection. Mrs. Binion herself was reportedly scarred for life by one of the huge Danes." That last part wasn't quite right. The mauling victim was a man who worked for the Binions.

Though silent on the matter of his dogs, Binion insisted that the shooting never happened. "The portly gambler himself has denied the reports," United Press wrote. "'Not a damn thing to it,' he said. 'This town is lousy with rumors. You can't believe anything you hear.'"

Rumor or not, such publicity could hurt a man trying to ingratiate himself with casino regulators, and Binion needed a rousing rebuttal. It soon appeared in the *Pioche Record*, the journal of a mining town to the north. "The various stories that have been appearing through press releases about Benny Binion are malodorous to put to shame the wildest efforts of a dime novelist," the *Record* wrote, adding that Binion was "the target of scatter-brained sensationalism."

The United Press account of the attempt to shoot Binion was "as stale as the opening of King Tut's tomb," the *Record*'s story asserted, and presented a "dither of misinformation." And those supposedly vicious guard dogs? They actually greeted strangers with "much tail-wagging and barks of welcome."

The *Record*'s writer knew this because his research included a visit to the Binion home on Bonanza Road: "Upon entering the Binion residence, our reporter would be instantly intrigued by the decorous atmosphere, Mrs. Binion's reserved charm, and a princely hospitality offered by Mr. Binion into which is insinuated the social traditions of the old South, including fried chicken by an imported colored cook."

Not only did he offer southern fried chicken, but Binion was generous to a fault with his cash, the *Record* noted. "Charitable organizations hail him as a philanthropist," the story said, "and unfortunate individuals look upon him as the sweet prince of 'touch.'"

On that last point, at least, the newspaper could be considered something of an impeccable source. About the time the story appeared, Binion bought the publisher of the *Record*, Nevada state senator E. L. Nores, a brand-new car—a Hudson Hornet. Or, as some sarcastically took to calling it, a "Binion Bullet."

Such a car cost about $2,500 in 1951. Binion's Horseshoe could grab that much on one sucker's roll of the dice.

The blind sheriff of Denton County and his deputies made little headway in their investigation of Noble's murder. The Texas Rangers were conducting their own probe but had turned up nothing in the way of solid leads, despite the assistance of the ever-present Lieutenant Butler of the Dallas police. Butler and the Rangers faced no shortage of hoods to interview, because by official police count, thirty-nine people "had been propositioned to kill or had attempted to kill Noble" since 1945. However, five of them were already dead and fourteen in prison. Some of the rest, in Butler's estimation, didn't appear capable of pulling off the complex bombing job. Still, "all are tough outlaws," he wrote. "Informants close to Binion state that he would not have anything to do with some of the lessor [sic] lights mentioned, but others state, equally as positively, that Binion did not care who made the money as long as Noble was killed; the quicker the better."

Butler and Ranger Bob Crowder initially focused on three men as their prime suspects: Bob Braggins, Finley Donica, and J. R. Gilreath, well-traveled journeymen Dallas burglars who knew their way around explosives. A witness told police that a few days before the bombing he had been in Donica's home and seen a "two-gallon pickle jar, full of dynamite sticks." The three men were spotted together less than an hour after the murder at a nearby café, where they looked, a waitress said, dirty, hot, and thirsty. In the classic manner of dimwitted criminals who hit it big, all three bought new cars right after the killing. But leads that looked promising fell apart. Polygraph tests of the men told police nothing. A witness who said he heard two of the suspects talking about the murder soon recanted his story, and had a good reason for doing so. "He is very muchly afraid of Gilreath killing him," Butler wrote.

Many of the usual rats had gone mute. "Most of the informants are afraid to do any talking," Butler wrote. "The word in the so-called underworld being to 'forget the Noble deal' if you want to get along."

Getting nowhere, Butler and Crowder decided to try a different, more aggressive strategy. They would go to Las Vegas, where they could question Binion in person. It would be two tough cops—one of whom was, after all, a Ranger—putting the heat on one simple gambling man. This, they believed, might finally crack the case—or, at the very least, produce some decent leads.

In the fall of 1951, the Nevada Tax Commission reversed itself and decided to grant Binion a new hearing on his Horseshoe license application. That worried Robbins Cahill, a commission official who thought that approving Binion would present big image problems for the state. "You left yourself open to the argument, 'Well, if a man with a background like that can get a license, who can't?'" Cahill said. "Who can you keep out?"

Practically nobody, as it developed, for other commission members seemed untroubled by Cahill's concerns. But before they could rehear Binion's case, they had to make a stab at appearing to do their duty. The commission dispatched two men to Texas to look into Binion's background. Commission member Paul McDermott and an agency supervisor flew to Dallas, where they talked to reporters, prosecutors, police, and business owners. They asked about the murders of Sam Murray, Raymond Loudermilk, and a few others, including Noble, and they examined some court records. They uncovered absolutely nothing that was new. Nor did they find any hard evidence that Binion was actively engaged in the gambling business in Texas, though he remained under indictment for that. They could have done as well if they had stayed home and read the newspapers.

The Nevada emissaries did accomplish one thing: they provided Dallas police with another good indication of Binion's heft in his adopted hometown when they related his treatment at a recent Branding Iron Dinner given by the Las Vegas Press Club. This was one of those gatherings in which local journalists and politicians poke fun at each other and drown any lingering resentments at the bar. One of the press club skits that night made light of the recently consummated Binion-Noble feud. This provoked much laughter from the audience. When the hilarity subsided, Binion was presented with a commemorative branding iron, a gift he accepted to much cheering. "Most of the prolonged applause," a memo noted, "came from the other big time gamblers who were present."

Not coincidentally, these were some of the same Strip casino operators who had written or called the Nevada Tax Commission urging that Binion be granted a license. "They all like Benny," McDermott said.

It wasn't only the local hacks and hustlers that Binion had finally managed to pocket. Some of the state's most powerful politicians were lining up behind him too. Governor Charles Russell said he had been in Las Vegas recently, and while many locals had told him they supported Binion's licensing, he couldn't find a soul who would speak ill of the man. "No one," he said, "has ever come to me opposing Mr. Binion."

Another of Binion's ardent advocates was Nevada's senior senator, Pat McCarran. Like Binion, McCarran had spent much of his youth in the wild, herding livestock, although in McCarran's case they were sheep. Starting small and local—the Nevada state assembly—McCarran built his political career brick by brick. He was not elected to the U.S. Senate until he was fifty-six. By turns sentimental and ruthless, he valued loyalty above all. In other words, he took care of his friends. He had intervened on behalf of Meyer Lansky and Bugsy Siegel so that they could procure scarce postwar construction materials for the building of the Flamingo, to the detriment of some deserving locals. Veterans home from the war couldn't find bathtubs and basins for their new homes, but they could "see hundreds of them stacked up in the lot where the Flamingo was building," Cahill recalled. And when Moe Dalitz faced some resistance in securing a gaming license in 1949, McCarran helped ease the way—after a meeting with Galveston mobster Sam Maceo, a Dalitz ally who had been Binion's landlord at the Southland Hotel in Dallas.

Now that McCarran's friend Binion needed help with his own license, the senator brought his considerable influence to bear. "McCarran never quit trying," said Cahill, who recalled years later that the "McCarran machine" removed a Binion opponent from the tax commission by arranging for him to get a better-paying job at another state agency.

Such machinations were hardly secret at the time. An editorial in the *Reno Evening Gazette* took disapproving note of a "well-organized propaganda campaign" on Binion's behalf. "Considerable pressure is being brought to bear on members of the tax commission," the paper said. "To put it mildly, this is a rare and unusual performance." That was a restrained way of saying what had become a general belief in the small world of Nevada casinos: the fix was in.

Before he could take advantage of that, Binion had to deal with the two inquiring lawmen from Texas.

On November 12, 1951, Butler and Crowder flew unannounced to Las Vegas and checked into a room at the Apache Hotel, one floor above the Horseshoe. When they learned that Binion couldn't see them right away—he was home asleep—the pair took a walking tour of Fremont Street's packed sidewalks. Glitter Gulch was enjoying record crowds that evening, thanks to Armistice Day celebrations. "The three-day holiday jammed the community to the gunwales," the *Review-Journal* reported. By the time the two lawmen reached the bright lights of the Golden Nugget, across the street from the Horseshoe, a couple of Las Vegas police detectives were on their tail. Finally the detectives approached the Texans and asked if they were in town for business or pleasure. The conversation was an amicable one, but it also served to inform the outsiders that Binion owned the local cops.

The next morning Butler and Crowder met Binion for breakfast at his customary booth in the Horseshoe restaurant. He greeted the pair by half joking that he had heard Butler had come to kill him. With this gangster version of small talk out of the way, the two officers took their seats and began firing questions about Noble's death. To judge from Binion's demeanor, they could have been asking about the scrambled eggs. He was "cool and collected," Butler and Crowder wrote in their report. "He seemed to be sure of himself, looked his questioner straight in the eye, and did not hesitate in his answers . . . Binion talked more freely than we expected him to."

He also didn't admit to any crime. The lawmen said numerous informants had told them that Binion stood behind the attempts on Noble's life. Never happened, Binion said. If he had wanted Noble dead he could have found professional killers to do the job for a couple thousand bucks, five thousand at the most. Not that he knew any such killers. "He denied knowing any of the West Dallas punks that we have known to discuss Noble's murder for money," Butler and Crowder wrote.

Well, he did know some of them. Binion acknowledged more than a passing acquaintance with Johnny Grisaffi and the departed Lois Green. This prompted Butler to recall a night when he stopped Green as he drove through Dallas. Green "jumped out of the car with a pistol," in Butler's account, but threw it down when he saw who had pulled him over. Green told Butler he was upset and anxious because of his failed attempts to dispatch the Cat, but that Binion was going to give him "all the time I need" to kill Noble. The anecdote caused Binion to stare in surprise. "Did that son of a bitch really say that?" he asked.

Next came more conversational pleasantries. Binion told them he had a new bodyguard, one Cole Agee, a former border patrolman and a crack shot. "He can knock the eyes out of a gnat," he bragged. He also announced that he had personally made "over a million dollars" since moving to Nevada, and that he had ten thousand acres of oil-producing land under lease in Wyoming. "He had paid 25 cents an acre for the lease and had just turned down $3.50 an acre for it," the lawmen's report noted.

When Butler and Crowder asked him about the recent shots fired at his car in Las Vegas, Binion laughed it off. Although he had previously denied it, he now dismissed the incident as little more than a prank, a bit of spirited recreation by some carousing soldiers or liquored-up cowboys. The two experienced investigators heard this fanciful tale from a racketeer who had been locked in a violent feud and swallowed it whole. "After this description by Binion," Crowder and Butler wrote, "we were inclined to agree with him."

Next they talked about control of the Horseshoe, and Binion's partnership charade with Monte Bernstein. For one of the few times in the interview, Binion turned candid. "He contended that his relations with the Jew were strictly business," the lawmen wrote. "It was clear that Binion ran the place."

And that was that. Two hotshot lawmen finally scored an interview with the notorious chieftain, the fugitive from justice, the prime suspect in a spectacular murder, and they came away empty. Over the course of several hours, Binion had evaded, dissembled, and denied, all while giving his questioners almost nothing in the way of actionable information.

Butler and Crowder couldn't get a flight out that afternoon. So Binion arranged for one of his favorite local lawmen to take his Texas counterparts on an after-dark excursion to the Strip. "That evening, Captain Ralph Lamb of the Las Vegas Sheriff's Department entertained us at the Flamingo Club," they wrote in their report. They didn't mention that the Flamingo remained one of the most mobbed-up casinos in town.

At least they had an escort who knew the ins and outs of Vegas. Lamb was, in Binion's estimation, "as fine a man as I ever seen." When Crowder and Butler met him, he had embarked on a long law enforcement career that would include years of taking thousands of dollars in cash under the table from Binion.

The two Texas investigators encountered another local cop luminary as well. "We met Sheriff Glen Jones, who was having breakfast at the Horseshoe Club," they wrote. The sheriff was in fact a regular at Binion's restaurant, where he ate for free, at least until his law enforcement career expired prematurely. Within a few years he would be caught in a sting operation and accused of extorting $1,000 a month in protection money from Roxie's, a brothel operating out of a motel on the Boulder Highway.

"A good man, Glen Jones," Binion said later. "But he drank a little whiskey, and they got him tangled up."

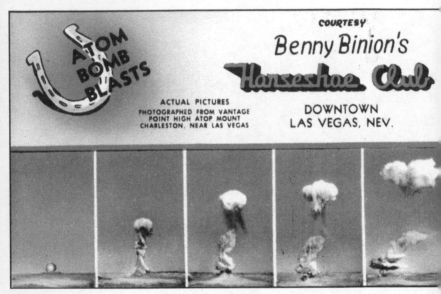

A Horseshoe postcard from the 1950s touting a new sort of tourist attraction.

# 15

# "THEY WAS ON THE TAKE"

Them dice just run in cycles.

—BB

If Las Vegas in the summer was a suburb of hell, albeit one with nearly naked chorus girls and all-you-can-eat buffets, the weeks of late autumn came close to compensating for the deadly heat. The nights dipped into a pleasant chill and the afternoons rolled in cool and dry, with a high, clear sky. Perfect weather for setting off some A-bombs.

In November 1951, after concluding a series of blasts, the federal government announced that it would soon resume the testing of atomic weapons at Frenchman Flat and Yucca Flat, a couple of forsaken patches of the Mojave sixty-five miles northwest of Las Vegas. The first of the bombs had been detonated ten months before at the Nevada Test Site, and the feds had been pleased with the results. The military and the scientists considered the test site a logistical godsend—isolated but accessible, reachable by road and rail but suitably far from prying eyes. Having such a proving ground on U.S. soil was "one of the best things that has happened to us," said Gordon Dean, chairman of the Atomic Energy Commission.

On the days that bombs went off, the Vegas gambler or tourist who timed it right could look to the horizon and see the remnants of a pinkish mushroom cloud against the cobalt-blue sky. Some casinos, including the Horseshoe, put pictures of the clouds on promotional postcards. Other clubs offered special "atomic cocktails" and detonation-watching parties from rooftops. A dancer at the Last Frontier performed as Miss Atomic Blast, described by a canny publicity agent as "radiating loveliness instead of deadly atomic particles."

Luckily for Las Vegas, the prevailing winds were westerly, as they swept the detonations' floating, irradiated dust and ash away from the city and over the scattered sheep ranchers, desert dwellers, and polygamists of eastern Nevada and Utah—unsuspecting people referred to in federal government documents of the time as "a low-use segment of the population." The radiation would do its work on them, but that would take a while. Not for years would hundreds of people, later known as downwinders, be diagnosed with cancers blamed on the fallout.

For now, Vegas welcomed the news that the tests would be starting again, because activity at the test site meant even more jobs for locals. These were the years when the city's economy seemed to hum. In addition to military spending, tourist numbers had been growing, and construction of resort casinos along the Strip continued apace. The Sahara was going up, with the $5.5 million Sands soon to follow. Coming next: the Showboat and the Riviera.

Even more developers with grand plans were descending on Las Vegas, for there were fortunes to be made. Hence Binion's urgency. Although the Horseshoe was doing red-hot business, he couldn't maintain the shotgun marriage with Monte Bernstein much longer. To really make this deal work the way he wanted, Binion needed his license.

On the Strip, bandleader Harry James and his wife, actress Betty Grable, were arm in arm, exuding furs-and-diamonds glamour at the Thunderbird. Back on Fremont, the Horseshoe continued to pull in the crowds night after night, and proclaimed its simple slogan in quarter-page newspaper ads: "Always Action." But on the morning of December 1, 1951, the real action could be found one block from the Horseshoe, at the federal building on Stewart Avenue, where the state tax commission had gathered for a hearing on Binion's license application. This was the same place where the Kefauver committee had gathered a year earlier. But this time Binion showed up, ready to make his pitch.

He strolled into the second-floor hallway about eleven thirty that morning, the heels of his handmade Willie Lusk boots knocking against the brown terrazzo floor. Binion waved to half a dozen newsmen as he ambled past four armed Nevada highway patrolmen, who were there to keep irate reporters and curious citizens out of the hearing. For the star witness, the padded leather doors, the color of port wine, opened wide. Inside the high-ceilinged courtroom, where the meeting was chaired by Governor Russell, Binion settled himself into a shiny wooden chair and—surrounded by twenty bas-relief eagles along the top of all four walls—wasted no time in turning on the ranch-house charm. "Binion had this very engaging style," said Robbins Cahill, then the commission's secretary.

Upon swearing to tell the truth, Binion first had to explain his shooting of Ben Freiden, the rival numbers operator, which he did with ease. "He was a bad man, a very bad man," he said. This not only satisfied the concerns of his questioners but also entertained them. Recalled Cahill, "He had the tax commission in stitches, just laughing at his killing a man." Next Binion justified his shooting of Frank Bolding, the bootlegger. "Just a nigger I caught stealing some whiskey," he said. Again laughter erupted. And so it went, for about an hour.

After Binion left the hearing, state senator E. L. Nores made an appearance. Whether he drove his new Hudson Hornet to the courthouse is unclear, but his support for Binion hit a familiar blaring note. "Binion is a man you can believe in," he said. "I have business dealings with him and have found him to be a man of high character." As to problems in Texas, Nores remained untroubled. The senator said he had a brother in Dallas who had assured him that Binion had a good reputation there. Nores offered no proof of his brother's investigative credentials; mere siblinghood was apparently sufficient. If his friend did not get a casino license, Nores told commissioners, "you are making a serious mistake."

That afternoon, they voted unanimously to approve Binion's application. (Cahill did not have a vote.) The commissioners did add a probationary requirement: if Binion were to "bring discredit on himself or the state of Nevada," the license would be revoked. Absent that, he was free to run the Horseshoe.

This represented a remarkable turnaround, even in a state known for creative approaches to regulation. While an ebullient Binion was slapping backs around his casino tables, the *Reno Evening Gazette* again shifted into high dudgeon. "Taking on extraordinary powers," the *Gazette* said in an editorial, "the Nevada tax commission in effect held a trial and granted an acquittal on a Texas criminal indictment, and overrode the charges of the Kefauver crime investigating committee." The paper also reminded readers that Binion "is still a fugitive from justice in the eyes of Texas law, and it is not likely that any other state but Nevada would grant him asylum."

A second *Gazette* editorial-page column piled on: "Maybe Binion's qualifications, reputation and past records were all carefully scrutinized by members of the tax commission, but if such was the case, the members and [Governor] Russell must have been benignly blind-folded at the time."

Binion—for once—kept his immediate public reaction truthful, concise, and diplomatic. "I am," he said of the licensing, "very thankful."

Years later, he was asked how he had swayed the commission. "They was on the take," he said. "There would've been some you could've bribed, if you'd wanted to, but I wouldn't give 'em nothing." This was in all likelihood another of his classic semantic denials, the Cowboy once again regarding payoffs as friendly gifts and painting stark corruption as beneficence. In contrast, a 1953 FBI report contained this blunt summation: "Reports were received from reliable Informants in the Las Vegas area that Benny Binion 'really put out' to the commissioners of the Nevada State Tax Commission."

Whatever it cost, it was worth it. Binion had risen so high now that within a few weeks he even made Walter Winchell's "On Broadway" newspaper column. From Manhattan, Winchell presided as the master of the snappy three-dot gossip dispatch. (". . . Imogene Coca back from a Cuban holiday with a cocoa-tan . . .") He dished out a frantic mix of celebrity news, political bulletins, and quick-release anecdotes, some of which might have been true.

"A wealthy Texan named Blondy Turner was in New York recently," Winchell wrote in his year-end column for 1951. "He telephoned Benny

Binion, prop of the Horseshoe, the newest gambling palace in Las Vegas, to wish him good luck." Blondy Turner placed a $10,000 dice bet with Binion over the phone, Winchell said, and Binion held the receiver close enough to the craps table that Blondy in New York could hear the stickman call his victory. Winchell continued: "'You win Ten Big Ones!' cheerfully informed Mr. Binion over the Long-Distance . . . 'Okay,' chuckled Blondy Turner in Manhattan. 'See you next week to collect it!' . . . When Mr. Turner, the Sportsman, arrived in Vegas, he made straight for the dice table . . . And lost $200,000."

In Vegas, even the fables were going Benny's way.

Life at the estate on Bonanza Road approached the idyllic, Vegas version. The Binion compound served as a mini-ranch and perpetual summer camp for the Binion children and their friends. They had a concrete swimming pool behind the house, and plenty of room among the groves of Chinese elms for them to ride horses with Gold Dollar.

Binion, as always, made it home for dinner most nights. Over a feast of, say, fried frog legs, he went around the table to each child, asking for thoughts on the day. "We could talk about anything, except we couldn't have any arguments," daughter Brenda recalled, which meant that one contentious subject—on which everyone had strong opinions—was off-limits. "We couldn't talk about horses."

With his two Cadillacs parked out front, Binion sat on a net worth that easily exceeded $2 million. The ranch in Montana alone was worth at least $722,000, and it supported a thousand head of cattle. And there were the oil leases he had mentioned to the Texas cops.

But the real gusher was the Horseshoe, where the cash money flowed seven days a week. Binion was forty-seven years old now, with nearly three decades of running gambling joints behind him, and he had made the most of his experience. Believing as always in loyalty, he had surrounded himself at the Horseshoe with trusted associates from his Texas days. As resistance from other casino owners had faded, he incorporated a primary lesson from his Dallas mentor Warren Diamond. He took the biggest bets, because the more the customers could bet, the more they could lose.

Other casinos imposed ceilings on craps bets to contain their own short-term loss exposure. But the Horseshoe was different, and ultimately this became Binion's Vegas trademark: the craps player's first bet, no matter how high, was his limit. A customer could put down a cool million if he had the guts and the cash. This appealed both to the fantasies of the casual gambler and the strategies of the high roller, and let a Wild West ethos blow through the room. It wasn't long before the Horseshoe was considered the center of the craps universe.

Binion also imported luxurious touches he remembered from Top O'Hill—free drinks and courtesy limo rides for gamblers were a Horseshoe trademark—but he democratized it as only a poor boy could do. Give them "good food cheap, good whiskey cheap and good gamble," all of them, from the scuffed to the shiny. Maybe you drove a Rolls and lived in Malibu, or maybe your suit came from Sears and the wife clipped coupons at the kitchen table. It didn't matter to Binion. The way to get rich, he loved to say, was to treat little people like big people.

With the Horseshoe's opening, Binion had shaken his Texas refugee status and secured a place of triumph. Years later he would routinely be referred to as the king of gambling in Vegas. This is where it started, at the corner of Second and Fremont on the southeastern end of Glitter Gulch. "I'm just a gambler," Binion said once. "I'm not a businessman." He wasn't a detail man either. He generally filed the fine points of business under the heading of a favorite phrase: "This, that and the other." He kept no calendar, and rarely consulted a clock. "I don't like too many appointments," he said, "and I don't like to be nowhere at a certain time." But every morning he checked the chili from the Horseshoe kitchen to ensure that it conformed to Bill Decker's jailhouse recipe. And he kept a sharp eye on the casino's operations, though not from an office or by poring over the books. Binion managed his entire enterprise from a booth at the Horseshoe restaurant, where his sole accessory of executive life was a table telephone. As he had always done, he went with his instincts, and success followed.

Gambling was now a billion-dollar-a-year enterprise in Nevada, and Binion pulled his bounteous share. Money poured into the Horseshoe's counting room so fast the staff couldn't keep up with it. "Their money management system is simple," one of their lawyers said. "Just pile cash on the floor until the pile gets too big, then start another one."

Binion left tabulating of the take to a close friend, one Robert "Doby Doc" Caudill, a cattleman and junk collector who dressed in bib overalls accented with a diamond stickpin, and carried a pearl-handled revolver in his boot. He had been a bootlegger during Prohibition and—some lawmen believed—sold narcotics and stolen jewelry. This was the kind of finance man to whom Binion could naturally relate. "He come here in 1906 and done been to college," Binion said, detailing Caudill's accounting credentials. His frugality was such that even a movie star couldn't bend it. "Sophie Tucker . . . went out to Doby Doc's to see all of his junk," Binion recalled. "So Sophie Tucker says, 'Doby, give me a souvenir.' He says, 'There's a 80-pound anvil you can have. Just pick it up.'"

At the Horseshoe, Caudill counted the cash after every eight-hour shift, before taking a nap in his room upstairs at the Apache Hotel. "Never got tired," Binion said, "because he slept three times a day."

Binion had the hottest dice tables in town, so why not bring in some card players to juice the scene that much more? Make it a contest between two of the most skillful poker players in the country. Pull them out of back rooms and put them on a world stage. It could be a marathon poker battle for the ages, and a publicity bonanza for the Horseshoe. Even the wily Binion couldn't foresee that this would turn into one of the most storied duels in modern American poker lore. Some possibility exists that the event might have resembled the legend.

In relating the intimate history of high-stakes poker, at least in the first three-fourths of twentieth-century America, professional card players employed oral history in the manner of lost jungle tribes. This was a hidden game with arcane codes of behavior and no institutional governance. A secret and isolated society with an aversion to outsiders tended to stay secret and isolated. Academic gumshoes exploring the folkways of the five-card-stud demimonde had yet to appear in any number, and players themselves avoided outside scrutiny because that would expose them to their worst enemies—hijackers and tax collectors. Any suggestion of broadcasting a poker game on television would have been considered dangerous lunacy. Books by insiders were rare. If a big-time poker master were somehow inclined to write about his profession, it would be quickly dismissed as counterproductive. Why waste time scribbling when you could be winning money at the table?

But the players did at least talk about the games and their heroic fellow gamblers—many of whom tended toward the dangerously exotic, if not psychotic—to each other, and maybe a few trusted associates. News of big pots, crazy bluffs, savvy raises, strong-arm robberies, and sensational wins made the circuit. And players gossiped like anybody else. Even on the mildest of days, such gossip spun itself into tall tales.

From this realm comes the story of the great Horseshoe battle: Nick "the Greek" Dandalos, international gambler of no small renown, was hanging around Binion's brand-new joint one day, and mentioned that he wanted to play in a poker game for the highest stakes ever. Binion got on the phone to an old pal from his youth, Johnny Moss, who had developed into one of the greatest players around. "I think you should come out here and have some fun," Binion supposedly told him.

The finely tailored Dandalos cultivated an air of mysterious aristocracy, and floated about with a beautiful woman on each arm as he dispensed the airy pronouncements of a daredevil patrician. "I would rather fall from a mountaintop than die of boredom on the plain," he liked to say. Another guy who went by "the Greek," the oddsmaker Jimmy Snyder, stood in awe of Dandalos's Continental savoir faire. "He made Omar Sharif look like a truck driver," Snyder said. This had been both bred and schooled into Dandalos. His godfather back in Greece was said to be a shipping magnate, and he claimed a university degree in philosophy.

To someone like Binion, this was tantamount to hailing from Neptune. "Well, Nick the Greek, he was the strangest character I ever seen," he remembered. "He was a kinky ol' guy. He'd put a snake in your pocket and ask you for a match." When flush, he kept stacks of cash—hundreds of thousands of dollars—in cardboard boxes in his unlocked Las Vegas garage or crammed under his clothes in bureau drawers in his bedroom. "Nobody ever knew where he got that money," Binion said.

Next to gambling and women, Dandalos loved poetry, and his favorite piece of verse was the finale of Henley's *"Invictus"*: "I am the master of my fate: / I am the captain of my soul." One starstruck girlfriend said Dandalos won bets by claiming he could "recite by heart any poem in the English language." She added, "I never saw him fail."

Moss, it can be safely said, never quoted poetry of any sort, although he was pretty good at conjuring some truncated, existentialist card-table haiku. "What good is money," he liked to say, "if you can't gamble with it?" His family had come to North Texas in a covered wagon in 1907, his mother dying en route of a burst appendix. When Moss was four, his father lost a leg after a telephone pole fell on him. Moss had to drop out of school—he managed to complete second grade—and help support the family by selling newspapers on the streets of Dallas. This led to more lucrative pursuits. "I learned how to gamble when I was about nine years old, shooting craps and playing dominoes," Moss said. "I made a living at dominoes by the time I was 15."

He received his early poker training at a Dallas dive called the Otters' Club, where he was hired as a "lookout man" to catch cheaters. After a series of scuffling jobs—in movie theaters, pool halls, oil fields—he finally found his niche as a poker professional. Moss stayed mainly in the Texas-Louisiana-Oklahoma circuit, playing in small-town Elks clubs and smoky motel rooms on two-lane highways. When not deep in the cards, he was hustling golf games or betting on horses, and he made and lost fortunes with barely a blink. In one high-stakes poker game in Dallas, he won $250,000 and instructed his long-suffering wife, Virgie, to go out and look for the nicest house she could find. She located the dream home, but Moss told her, "Sorry, you looked too long." He had blown all the money at the track.

When Binion called him, the story goes, Moss—doughy, pasty, expressionless—was wrapping up a three-day, nonstop game in Odessa, Texas. Without delay, he flew to Vegas, grabbed a cab to the Horseshoe, handed his luggage to a porter, and waltzed into the casino ready to play. He and Dandalos shook hands, then sat at a kidney-shaped, felt-topped table on the casino floor and commenced a game of cards that turned into a poker death march.

Back and forth went Moss and the Greek, for days, weeks, like two great armies seizing then ceding territory. They drank gallons of water and coffee as they played, and consumed countless sandwiches from Binion's restaurant. Spectators crowded six-deep at the rail. Moss never looked up from his cards long enough to see if it was day or night. The two players adjourned for sleep only once or twice a week. After Moss returned from one nap, the Greek greeted him with, "What are you going to do, Johnny? Sleep your life away?"

Superhuman stamina was a badge of honor for professional players. Dandalos once boasted to a friend of having won a weeklong game despite suffering a "severe" heart attack halfway through. He barely paused long enough to clutch his chest, in his telling, before raking in a pot. At the Horseshoe, he felt little need for rest and found lively activities to fill the breaks. One account has him escorting a visitor, none other than Albert Einstein, on a walking tour of Fremont Street, introducing him as "little Al from Princeton—controls a lot of the action around Jersey."

At the table, the play brought many moments of high drama as Moss and the Greek engaged in five-card stud, which is considered the classic of poker games. The first card is dealt facedown, with the next four faceup. Bets are made after each round. In one game, the Greek's reserves had dipped to $250,000, putting his back to the wall. The cards came, and as the players kept betting, the Greek's bankroll shrank.

Moss had a nine in the hole, with a six, a nine, and a two showing: a pair of nines. The Greek's up cards were an eight, a six, and a four. Moss figured his opponent was banking on that slimmest of hopes, an inside straight. The dealer gave Moss his last card faceup—a three. The Greek's final card was a jack. He bet $50,000. Moss believed he was bluffing, and raised the bet. Dandalos, who had only $140,000 left, put it all in the pot.

"I guess I have to call," the Greek said, "because I have a jack in the hole."

Moss answered, "If you have a jack in the hole, Greek, you're going to win one hell of a pot."

Dandalos flipped his hole card over: jack of diamonds. He reached across the table and with both arms collected a pot of more than $500,000. Though Moss had lost a bundle, his gambler's intuition told him he would prevail in the end, because the Greek had revealed an excessive fondness for the long shot. "It was just a matter of time," Moss said.

A lot of time. The epic clash finally ended after five months, when

Dandalos is said to have folded his hand, risen from his chair, and resigned with, "Mr. Moss, I have to let you go."

By some accounts, Moss walked away with as much as $3 million cash. A few versions of the story have him, as he basked in the glow of victory, immediately migrating to the other Horseshoe games and financial catastrophe. "Moss went over to the dice table and dropped most, if not all, of the money he won from the Greek," said poker player Doyle Brunson. "That illustrated just how cunning Benny Binion could be."

Did the Moss-Greek war really happen? No definite proof exists, one way or the other. Not a single photograph of it has surfaced, and the local papers didn't mention it at the time. But it's a pretty good tale, and it's still being retold as part of the modern game's creation myth—the chrysalis stage of professional poker as spectator sport.

If such a contest occurred, and if it stirred no small degree of excitement, with hundreds craning for a glimpse of two legendary gamblers playing cards, then Binion would have remembered that. He would have recalled the buzz, the attendant casino revenue, and the way Vegas was alive for months with talk of the big poker game at the Horseshoe.

That would have been a powerful enough memory to survive Binion's near destruction, which was—and of this there is no doubt—about to unfold.

Benny, Teddy Jane, and the children, along with some friends, out for a night on the Strip.

# 16

# "NO WAY TO DUCK"

Believe in justice. But spell it "Just Us."

—BB

**B**ack in Dallas, Henry Wade had been elected district attorney in 1950, succeeding Will Wilson, who had moved on to the Texas Supreme Court. Wade was a short, powerfully built former FBI agent who chewed cigars and enjoyed passing afternoons at the Lakewood Country Club playing dominoes. In the courtroom, he embraced the persona of a drawling avenger—another unforgiving, cagey Texas farm boy—and later in his career persuaded a jury to sentence a pair of kidnappers to 5,005 years in prison, then the longest punishment in the history of American jurisprudence. Wade hired and promoted assistant DAs who followed his merciless, scorched-earth approach to prosecution, and this win-at-all-costs ethos made him a revered figure in the deeply conservative precincts of Dallas.

Now, in early 1952, Wade found himself disturbed by an old, unresolved, and frustrating case, so he made straight for one of his newly hired assistants, Bill Alexander. Tall and rail thin, Alexander had been a decorated infantry captain in World War II, and wore the perpetual look of someone searching for something to shoot. On this morning he sat at his gray metal desk in the DA's offices on the sixth floor of the county criminal courts building, puffing an unfiltered Camel. Black rotary-dial phones rang and secretaries' manual typewriters clattered. Alexander glanced up to see Wade approaching across the linoleum with a cigar in his mouth and a thick stack of papers in his hands. One peek at the stack and he knew what he had inherited: Benny Binion's criminal file. Wade dropped the papers on Alexander's desk and said only, "Get him."

Authorities in Nevada had justified their refusal to extradite Binion with the rationale that gambling was legal in that state. Murder, however, was not. If Alexander could reinvestigate Binion's Dallas years and develop a plausible homicide case against him, Nevada's argument would be moot. After studying the file—it contained years' worth of reports, witness statements, and police investigative memos—Alexander hit the streets. For days he haunted the old hotels where Binion's gambling halls had operated and the shabby bars that had hosted his policy games. Although Binion had been gone for more than five years, Alexander had no trouble finding people who remembered him, and who retained deep knowledge of his assorted, alleged misdeeds. "The only problem was, nobody would talk," Alexander recalled. "Binion had more friends than Wade did."

Eyewitnesses to Binion's Dallas mayhem combined their clear memories with a strong aversion to sworn statements. "They'd say, 'Mr. Bill, I was there, but I'm not going to testify against Mr. Binion,'" Alexander said. Like many in his line of work, Binion had kept most of his bloodshed within the outlaw family. "He may have been tough," Alexander said. "He may have been criminal. But he didn't bother anybody."

In general, those who had known Binion still liked and respected him. And they still feared him. More than once, Alexander said, potential witnesses recalled vividly that "people who screwed with Binion's business developed problems."

Alexander was not one to coddle criminals. Some years later, as a prosecutor, he told the mother of a murder defendant who begged him for mercy on her son, "Lady, I'll step on your boy like he was a cockroach." But now he was forced to admit that the new Binion investigation had no muscle. Though Alexander's lack of success disappointed Wade, the district attorney was determined to keep pushing. When he wrote an angry letter, it all turned.

More than two years after Will Wilson had instigated it, the federal tax investigation of Binion remained alive but close to dormant. The file had passed from agency to department, functionary to bureaucrat, until early 1952, when the Dallas office of Internal Revenue referred it to the local U.S. attorney's office, attaching the label "racketeer case." Frank Potter, U.S. attorney for the Northern District of Texas, didn't believe he had enough to convict Binion—he privately characterized the evidence as "rather slim and doubtful"—but he knew that dismissing the case would set off a political storm in Dallas.

Potter convened a federal grand jury and presented evidence from Binion's 1949 tax returns, despite the prosecutor's own serious misgivings. The case against Binion was "very weak," Potter again acknowledged. "A great deal of our case was based upon testimony of gamblers . . . who were certainly not very credible witnesses."

Grand jurors nonetheless indicted Binion for tax evasion, which Potter attributed to the Cowboy's notoriety. If the case had been brought against "any ordinary defendant," he said, "we could not have secured an indictment." The government's chances of succeeding at trial were about 50 percent, he calculated, and only 25 percent in appellate court. Because of that, and the potential cost of a lengthy trial, Potter reached an agreement with Binion's lawyers to have him plead no contest in Nevada. In return Binion agreed to pay a $15,000 fine and $20,000 in back taxes.

This represented, for Binion, a most desirable outcome—a penalty that amounted to pocket change, required no prison time, and forced no return to Texas. All he had to do was enter a plea and turn over a cashier's check, and he would be free of this legal matter that had dogged him for years. Likewise, the U.S. attorney reasoned that because Binion had been cited and punished, all parties would now be satisfied. Potter, in fact, believed he would be congratulated for a job well done under difficult circumstances.

The plea agreement surprised District Attorney Wade—he was not consulted in advance—and set him fuming. Allowing Binion to cop a plea in Nevada meant that the State of Texas's case couldn't proceed. Justice was being thwarted, Wade believed, as were certain ambitions for higher office. In July 1952, he wrote the U.S. Department of Justice and asked that Potter's decision be overruled. "As you can readily see," he argued, "law enforcement in this area has suffered in not being able to bring Binion to trial in almost three years, since he is acknowledged to be or to have been the biggest gambler in this area in some time."

The letter blindsided Potter. He learned of it "to my utter surprise and astonishment" when he read about it in a Dallas newspaper. The reaction to it surprised him even more. It was highly unusual, if not unprecedented, for Justice to overturn one of its own ranking officials because the local DA had thrown a tantrum. But that appeared to be happening, and Binion's lawyers soon got wind that their plea deal might be falling apart.

In Las Vegas, Binion's happy satisfaction turned to dread. "Oh, the heat just built up on me," he recalled.

Binion may have sensed the heat, but he had no way of knowing the power of its source. On August 8, 1952, James P. McGranery, attorney general of the United States, sent a memo to FBI director J. Edgar Hoover. "The Binion case," McGranery told Hoover, "has been the subject of my personal attention." He ordered a full FBI investigation into the matter.

Five days later, FBI assistant director Al Rosen wrote an internal memo regarding Binion with the subject line "Obstruction of Justice." He reported that confidential informants "whose reliability cannot be evaluated" had told FBI agents that "pressure was allegedly brought to bear" on U.S. Attorney Potter by a member of the board of directors of the First National Bank of Dallas. First National owned a controlling interest in Hillcrest State Bank, where Binion had deposited hundreds of thousands in policy game proceeds. The bank official told Potter that if he could persuade the grand jury to no-bill Binion, his reward would be a federal judgeship. "Potter allegedly declined to use his influence," Rosen wrote.

Hoover sent a telex to the bureau's offices in Dallas and Salt Lake City, which oversaw the FBI's Las Vegas operation, three days after Rosen's memo. The Binion investigation, the director said, "must be given preferred and continuous attention."

Though he kept the FBI on the case, the attorney general had already seen enough to make a decision. McGranery ordered that the plea agreement with Binion be withdrawn, and that he be brought back to Dallas to face charges.

But the legal wheels were already turning, and Binion's lawyers insisted that their deal, once struck, couldn't be undone. While waiting for the federal court to decide this matter, Binion was ordered to jail by a judge. "Well, I guess nobody will have any trouble finding me for the next ten days or so," he said before book-in at the Reno lockup. He assured reporters he would receive no special favors during incarceration. "I'll eat jail chow just like everybody else." As usual, he made friends, this time with two young runaways next door. "And there's two little ol' girls in the next cell to me that stole a automobile in Kansas City and came out here," he recalled. "They was fifteen years old. So I knew from their conversations that they never were going to get in no more trouble. So I sent word to the judge to turn 'em loose and send 'em home, and I'd pay for it."

The judge did not accept that offer, but he did give Binion exactly what he wanted in his own case: the Honorable Edward P. Murphy denied the attorney general's motion, and allowed Binion to enter a no-contest plea to tax evasion. He would not have to go back to Dallas to face charges.

On September 3, 1952, in Carson City, Nevada, Binion was fined $15,000 and placed on five years' probation, and when the final gavel rang down, he showed the relief and ecstasy of someone who had eluded a firing squad. "Now don't that beat all," Binion exclaimed. He turned to his lawyer, smiled—displaying a "wide Texas grin," according to one newspaper—and said, "Man, I'm glad that's over."

Yet it wasn't. "Binion Freed," a Dallas headline declared, but added, "Wade Has Ace." Which Wade then played: Less than a week later, the Dallas district attorney traveled to Washington for a personal meeting with McGranery in which Wade pointed out that Binion's case had been based on his 1949 tax returns. His 1948 returns, Wade argued, offered a much richer chance for a successful prosecution. Evidence from Harry Urban's trial showed that Binion owned 66 percent of the Dallas policy wheels, and that the total take in 1948 exceeded $1 million. But Binion had reported making only $2,000 from the policy games.

Federal prosecutors in Dallas vehemently disagreed with Wade about the value of the 1948 returns. "This is positively untrue," one assistant U.S. attorney told the FBI, insisting that "1949 is the only year which would even support indictment, to say nothing of conviction." But the attorney general listened to Wade, and forestalled any internal dissension in the ranks by appointing a special prosecutor. Back in Dallas, a new federal grand jury was impaneled for the singular purpose of indicting Binion.

Just when he thought he had escaped, Binion found himself in extreme jeopardy. He didn't know the law especially well, but he did understand that he was under a pursuit unlike any he had seen. "The whole outfit was stalking me," he said years later. "I just didn't have no way to duck."

McGranery left no doubt that he wanted Binion handled in such a way as to produce favorable notice for the Justice Department. A Philadelphia lawyer with a regal bearing—he was a former congressman and federal judge— McGranery had been appointed attorney general by President Harry Truman in May 1952. He was a lame-duck AG on the day he took office, for Truman's term would end in less than nine months. But he saw himself as a reliable, if temporary, moral compass.

He conducted daily staff conferences in his office at the Department of Justice Building in Washington, DC. The imposing seven-story Justice headquarters covered a full block along Constitution Avenue, five blocks from the White House. As with many federal buildings in the District, governmental homilies had been chiseled into its limestone, and one near the Tenth Street entrance proclaimed "To Render Every Man His Due." The new AG made it clear that Binion would get his.

The staff conferences were attended by various assistant attorneys general and a delegate from the FBI, usually assistant director L. B. Nichols. Shortly after each session with McGranery, he produced a memorandum to FBI director Hoover, some of which ran to six typewritten pages, single-spaced. The talk at these meetings often turned to some of the bigger names of the era. The officials discussed, for instance, the illegal immigration status of a Swedish nurse working in the home of Richard Nixon, then a member of Congress and soon to be vice president of the United States. A possible solution would be to alert Nixon and let him introduce a "private bill" in Congress that would right the nurse's status. But that would be wrong, McGranery said, and he dismissed the idea. "The attorney general then commented on Nixon and referred to him as being a 'hypocrite,'" Nichols's memo noted. Nixon routinely did favors for campaign contributors, McGranery said, and "was not telling the truth when he said no one who had contributed had ever asked him to do anything."

The AG and his assistants also talked of hiring an ambitious, not to say rapacious, New York lawyer named Roy Cohn to "set up a new unit . . . in the Internal Security Section." The attorney general thought Cohn "had many admirable qualities," Nichols wrote, and "could be used for constructive purposes." One of his assistants disagreed, dismissing Cohn as a publicity seeker. Cohn later found work—and no small degree of infamy—as counsel to red-baiting senator Joseph McCarthy.

The Justice staff conferences occasionally dealt with sub rosa international matters, such as a proposal to reverse, via high-level bribes, the nationalization of the oil industry in Iran. McGranery told his staff he had sent a memo to Secretary of State Dean Acheson's home on a Saturday afternoon regarding a plan to have four oil companies borrow several million dollars to pay off Iran's prime minister. "The Attorney General said the whole idea was wrong and he would not be a party to it; that if a higher level wanted to take the responsibility, that was perfectly okay," Nichols wrote. Higher authorities did indeed take charge: Two years later, the CIA helped depose the troublesome—and democratically elected—prime minister in a coup code-named Operation Ajax. He was replaced by the U.S.-friendly and torture-condoning shah, Mohammad Reza Pahlavi, and the unintended consequences of that move unfold yet.

Amid such inflammatory topics, one matter that arose repeatedly that summer was Binion's case. Nothing could enrage the nation's chief law enforcement official faster, it seemed, than a subordinate's reluctance to pursue Binion. When an assistant said he "has his doubts as to whether they can get a prosecution," one memo reported, "the Attorney General literally hit the ceiling."

McGranery clearly had no patience for such discouraging talk. "He cannot understand this defeatist attitude: that Binion was one of the bigtime racketeers," the memo said. "As far as the Attorney General was concerned, even if they could not get a conviction there was a prima facie case; to get an indictment and get him back to Dallas and the ends of justice would be met." McGranery hadn't quite finished hitting the ceiling. "The AG then lambasted the Criminal Division and the attitude of the Criminal Division."

The pleadings by the Dallas DA had an obvious effect. McGranery told his staff that the first Binion prosecution had been based on inferior evidence, which was Wade's argument. "The Attorney General further commented . . . that this is the weakest of the cases they could possibly present. He now understands the Treasury Department has worked up a much stronger case . . . He wants this case presented in Dallas as quickly as possible."

If McGranery's enthusiasm for prosecuting a distant tax case puzzled his assistants, he explained his zeal in a meeting on August 25, 1952. An unidentified congressman had called about the matter, McGranery said, and suggested the convening of a special grand jury. "The Attorney General stated the President would very much like to have this done," Nichols wrote to Hoover.

As Binion described it, the feds' design was to "get publicity to keep the smoke screen to cover up their own damn doin's . . . I was furnishing 'em smoke." It was undeniably true that the Truman administration could have used some good public relations on tax matters. The scandal that ensnared assistant attorney general Theron Lamar Caudle—who had promised to prosecute Binion but never did—had spread throughout the Bureau of Internal Revenue. There were, the Associated Press reported, "charges of widespread graft, corruption, irregularities and inefficiency in the nation's tax-collecting system." Lavishly publicized congressional investigations led to the firing or resignation of some 166 tax agency employees, including the bureau's chief counsel, who was accused of participating in a half-million-dollar shakedown scheme.

Perhaps this pursuit of Binion was a diversionary action, or maybe it sprang from a simple desire to righteously hammer a high-profile gangster. The motives may have been hidden, but the power behind them was clear. As the attorney general revealed, the question of how to bring down Benny Binion had now reached the White House.

———

If President Truman wanted Binion brought to trial in Texas, then McGra-nery would hear of nothing else, as he demonstrated one late summer after-noon in Philadelphia. Michael L. Hines, a lawyer and friend of the Binion family, had flown from Las Vegas and requested, via a mutual acquain-tance, a conference with the attorney general. McGranery agreed to the meeting in his apartment at the Warwick Hotel, but secretly stationed an FBI agent in an adjoining room for security, and to eavesdrop.

Hines said he simply wanted to give Binion's side of the story. As the FBI man listened and made notes, the Vegas envoy said he knew the Bin-ions well, and that he made his visit strictly as a personal mission. "No one could hire me," Hines said. "I came out of pure friendship." He neglected to mention that he was a partner of Binion's boon companion and legal counsel, Harry Claiborne.

Binion had been caught in a Texas power struggle, Hines told McGra-nery. "They are afraid that Benny will come back and take over things in Dallas," he said. "They are doing everything they can to put him away." Binion feared for his life if he returned, Hines said. "He's afraid they will bump him off if he goes back . . . Either bump him off or give him a long stretch."

Though the meeting was cordial, McGranery showed little sympathy for Binion's plight. "I don't suppose there's anything you can do," Hines pleaded. McGranery replied that he was sorry that he could not make his visitor's trip more pleasant, but knew of no legal reason that Binion should not be brought back to Texas.

Hines thanked McGranery and, as he departed, made one last entreaty on Binion's behalf. "Is there anything *I* can do," Hines asked, "to help him out?"

Yes, the attorney general answered. "Tell him to start praying."

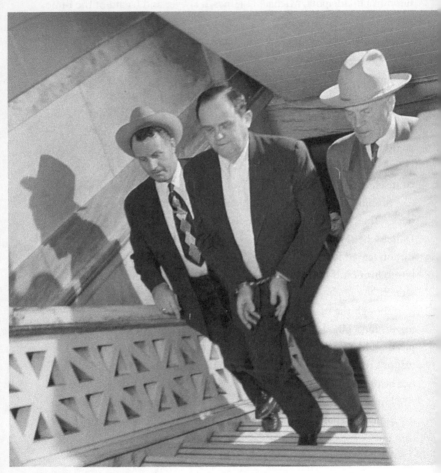
The cops finally put Benny in cuffs.

# 17

# THE GREAT BONANZA STAKEOUT

Never follow an empty wagon.

—BB

**B**inion wasn't planning to rely on mere prayer for a fight with the feds. He had earthly friends, and he intended to use them. They were powerful, and they were in his debt. At least one of them, Hank Greenspun, had both the gift of hyperbole and the means to display it. And he owed Binion big.

Greenspun, a New York lawyer looking to remake himself out West, had come to Las Vegas a few months before Binion, in September 1946. After a stint as a publicity agent for Bugsy Siegel, followed by several episodes of smuggling machine guns to Israel—he later pleaded guilty to violating the federal Neutrality Act—Greenspun bought a small newspaper that he renamed the *Las Vegas Sun*. A crusader by nature, he went after Senator Joseph McCarthy, calling him, among other things, "the queer that made Milwaukee famous." He also declared editorial war on McCarthy fellow traveler Pat McCarran, accusing the Nevada senator of destroying democracy via a corrupt political machine. Major Vegas casino owners, all of whom were beholden to McCarran for political favors, pulled their advertising from the *Sun*. The lone exception was Binion, who refused to yank his ads. Much later, he recalled the pressure from Gus Greenbaum, the Phoenix mobster who was one of Siegel's successors at the Flamingo, to put the *Sun* out of business. "Greenbaum said, 'We gonna bust him,'" Binion remembered. "I said, 'You gonna have to bust me, too.'"

Part of this grew out of Binion's sense of decency. "I didn't like that kind of stuff... People puts too much importance on theirself." But he also sensed that Hank Greenspun could be a valuable, rising ally, while McCarran—although he had helped Binion obtain a casino license—had now passed the peak of his power. "What the hell," Binion said of McCarran. "He wasn't going to be here forever." For this, Binion earned Greenspun's deep and abiding loyalty. And Greenspun, who penned a regularly bumptious column on the *Sun*'s front page titled "Where I Stand," rarely disguised his sympathies—as seen on October 1, 1952, when he addressed his friend's treatment by authorities.

"I sometimes wonder," Greenspun mused, "if the President of the United States is aware of the fact that agencies of the federal government are being used to pillory and harass private individuals at the whims and dictates and for the personal satisfaction of some elected autocrat." He went on to deplore the "cheap, rotten political treachery" directed at Binion, who had been a "model citizen" in Las Vegas. "Either the Attorney General of the United States is being hoodwinked by some corrupt Dallas officials in a nefarious political scheme," Greenspun wrote, "or else the attorney general is taking pressure from some high government official who has personal reasons for 'getting Benny.'" Probably both, he concluded. For good measure, he compared the feds to a lynch mob and the Gestapo. "No man," he added, "does more for the good and welfare of the community than this man whom the federal government and a few politicians in Texas are trying to shackle."

In Washington, FBI director Hoover read the column, and decided McGranery needed to see what was being said about him. The director uncapped his pen and wrote at the bottom of the page, "Send copy to A.G."

Potter, the U.S. attorney in North Texas, also had serious reservations about Binion's treatment. "I do not believe it is the policy of the Department of Justice to resort to subterfuge to return a defendant for prosecution by State authorities," he wrote to his bosses in Washington. But his protest had no teeth, because a special prosecutor appointed by the attorney general was running the show in Dallas now. That prosecutor got some help from the federal judge who impaneled the grand jury to consider Binion's case. Judge T. Whitfield Davidson reminded jurors that Herbert Noble had recently been "blown to pieces at his mailbox," and that Mrs. Noble was "blown to pieces as well." The judge added, "And not long before that you read where another man was killed, and another man was killed, and another man was killed." Lest the panel still not get the point, Judge Davidson told them that sometimes income tax cases were the only feasible way to punish those who had hired killers, "as was done in the case of Al Capone." The grand jury promptly indicted Binion for tax evasion.

He got the news at the Horseshoe, and seemed close to dumbstruck. "I don't see how they could have done it," Binion said when a reporter called. "I swear I don't." Six weeks later, at a court hearing in Las Vegas, he removed his white Stetson and told a judge that officials in Texas wanted him dead. "I don't fear the federal government," Binion said. "But I fear if I fall into the hands of Texas authorities, I will be murdered." The judge, though apparently sympathetic, said he had no alternative, and ordered that Binion be returned to Dallas. Then the problems compounded: in December, the government filed a tax lien against Binion, claiming that he owed $862,532.

Binion's lawyers appealed his case to the U.S. Supreme Court. His indictment on tax charges, which had come after he had already been sentenced for tax fraud, arose from "a political conspiracy to persecute and oppress" Binion, his lawyers argued. Such treatment was "an abuse of federal process in aid of state court prosecution." They also alleged that Judge Davidson's remarks about Herbert and Mildred Noble, not to mention his reference to Al Capone, were absolute proof of prejudice and "willful disregard of the rights of the accused."

If Binion's attorneys thought that was harsh, they should have seen the confidential memo that Lieutenant Butler of the Dallas police wrote for the FBI. The bureau had asked Butler for an up-to-date summation of Binion's criminal career. His lengthy essay included the usual dead people—Loudermilk, Freiden, the Nobles, et al.—but also offered this tidbit: Binion had "a private cemetary [sic] equipped with a lime pit in which he disposed of bodies," a boneyard that police had never quite managed to find. Butler also reported that Binion, in partnership with Mickey Cohen, "was very interested in getting a policy operation started in the Los Angeles negro sections."

The Dallas investigator, who knew what his audience wanted, went on, page after page, with descriptions of Binion's wealth and resultant political influence: "For an illiterate Binion has acquired a vast fortune," he wrote. "He early learned what power money had, and what he couldn't steal, he bought." Butler also warned the feds to take special care with their informants. "Some precautions should be taken to protect all important witnesses for the Government," he said. "It has been proven beyond a doubt that Binion will not hesitate to kill anyone that becomes a threat to himself, his money or his freedom."

In January 1953, Attorney General McGranery began to worry that Binion would flee Nevada to avoid prosecution. He instructed FBI director Hoover to begin a "discreet" twenty-four-hour surveillance. An assistant to Hoover phoned Arthur Cornelius Jr., the agent in charge in Salt Lake City, and ordered the stakeout. Binion might try to leave the country, the assistant warned Cornelius. He must be watched at all times, and any suspicious movements had to be reported immediately to bureau headquarters. Cornelius asked if he should place a wiretap on Binion's phones. Just watch the man, he was told.

FBI agents rented a house across the street from Binion's residence, and positioned cars at the end of the street. Hoover personally phoned McGranery that afternoon to tell him that the operation had commenced. "The attorney general," Hoover wrote to his senior staff, "was most appreciative of the work of the Bureau in this regard."

That's because the attorney general had no idea how poorly the operation was proceeding. The AG's orders aside, this was not a subtle surveillance. Crew-cut G-men sitting idly in plain Ford Fairlanes, pretending to read the newspaper all afternoon, were pretty easy to spot on Bonanza Road. Even the kids were laughing at them. "If we didn't have anything to do we'd jump in the car and let them follow us," said Brenda Binion Michael. She was eleven then, and her brother Jack, almost sixteen, would drive the family Buick. "I'd be on my knees looking out the back window," she remembered. "I'd say, 'Here they come, Jack.' As soon as they figured out my Dad wasn't with us, they'd turn around and go back."

Although the stakeout amused his children, it angered and worried Binion, and he was determined to halt it right away. He tried to flag down one FBI car as it drove past his house, but the driver wouldn't stop. Binion climbed into his baby-blue Cadillac and told Gold Dollar to take him downtown to the county courthouse.

Later that morning the phone rang in the FBI's Las Vegas operations: Captain Ralph Lamb of the sheriff's department calling. He explained that he was at that very moment sitting in the district attorney's office with Binion. He wanted to know if the FBI had initiated a surveillance. This was no small matter, Lamb said, because hostile racketeers often tailed Binion, and he couldn't tell the agents from the hoods. "There are people who want to bump him off," he said. "He's scared to death." Lamb proposed an alternative: if the FBI wanted to know where he was, Binion would be happy to keep them fully informed.

Agent Cornelius called FBI HQ with this news. But when Hoover learned of Binion's offer to self-report, he was less than grateful: "We want no favors from him." Cornelius also warned his supervisors about Binion's close ties to the sheriff's department, suggesting that Lamb's officers might disrupt the surveillance in the guise of investigation. For some reason, FBI brass thought they could handle that by letting Lamb know that the men following Binion indeed hailed from the FBI. Cornelius did as ordered, phoning Lamb and confirming the surveillance. This was "strictly confidential information," he told Lamb. Which meant, don't tell Binion.

The FBI might as well have put it on a billboard. The information immediately made its way to Lamb's good friend and benefactor, and from there it was soon in the hands of Binion's pal at the *Las Vegas Sun,* Hank Greenspun.

Hours after Cornelius's call to Lamb, as the agents continued their stakeout, a 1948 Pontiac approached one of the FBI sedans from the rear. There was a flash of light—from a camera, not a gun—and the Pontiac sped away. Later that same day, radio station KENO, a Greenspun property, broke the news: Federal agents had put Binion and his family under twenty-four-hour watch. The order for this surveillance, the radio station said, had come from the U.S. attorney general himself.

The broadcast made for some deeply unhappy FBI officials in Washington. Cornelius got on the phone in a desperate attempt to placate his bosses. The license plates on the surveillance cars had been changed, he told them. Agents were making "every effort" to keep the stakeout discreet, but the bureau's top brass had to understand that Las Vegas was a small town where such matters proved difficult to hide.

Hoover seethed at Cornelius's excuses. "This job is to perform, not constantly grouse about the difficulties," he wrote at the bottom of one report. "Tell him so when he calls in."

The bureau's situation worsened the next morning, when the *Sun* gave the story a full front-page ride. A headline screamed, "'I'm Not Running Away,' Says Binion as Federal Agents Cover Residence." The *Sun* ran two accompanying photos of FBI agents sitting in their cars as they conducted their "not-too-obvious" surveillance. One of the agents had ducked as his picture was taken. "Camera shy," the newspaper remarked.

The ridicule traveled fast and well. Hoover sent a memo to Attorney General McGranery that day with details of the *Sun*'s coverage. Three days later, on the evening of January 19, 1953, McGranery phoned Hoover. This was McGranery's last full day in office; Dwight Eisenhower would be sworn in as president the next morning.

Hoover was out, so McGranery spoke to the director's assistant, L. B. Nichols. The attorney general said he had been giving the Binion case some thought. What do you think, he asked Nichols, of this "rather silly" surveillance of Binion? Nichols dodged, claiming he had been out of the office for the past few days and wasn't current on developments. The stakeout, the attorney general mused, seemed to serve no further purpose and had become an embarrassment "to the agents." Perhaps it might be best to call the whole thing off.

Within hours of McGranery's caving in, Hoover ordered the agents to leave their posts on Bonanza Road. The FBI's operation had lasted all of six days.

Binion had deeply embarrassed the U.S. Department of Justice, and it was not in the agency's nature to shrug off insults from gangsters. A new attorney general had taken office—Herbert Brownell—but the desire to nail

---

Binion endured. As Brownell told his freshly hired staff, high-profile criminal cases represented the department's best chance to generate good publicity and erase the memories of scandal. Two months after the botched stakeout, Hoover was advised by his agents that a couple of Justice investigators—not from the FBI—had been appointed to probe Binion's affairs. "The original request apparently came from the Attorney General himself," a memo to Hoover said. "He is placing two undercover officers in the Las Vegas area for the purpose of developing information as to whether Binion carries a firearm on his person."

That was like asking whether Binion wore a hat. He had carried handguns in his pocket or his boot since he was a teenager. Now an assistant attorney general, Warren Olney III, believed Binion—a "vicious character," in his estimation—could be prosecuted for violating the Federal Firearms Act, which prohibited anyone convicted of a violent crime from taking a gun across state lines. This was the same Warren Olney who had warned Texas legislators in 1951 against gangsters' infiltration of the oil business.

His new idea found an advocate in Al Rosen, one of Hoover's top-ranking assistants. "If he [Binion] went into Montana," Rosen advised Hoover, "we could arrange with local cooperative police to make an appropriate check of his person on some subterfuge." Or if Binion happened to drive across the Hoover Dam into Arizona, "we could have the national park rangers shake him down."

This seemed a bit much, even to the FBI director. "No," he wrote. "While I would like to bring Binion to justice, we do not have jurisdiction in this matter. It is a straight Treasury responsibility."

The bureau already had its own campaign against Binion. For a while the FBI believed he had hired someone to kill Dallas DA Wade. "You are instructed to give this investigation urgent priority," Hoover cabled to agents in Dallas, Los Angeles, and Salt Lake City. That business died after some research revealed the source of the allegation: a sad-sack mob pretender who had first gone to the police to complain that he had been the victim of a theft—$16 by an Amarillo prostitute. He had thrown in the Binion story as a bonus. "A quote screwball end quote," one subsequent bureau report explained. "Apparently likes to be considered a quote big shot unquote."

The FBI was also sweating Binion's political connections. Hoover sent a memo to Attorney General Brownell noting a "report that Senator McCarran of Nevada had assured an associate of Binion that he would not be returned to Texas." In another memo to the AG, Hoover warned that an informant "has advised that it is Binion's desire to get political control of Las Vegas and the entire state of Nevada . . . He also has advised that such action is dependent upon whether Binion is successful in defeating the prosecution pending against him." That investigation fizzled too.

A separate FBI "radiogram" said that according to an informant, Binion's Las Vegas employees had undergone special firearms training for undisclosed purposes. It added that Binion "had been responsible either directly or indirectly for a number of murders and that he [the informant] had now received some information indicating that Binion had allegedly spent $300,000 in an effort to have his case with the Internal Revenue Bureau fixed." Another bureau memo to Hoover reported that Binion was "very worried" about whether he had reported income from his gambling operations at the Top O'Hill Terrace. Once again, the FBI demonstrated a tenuous grasp of Binion-related matters. The memo placed the notorious casino in a city on the Texas coast, about 320 miles south of its actual location.

Hoover and his subordinates need not have worried so much, because on April 13, 1953, the U.S. Supreme Court refused to hear Binion's appeal. And one month later, the justices rejected his motion to rehear the case. Aside from some minor courtroom maneuverings, Binion had exhausted his legal remedies. He was headed to Texas to stand trial.

Binion had been ordered to appear in Texas on June 8, 1953, for arraignment on federal charges. Imaginative lawyers in the U.S. attorney general's office began to fear once more that he had nefarious plans. On June 4, an assistant attorney general stopped by the office of assistant FBI director Nichols and said he was worried that Binion might try to leave the country. He requested that the bureau put Binion under a twenty-four-hour surveillance until he actually walked into the federal courthouse in Texas. Nichols recalled that the last Vegas stakeout had not gone well. As he diplomatically described it, "There was some aura of embarrassment to our agents out there." But after initial hesitation, Director Hoover came to agree with the attorney general's office. "I think we should do it," he wrote.

Under the supervision of Special Agent in Charge Cornelius—again—FBI men began watching Binion around the clock. That wasn't all: They set up checkpoints along all highways leading out of Las Vegas—south to Phoenix, west to Los Angeles, east to Amarillo, and north to nothing but desert. Agents patrolled the downtown train station, and the bureau ordered all four airlines that serviced Vegas to notify it if Binion boarded a commercial flight. Should Binion try to leave on a private charter or a friend's aircraft, the agents had that covered too. "Arrangements were made," the local office reported to FBI headquarters, "for a privately owned airplane and pilot to be constantly available for use of the surveilling agents for pursuit purposes if needed."

Determined not to botch it this time, Cornelius believed his men had blanketed every possible way out of town. "Agents are to survaill [sic] him wherever he goes," he assured Hoover in a telex.

The mission was working perfectly—until it actually had to work.

On June 5, one hour after midnight, Binion and his son Jack walked from his house and climbed into the backseat of his 1952 Cadillac. The car—an Imperial sedan—was a deco luxury masterpiece with a curvilinear body and a grand, aerodynamic sweep. The front bumper, a muscular brace of gleaming chrome, led the way with twin nose cones, known as Dagmars, in honor of an amply proportioned female television personality. The cabin, with room for eight, felt as spacious as a Pullman sleeper. All of it rolled on wide tires whose broad whitewalls were evocative of a rich man wearing spats. And it went fast—a machine that could hit 125 miles per hour on the open highway without breaking a mechanical sweat. It was, in fact, the most powerful mass-produced car built in America.

Now Gold Dollar drove as the car shot through Binion's gate, turned onto Bonanza Road, and headed west. FBI agents in three separate sedans followed. Once on the highway, going toward Tonapah, the Cadillac cruised at 85 miles per hour. One of the FBI men stopped to call his office. The other two agents, driving in six-cylinder Fords, struggled to keep pace with the

V-8 Caddy. Binion said something to Gold Dollar, who braked hard and made a sharp turn onto a dirt road that led into the desert.

The two agents went that way too, their cars bouncing over the washboard road, but they were blinded by the cloud of dust in the Caddy's wake. This continued for five miles, the agents pursuing the cloud and doing their best not to veer off the road and into the scrub. "Agents were driving at risk of their lives," a bureau report said. Then the dust vanished, the air clear again, as the agents came to an intersection with a paved road. The two FBI cars idled in the deep desert night as the bureau men scanned the horizon: nothing in all directions except to the south, where the lights of Las Vegas faded the blackness. To their dismay, there was no sign of Binion's car. They had no choice now but to split up. The first agent drove left on the paved road, and the second went right—"at top speed," the FBI noted—but neither one caught sight of the Cadillac again. One of them stopped to call Cornelius with the dread news: ten minutes into the tail, their man had escaped.

For the next five hours, Cornelius and his agents combed Las Vegas in a frenzy, searching for Binion, or at least his car. They checked his house, and they checked the Horseshoe. The airport and the train station too. Cornelius also contacted his men at the highway checkpoints. Agents phoned confidential informants who had spied on Binion in the past, hoping for a shred of a clue to his whereabouts. All of it came up empty.

Finally, at ten thirty that morning, Washington time—a full six hours after the operation fell apart—Cornelius called bureau headquarters and talked to assistant director Rosen. They had lost Binion, Cornelius admitted. Even worse, they had no idea where they should look now. As was customary, Rosen immediately typed up a memo, and attempted to obscure the depth of the calamity. "Cornelius called to advise that Binion is presently not under surveillance," he wrote.

The director of the FBI was in no mood for mincing words. Only minutes before Cornelius's call, Hoover had notified the attorney general's office that the surveillance was proceeding perfectly. Now he would have to phone the AG back and admit disaster, something he did not do well. "This is atrocious," he wrote to his assistants. "Get facts promptly."

Cornelius again tried to defend the actions of his men and himself. The surveillance had been assembled on "very short notice," he said. The agents were working on little food and no sleep. And that chauffeur of Binion's could drive really fast. This failed to mollify Hoover, in part because Cornelius had already seen his share of professional difficulties. In July 1952, when he was in charge of the bureau's Philadelphia office, his supervisors put him on probation for his "failure to develop a satisfactory criminal informant program." The probation continued when, three months later, managers found "delinquencies" during an office inspection. Cornelius was transferred to the Salt Lake City office, the FBI's Siberia, where he had presided over the first catastrophic surveillance of Binion.

Cornelius had rallied briefly in February 1953, when he happily announced, via a press release, the arrest of a high-profile suspect named Charley Finn. As one half of a notorious duo known as the Flying Finn Twins, Charley Finn was wanted for stealing an airplane. Unfortunately for Cornelius, he had arrested the wrong Finn twin—he mistakenly nabbed the identical George—and the mix-up caused the bureau no small shame. The special agent's probation continued, and when another office inspection the next month found more procedural violations, it was extended once again.

And now this debacle. Not only had they lost Binion, but Cornelius and crew had not thought to record the license number of his Cadillac. They had to wake up the superintendent of the Nevada Highway Patrol, who went to his closed offices in Carson City and pulled the information: Nevada 41-151. At least they had the tag number. All they had to do now was find the car attached to it.

There it was, some thirteen hours later, a baby-blue blur: Gold Dollar topping 100 miles per hour as he neared Grants, New Mexico, on Route 66, at two in the afternoon. They were five hundred miles southeast of Las Vegas, traveling in the general direction of Texas. "Observed in instant car," an agent wrote, "was a heavy set Negro who was driving." Binion was lying down in the backseat, probably asleep.

FBI men in three cars picked up the chase, and this time they managed to stay with the Caddy, all the way into Albuquerque. Binion and Gold Dollar made a brief stop at a downtown boot-and-saddle shop, then paused for twenty-five minutes at the Owl Café, where, the FBI noted, "they apparently had something to eat." Then they hit the highway again, making their way to Clines Corners, New Mexico, "at a progressively higher rate of speed," in the FBI's opinion.

On they went, through a string of dusty, sun-blasted New Mexico towns: Encino, Vaughn, Fort Sumner—passing the grave of Billy the Kid— and Clovis. They crossed into Texas, blowing through Muleshoe, Sudan, and Littlefield, with the bureau men trailing. It was after nine, the sun finally down, when they made Lubbock. Binion's first stop there was Willie Lusk's custom boot store, the shop he had helped bankroll many years before. In the parking lot, Binion stepped from the Cadillac and stretched in the warm night air. FBI agents peered from their cars a half block away as he turned, stared, and began to walk toward them.

All agents on this chase knew that Binion had been branded in a number of bureau reports as an armed and dangerous hoodlum, a vicious racketeer who had shot and killed at least a couple of men. Now he was coming for them. They could turn and flee, they could step out to confront him, or they could wait in their cars. They waited.

When he finally reached them, Binion leaned into the window of an FBI Ford and looked the agents over. Smiling, he said, "Aren't you boys getting tired?"

He had spotted the FBI tail from the moment he left his house, Binion told them. And that side trip into the desert outside Vegas had been made "just for fun." Even fun had its limits. Binion felt nothing but contempt for high-ranking bureau officials, but he knew a bunch of beleaguered working stiffs when he saw them. There was plenty of room in the Cadillac, he told the agents. The seats were soft, and a man could stretch out and relax if he wanted. Why didn't they pile in the back of his car and ride with him all the way to Dallas? Make it easier on everybody.

"This offer," a bureau memo later said, "was declined."

The next stop for Binion and Gold Dollar was Neil's, "a barbecue place," the G-men made sure to record. Then they hit the road again, and by sunrise they rolled into Fort Worth with the bureau cars still trailing. Binion checked into the Texas Hotel downtown and stayed in his room for the next twelve hours while the agents sat. That evening Gold Dollar drove him to Dallas, where he laid some flowers on his mother's grave as agents watched.

Binion waved one of the bureau men over, and began to talk about how much the city had grown since 1947. Then he disclosed his itinerary: After this cemetery stop, he planned to visit a friend. When that was done, he would go downtown to surrender to authorities. Binion hoped no one would be there to see it, but he predicted otherwise. "My damn attorney is so publicity hungry he probably called the newspapers," he said.

The reporters and photographers were indeed waiting when Binion walked into the Dallas County Jail building through a back door, wearing white cowboy boots and smoking a fat cigar. It was nine o'clock on a Saturday night. "I ain't talking," he said to their shouted questions. He was, some bystanders noted, paunchier than they remembered, and his hair was a little thinner. A couple of the reporters thought he looked a bit dusty and unbathed, not what they expected from Vegas royalty, and he could have used a shave. They fired more questions. "I said I ain't talking," Binion answered.

In the sheriff's office, against a backdrop of jail bars, Binion greeted his old friend Bill Decker, who appeared crisp and photo ready in a cream-colored fedora and a neatly knotted silk tie. With a lit cigarette dangling from his half smile, Decker served Binion with warrants for his arrest on state gambling charges. Next, deputies officially photographed, fingerprinted, and weighed Binion, who clocked in at an even two hundred pounds. "It's awfully hot down here," he said, pulling at the sweaty white shirt sticking to his skin.

The whole process didn't take more than ten minutes, and after posting a $15,000 bond, Binion was free to go. Outside the courthouse, Gold Dollar waited with the Cadillac as FBI agents stood nearby. "They sure gave us a run, those government men," Gold Dollar told one reporter. "A couple of them followed me out of Las Vegas, but we shook them in a hurry. Another pair caught up with us in New Mexico, and we never could shake them." The agents chose not to comment.

From Dallas, Binion and Gold Dollar drove to Austin—observing the posted speed limit all the way, the FBI pursuers noted with gratitude. There, two days after his Dallas booking, Binion appeared in federal court to face tax charges. He was, one newspaper writer observed, "nattily dressed in a coral green suit, pale green tie and fawn-colored mesh cowboy boots with sharply pointed toes." No dust or grime this time.

As the charges against him were read, Binion responded "not guilty" to each one. The judge set trial for September. Binion posted a $20,000 bond, climbed into his Cadillac, and rode—without an FBI escort—back to Las Vegas, where he hoped to keep from losing everything.

Binion on the witness stand in Dallas, pledging to quit the gambling business forever.

# 18

# "WHACKED AROUND PRETTY GOOD"

*The damn government's been getting bad for a good many years.*
*They'd put it on you.*

*−BB*

ederal prosecutors, preparing for a courtroom battle, cataloged Binion's assets and liabilities. Cash and real estate had a market value of $2.4 million. The Montana ranchland and the cattle on it accounted for more than half of that. His ownership of the Horseshoe was valued at $757,087, and the house and property on Bonanza at $67,500. Binion also owned the old family farm in Grayson County, Texas, where he was born. Its worth: $6,500. In addition to calibrating Binion's property, the government subpoenaed 102 witnesses. Among them were George Wilderspin, who had run Binion's Fort Worth operations, and Fred Browning, his former partner from the Top O'Hill club. Both of them had presumably seen Binion pocketing fair amounts of unreported—and untaxed—cash over the years. In early September 1953, a federal prosecutor announced the government was ready for trial.

One day after the feds made a public show of champing at the bit, Binion surprised everyone—from press to prosecutors—by appearing before Judge Ben Rice in San Antonio and pleading guilty to four counts of tax evasion. He and his lawyers provided no public explanation, but they believed a trial would inevitably result in a conviction and years of prison time, while a plea might allow the judge to pass sentence with some leniency. Judge Rice accepted the plea, and gave Binion several months to settle his affairs before imposing punishment.

As he returned to Las Vegas, Binion now had two tasks before him: he had to raise enough cash to pay his back taxes, and he had to deal with a looming casino license problem. The tax commission had allowed him to run the Horseshoe provisionally. If he brought discredit on himself or the state, his license could be revoked. Pleading guilty to a federal felony was considered a mark of discredit, even in Nevada.

He found a solution to both of his problems in the form of an old friend, Joe W. Brown, a gambler from New Orleans with lucrative interests in thoroughbreds and oil fields. Brown was loaded with cash. "He had $200 million," Binion said, "and I just welcomed any part of it." Brown also declared himself willing to take over the Horseshoe.

Binion and Brown publicly announced their deal. For $858,000, Brown would purchase a 97 percent interest in the Horseshoe and run the place. This was, in no small part, a fiction, for Brown's true stake fell closer to 25 percent. But as Binion liked to say, "Don't ever tell a lie, unless you have to." This simple fabrication had one purpose: to fool the state tax commission.

Not only did Brown have enormous wealth, he arrived scandal free, though he had been placing big bets for decades. "I'm one of the few people who ever made a million dollars gambling who never got his name mentioned in the Kefauver reports," Brown declared. He could honestly assure regulators that he had no unsavory entanglements, gangster-related or otherwise. "Just me, Mrs. Brown and Christ," he said. "That's the only people in my business." The thought of a New Orleans oilman, his wife, and Jesus running a Glitter Gulch casino appeared to soothe the nerves of the tax commissioners. "He was a very, very straightforward man," recalled Robbins Cahill. "He had all the money he could ever want, or ever need, and he wasn't obligated to anybody . . . He had no record of any kind that could be held against him." Commissioners granted Brown a license with little debate.

Binion had now installed at the Horseshoe a friend who would be happy to give the reins back to him when the time was right, and he hoped that time would be soon. Next he set about assembling the balance of the cash he would need to pay his taxes and penalties, and he heard the clock ticking. "I'm getting the rest together as fast as I can," he said to an inquiring reporter. "I been under such a strain I ain't had time to get everything done. They [federal authorities] got a date set on me, and they don't trade much."

Other friends stepped in, providing ready coin in exchange for their own pieces of Binion's casino. But these pals weren't so clean as Brown; they and Binion issued no happy public announcements of new partnerships. Meyer Lansky bought in. So did his mob associate Joseph "Doc" Stacher, a Kefauver committee target who had been a boyhood companion of Lansky's and was now running the Sands in Vegas. Abner "Longy" Zwillman, known as the Al Capone of New Jersey, managed to hook a percentage. Gerardo "Gerry" Catena also walked away with a slice of the Horseshoe. Catena ultimately rose to be underboss of the murderous Genovese crime family.

It was, in other words, business as usual in Las Vegas.

When at last Binion had pulled together the necessary bankroll, in early December 1953, his lawyer took a check for $516,541 to the Las Vegas office of the Bureau of Internal Revenue. This—after some adjustments to the government's original claim—paid the tax liability in full, but Binion still faced sentencing later that month. He retained hope that he would receive probation. If so, he could perhaps regain his casino license, though it might take the usual combination of favors and payoffs, so that he and the Horseshoe could stay in business. As for pending state gambling charges, late news out of Texas provided some grounds for optimism. The conviction of his partner Harry Urban had been reversed by the state court of criminal appeals. The prosecution had erred when it introduced evidence about Urban's long and colorful history with Binion. Such information, in the court's opinion, would have prejudiced jury members by causing them to believe not only that Urban was a gambler, but that he was "a very bad man" as well.

Dallas district attorney Wade said publicly that the court's ruling would make it difficult to prosecute Urban anew. This gave Binion some belief that he could plead to the state charges and possibly pull probation for that too.

Such were his designs as he left Las Vegas to face the federal judge for the final time.

Binion took Teddy Jane and four of their children to San Antonio, Texas, for the sentencing. They booked a suite at the St. Anthony Hotel, across the street from a park named for William B. Travis, a hero of Texas independence who wrote a famous letter from the Alamo pledging "Victory or Death." If this was to be Binion's own last stand, it was a contrite one. The night before his court date he received a local newspaper reporter at his hotel room, where he expressed his dilemma in familiar, if defeated, terms. "I gambled and I lost," he lamented. But this last-gasp attempt to present himself as a chastened man didn't quite hit the mark. As the newspaper story put it: The "portly, long time gambler . . . was ill at ease in his comfortable hotel suite. He was surrounded by his wife and four children as he talked." Getting little from his main subject, the reporter turned to Mrs. Binion, but he found Teddy Jane in no mood for conversation. She refused even to give the paper her kids' names. "The children had nothing to do with this," she said, bristling.

The family accompanied Binion the next day to the downtown courtroom, and sat behind him as Judge Rice allowed the defendant one final statement. Binion—freshly barbered and in a dark suit—rose and, between gulps, took the humble route. "I just didn't intend to cheat the government," he told the court. "I'm kinda ignorant and I got to gambling around and, well, you know." He hinted that he might even leave the casino business if he could stay out of prison. "Now, Judge, what I'd like to do is go on to Montana, and raise a fine head of cattle. I've got a pretty good-sized family started," he said. "And, Judge, you know, I've paid all the taxes I owe." This entreaty poured from a man who had previously avoided all manner of serious legal trouble through connection, action, combustion, and intimidation. Now it revealed someone deeply humbled and out of gas.

Worse, it didn't work. Judge Rice had before him Binion's presentence report, written by a probation officer, which depicted the defendant as a long-time, large-scale, fully cognizant tax evader who had refused to cooperate with investigators. "Investigation has disclosed that defendant kept large amounts of currency which he did not run through his bank account," the probation officer wrote. In addition, the report said, Binion was a killer with a "lengthy prior criminal record all of which has grown out of his activities in the bootlegging days and in his gambling."

This left the judge with little inclination toward mercy. "I am sorry I cannot grant your plea," Rice said. He delivered this declaration, the *San Antonio Express* observed, "with all the dignity that becomes a federal court official." Looking down at Binion from the bench, Rice pronounced sentence: five years in prison and a $20,000 fine. Binion was remanded to the custody of the marshals, and a sharp rap from the gavel brought the proceedings to a close.

The severity of the sentence stunned the defendant, his lawyers, and his family. "He thought he was going to get out of it," daughter Brenda recalled. He was a forty-nine-year-old husband with five children to raise and a business to run, and now a man with a government badge was placing him in handcuffs. Before authorities escorted Binion from the courtroom, the marshal in charge allowed him a few minutes in an adjoining office to say good-bye to Teddy Jane and the children. "All of us were crying," Brenda remembered. She mistakenly believed her father had been sentenced to forty years. "I thought, my god, I'll never see him again." He hugged them all—at least as well as he could while cuffed—and then was taken away.

Reporters and photographers waited in bright afternoon sunshine on the sidewalk outside the courthouse, hoping to catch a shot and a few words. Binion approached, flanked by two U.S. marshals who were taking him to the county jail. The crime boss had regained his composure. With his cowboy hat cocked at a jaunty angle and his wrists shackled in front of him, Binion gave the men with the cameras a confident smile. "Get a good one, boys," he told them as the shutters clicked. "From now on you're going to have to find a new subject."

The marshals drove Binion 275 miles north to Dallas for another court appearance a few days later, this one on state gambling charges. By then, his lawyers had reached a deal with District Attorney Wade: if Binion would plea guilty, the sentence—four years—would run concurrent with the federal prison time. The courtroom was packed, with spectators squeezing into every bit of space on the shiny wooden benches, but this was an anticlimactic affair, finished in less than half an hour. Perhaps the only bit of news emerged when a woeful-looking Binion was asked what he would do after he served his time. "I don't intend to go back into the gambling business," he said. It was a prudent answer. Another gambling indictment in Texas, Wade noted, would allow prosecutors to charge Binion as a habitual criminal and make him eligible for a life sentence.

When it was done, all traces of swagger had vanished. Later that week, marshals reported, Binion suffered "some type of minor heart attack" while in custody. It was, more likely, an episode of debilitating anxiety.

Just before Christmas, on a bitter-cold night with howling wind and blowing snow, Binion entered the federal prison at Leavenworth, Kansas. "He will find prison life far different from his past experiences," a United Press reporter advised readers. There were other federal prisons to which Binion could have been sent, including some much closer to Las Vegas. But U.S. Attorney General Brownell had ordered that he go to Leavenworth, which had already seen its share of famous criminals—Machine Gun Kelly and Capone enforcer Frank Nitti among them. The warden announced to the press that Binion would be treated like any other inmate. "Prison Doors Clank Shut on Benny Binion," said a front-page headline in the *Nevada State Journal*. "Interesting Career Interrupted by Uncle Sam." This proved that somewhere in Reno a copy editor had the gift of understatement. The labyrinthine kingdom of riches that Binion had built over the decades—through brutality, guile, loyalty, and skill—wasn't merely on pause. It now teetered on the edge of collapse, and the only person who could save it wouldn't be eligible for parole for two and a half years.

"I got whacked around pretty good," Binion said.

The FBI certainly believed it had done its share of the whacking, and wasted little time in crossing Binion off its "Top Hoodlum" list. In the bureau's Who's Who of thug-land, he was now a nobody.

Down in Texas, Lieutenant Butler of the Dallas police still looked for leads into the Noble bombing. He went so far as to persuade several of the original suspects to take shots of Sodium Pentothal—truth serum—and submit to questioning. In one session, Butler asked a doped-up Bob Braggins who paid the generous bounty on Noble. "I don't know," Braggins said.

"Do you think it was Binion?"

"You ask me what I know," Braggins said, "or what I think?"

"What do you think?"

"Binion," Braggins said.

But Butler got no closer than that to making a solid case. Even under truth serum his suspects dodged, evaded, and lied.

There was another reason the investigation had slowed. W. O. Hodges, the blind Denton County sheriff who had pursued the Noble case with vigor, had taken his new guide dog, named Candy, out for a walk in the early-morning darkness. The sheriff and the dog wandered into the street, and were hit by a car and killed. It was by all indications an accident, but it had the effect of ending Denton County's role in the probe. Noble's death went on the books as an unsolved murder, and stayed that way.

As for Wade, the Dallas district attorney basked in triumph for his handling of the Binion pursuit. Soon he would be contemplating a run for Congress. He also gave local reporters a surprising admission: his case against Binion had really not been all that sound. Two of the gamblers who would have provided crucial testimony were dead, and others were unreliable, he said. If Binion had gone to trial, the DA calculated, he would probably have been acquitted.

This meant that Binion had pleaded no contest once and guilty twice in cases where prosecutors doubted they could have convicted him at trial. Although he didn't know specifically of these admissions, Binion believed he had been swindled in court, and he never lost that suspicion. He had been conned into giving up without a fight, and got next to nothing in return.

Though he would not have used the term, irony attached itself easily to his case. He had paid his taxes but still had to serve time. He had flouted the law for decades; only after he went straight, Vegas-style, did he wind up in chains. He was being punished not for his own spectacular crimes, but to cover the corruption of others. And he—the wiliest of operators—had been catastrophically hoodwinked. "I could've beat this damn case if I hadn't got tricked into pleading guilty," he said years later. "I got tricked all the way around by the government."

Binion had faced many hardships and setbacks in life, but this was the harshest so far. Yet it wasn't long after the Leavenworth cell doors closed behind him that, once he had recovered from his shock, he began to plot his return to Las Vegas and his ultimate redemption. Doing so, he reverted to his lifelong pattern: He had survived a lost childhood by learning the cunning skills of larcenous adults. Then he had grieved the death of his beloved mentor Warren Diamond, but seized the chance to succeed and exceed his criminal father figure. And when he was cast out of Dallas, he had emerged even stronger and richer. Now he had to climb back again. There would be no wistful waiting for fortune to turn his way. That was for suckers. This would happen because he drew upon himself to make it happen.

"There ain't no such thing as luck," said the man who had benefited from plenty of it. "It's unseen talent. I've just got talent they don't know about. Lot of damn ways." His talent, Binion believed, would propel his resurrection. That, along with some friends in high places, and the continuing string of unfortunates who turned up dead.

# THE RIDE BACK HOME
## 1954-1989

Binion, his children, and Fred Merrill Jr. (in denim jacket) before his incarceration. Daughter Barbara is to Binion's left.

# 19

# THE FIREMAN GETS RELIGION

When you quit learning, I think your damn light's went out.

—BB

eavenworth, Kansas, did not impress many with its beauty even on the nicest days. The winters could be especially bleak, with a cold prairie landscape of brown stubble and bare trees, and heavy gray skies that never seemed to lift. The prison itself broke the horizon with twin cellblocks that rose seven imposing stories. They adjoined a rotunda topped by a silver-colored dome that towered 150 feet, a complex known as the Castle. "A giant mausoleum," an inmate wrote of it in 1929, "adrift in a great sea of nothingness."

Convict laborers from the nearby military stockade built this, the first federal penitentiary, out of limestone from a nearby quarry. Starting in 1897, they worked twelve hours a day, seven days a week, in conditions harsh enough to provoke the occasional riot. Misbehaving inmates were forced to haul a twenty-five-pound ball and chain as they labored, which they called "carrying the baby." In the early years, prisoners who were caught stealing were branded on the face with a T. Those who tried to escape got a D brand, for deserter. As one of the first wardens put it, "Leavenworth is hell." Few who attempted to flee actually succeeded in breaking out. A brick wall, also built by inmates, surrounded the prison yard and out-buildings; it stood forty feet high, to thwart climbers, and extended forty feet belowground, to block tunnelers. The only escape for most came via parole, transfer, or death. Though conditions had improved markedly—the prison now had furniture plants and shoe factories with modern equip-ment, an array of educational classes, and musical performances by inmates—Leavenworth still meant hard time, and carried a reputation as the toughest of federal pens.

When Binion arrived, his hair was dirty and uncombed, his gaze had gone blank, and his jowly face showed the weary sag of a man who had gambled away his last shred of hope. Like every inmate, he underwent physical and mental exams during his first few weeks of confinement. The prison doctor reported that he had flat feet, four missing teeth, and "mod-erate obesity," but was otherwise in good health and "suitable for regular duty." Binion cautioned that such duty shouldn't be too rigorous. "He says he is unable to do hard work," the doctor said, "because he is not used to it." Deprived for the first time in decades of custom-made cowboy boots, Binion also complained that the prison shoes were too tight.

His performance on drills of mental acuity reflected the skills of some-one who had forsaken a backcountry school in the second grade. "He has very limited ability in reading and writing and claims not even to know his multiplication tables," wrote one interviewer. An intelligence test pegged Binion's IQ at 89, or low average. Regarding his emotional state, exams showed he had rallied from his initial despair. There were, however, linger-ing financial worries. "The inmate claims that he is worth about $800,000, but that he is in debt in the amount of $600,000," an examiner noted. "The wife has informed us that she plans to sell the home and operate a ranch, that she will receive approximately $175 a month while he is incarcerated."

Even in prison, Binion summoned his remarkable skill of bounce. He adjusted well to con life within a few weeks. "The inmate seems to have a satisfactory attitude toward his sentence and confinement," an associate warden observed. "He keeps himself clean and his quarters orderly." Though he asked to be assigned to Leavenworth's Honor Farm, officials conferred and decided otherwise. The former big boss of gambling would now work in the prison fire department as a maintenance man.

Back in Las Vegas, mob money kept building resorts and importing Hollywood stars. The nine-floor Riviera opened in 1955, the first high-rise on the Strip. Liberace performed for $50,000 a week as its headline act—though he had not yet taken to wearing capes of ermine and rhinestones—and former Phoenix mobster Gus Greenbaum ran the place. At the Sands, gamblers could combine sunbathing with dice: the pool had a floating craps table. Dean Martin and Jerry Lewis could be found playing blackjack in the hotel's casino, and Frank Sinatra cavorted with Doris Day and Lauren Bacall.

With such material, all the chamber of commerce needed was a public relations apparatus to position Vegas as a desert Xanadu. Enter the Las Vegas News Bureau, which circulated the pictures of the stars, the swim-up craps table, and the showgirls worldwide. If some heartland burgher opened his hometown newspaper to find a photo of three beauties in bathing suits straddling a phallic fake rocket in a Strip parking lot, Vegas businessmen had the news bureau to thank.

Even Noël Coward, the sophisticated British playwright and performer, signed up for a monthlong gig at the Desert Inn in 1955. "This is a fabulous, extraordinary madhouse," he wrote in his diary. "The gangsters who run the places are all urbane and charming . . . Their morals are bizarre in the extreme. They are generous, mother-worshippers, sentimental and capable of much kindness. They are also ruthless, cruel, violent and devoid of scruples." He noted the presence of many beautiful women, but added, "Every instinct and desire is concentrated on money." Coward, by the way, had a great run in Vegas. "It has all been," he wrote as he left, "a triumphant adventure."

Not everyone departed in victory. A fading Hollywood star named Ronald Reagan, seeking fast cash and a career turnaround, launched a two-week run at the Last Frontier. For $30,000 he emceed a show full of silly costumes, slapstick humor, and sentimental pieties. Critics savaged the show, and Reagan's contract was not renewed. He left Las Vegas contemplating a career in politics. But the Gipper was an exception. For most, Las Vegas offered unlimited opportunity.

Binion's former establishment now had a longer name: Joe W. Brown's Horseshoe Club. Brown put his name on much of the casino kitsch, such as ashtrays and matchbooks, and scratched Binion's name off the chips. The place featured a new attraction, which had been envisioned by Binion but executed by Brown: a big plastic horseshoe displaying $1 million in $10,000 bills. Tourists lined up to have their photos taken next to it. And night after night, the casino seemed to bulge with gamblers. With the real proprietor gone, the mobsters who had been allowed into the Horseshoe's ownership structure wasted little time in figuring out how much of this handle they could steal. The answer: millions.

The mood had darkened on Bonanza Road. For the Binion family, the adjustment to life without a wealthy and powerful patriarch proved to be a series of financial and legal obstacles. Teddy Jane canceled any plans she might have had—however slight—to sell the Las Vegas house. This created cash-flow problems. Gold Dollar soon left for another job, and the Binions' cook—so famous for her fried chicken—was discharged. Other employees drifted away, and Teddy Jane began cutting the lawn herself, operating a power mower while wearing a large diamond ring and Spring-o-lator high heels.

The family tried to visit Leavenworth several times a year, but they often made the fourteen-hundred-mile trip by bus only to see Binion for an hour in the prison visiting room. "They'd frisk him in front of us," daughter Brenda said. "Jack would say before we'd go in there, 'Brenda, don't you cry, because it upsets Daddy.' Of course I'd start crying, and so would Daddy."

After Thanksgiving 1954, eleven months into his sentence, Binion took a pad of lined paper, like something a schoolboy would use, and composed a letter to his daughter. He wrote with a fountain pen, in blue ink. "Dear Brenda," he began, "my favorte [sic] cowgirl."

Binion had long claimed to his gambling associates that he was illiterate—he found advantage to being underestimated—but he had limited abilities to read and write. His missive to Brenda was full of misspellings, grammatical crimes, and run-on sentences, but he could say what he needed to. "I Know you all had a nice Thanksgiving I had a nice dinner and enjoyed It very much good turkey," he wrote.

Mainly he wanted to tell his children that he missed them. "You Kid's are growing to fast I just cant get usto Knot having any baby Becky will be a big girl before long," he wrote. "I Have been Fortunant for fifty year's to have a fine famley as I have you all are the best and I love you all More eatch day and I thank God for being so Good to me."

Binion also announced he had been losing weight. "I am not so fat Know I am 180 pound's Mother called me slim I liked that." He asked Brenda to say hello to his friends Doby Doc and Gold Dollar, and to tell Teddy Jane he would write soon. "Just Keep Being good and we will all Pray and we will Be happy toghter agan."

He ended it with "cowgirl your dadie loves you." Then he signed it L. B. Binion, adding his inmate number, 70732.

More than a year into his sentence, Binion had done about as well as could be expected in prison. As he noted in his letter, he had lost twenty or thirty pounds. He looked lean, healthy, groomed, and sharp-eyed now. He slept in a bunk in the fire department dormitory, a far better berth than the oppressive cellblocks that housed most prisoners, and he had been promoted to assistant lead fireman. This assignment carried some responsibility—he spent part of his time monitoring the prison factories for fire safety—and little in the way of actual labor. The job had other advantages: he sometimes used an empty fire extinguisher to sneak hard-boiled eggs out of the prison kitchen for use as barter.

Leavenworth officials happily noted that Binion had completed a religious education course, and had been baptized a Catholic. Since then, an entry in his file said, "he has been most faithful in receiving the sacraments regularly." For the first time in his life, Binion attended services every Sunday. "My family's all religious," he explained years later, "and I didn't have nothing else to do." He also tried something else new—reading a spiritual tract. "A book wrote by a monk in 1500 and something. Old priest give it to me," Binion recalled. "And it's just little sayings that he thought of every day that he wrote down. They's one there, he says, 'Don't censure no man for his shortcomings.' Says, 'We're frail creatures.'"

This awakening of the soul also delivered an earthly reward. A priest smuggled steaks, which he brought into the prison in his briefcase, to Binion. When Teddy Jane visited Leavenworth, she carried cash to pay back the clergyman.

These adventures in contraband went undetected, and the great racketeer experienced only one run-in with prison authorities. Guards conducting a routine search found four extra pairs of socks in his laundry bag. Binion was merely reprimanded for this offense, an associate warden wrote, because "it is felt that control has been somewhat lax with regard to the issue of socks." Beyond that, he had behaved—as far as prison officials were concerned—as the model inmate. "His conduct," wrote Warden C. H. Looney, "is outstanding."

Unfortunately for Binion, his hope to see more of his family rested not with Warden Looney, but with the Bureau of Prisons officials in Washington, who showed him little sympathy. In 1955, he requested a transfer to the Terminal Island federal pen, near Los Angeles, which would put him more than a thousand miles closer to his wife and children. Leavenworth's warden backed the transfer with no hesitation, writing: "Binion is a cooperative and pleasant individual . . . and should have no difficulty adjusting at Terminal Island . . . He exerts whatever influence he has for the benefit of inmate morale." Because of Binion's long separation from his family, the warden added, "this man is beginning to show signs of depression."

But the director of the Bureau of Prisons, James V. Bennett, turned the request down flat. The decision was based in no small part on what prison records called "the notoriety angle."

Over the course of fifteen months, beginning in 1955, Binion came up for parole twice. Given his nonviolent offense and his good prison record, he and his counsel believed he enjoyed a good chance at release, and they called in favors to put some not-so-subtle pressure on the parole board in Washington. They persuaded the U.S. attorney who had prosecuted him, Charles F. Herring, to inform the board that he did not object to setting Binion free. "Were I in a position to make a decision," Herring wrote, "I would grant the parole as requested." Ben Rice, the federal judge who had passed sentence, agreed. "I have no problem whatever to parole being granted to Mr. Binion," he said in a letter.

A Nevada state senator, meeting a parole board member at a Washington reception, happened to mention that everything that Binion had done in his state "was legal at the time it was being done." The state's lone congressman, Cliff Young, reminded the board in a letter that Binion had "achieved a widespread and well-deserved reputation for participation in civic activities" in Las Vegas. One of the U.S. senators from Nevada, George W. Malone, called to say that Binion's record in the state was good and he had a "fine family." Several letter writers informed the board that Binion's official parole adviser, who would make sure that all rules were followed, was to be none other than the lieutenant governor of Nevada—and cowboy movie star—Rex Bell.

Binion's lawyer, Emmanuel M. Stern, also wrote and called repeatedly, praising his client as a man of good habits, including a fierce devotion to his wife and children. "He has never drank to excess," Stern said. "He has never kept company with women other than his wife, since his marriage." And, he insisted, Binion no longer held any public relations value for a federal government that wanted to show off its crime-busting ways. "This case," he wrote, "long ago lost all of its publicity feature."

U.S. attorney general Brownell put the lie to that last part five weeks after the lawyer's letter. Delivering a speech to the Republican National Convention in August 1956, Brownell reeled off the Justice Department's recent wins, including tax evasion prosecutions of "well-known racketeers." They included Frank Costello, the so-called Prime Minister of the Underworld, and Albert Anastasia, reputed head of Murder, Inc., the notorious squad of New York hit men. And, Brownell made sure to mention, the department had buried Binion. A clipping of a newspaper story about Brownell's remarks went into Binion's Washington file. Not long after the speech, a parole board member handwrote this note regarding Binion's case: "Has received nationwide publicity . . . Much pressure on case." And later, in another memo, he wrote, "Was cited publicly as a racketeer by Atty Gen . . . A hot case."

Board members weren't inclined to buck the top boss on hot cases. So it came as little surprise when they turned down Binion both times for parole.

In November 1956 a man named Samuel Block came to the parole board offices in Washington to make the case for Binion, whom he knew through the oil business in Montana. Block told officials he had recently visited the

Binion home on Bonanza Road, and came away troubled. "The family is going to the dogs," he said. "They need their father."

Block lodged his appeal less than a month after a violent but initially unremarkable crime in the tiny Death Valley town of Baker, California, where two young men broke into the home of a highway café operator. They beat the victim—breaking his nose—and wounded him with a gunshot to the back as he tried to run away. Then they grabbed some cash and fled. These two might have been expected to be smarter than the usual strong-arm robbers, for they had met as students at Nevada Southern University in Las Vegas. They were foiled by one of those catastrophes that have destroyed any number of otherwise brilliant holdup schemes—bad wheels. Their getaway car broke down, so the robbers tried to flee by bus. This led to their arrest.

Such a crime would not ordinarily excite much interest outside the town where it occurred, but after the two suspects began singing to police, this one went nationwide. The *Las Vegas Review-Journal* ran a banner headline on the top of the front page: "Nab Vegas Girl as Rob Ring Head." And not just any Vegas girl. A dispatch from its newswire had details: "The gorgeous young daughter of millionaire gambler and tax evader Benny Binion was accused in Las Vegas today of being the 'brains' of a two-state robbery gang."

She was indeed gorgeous—the papers ran a school yearbook photo of a wavy-haired beauty in a lace collar—as well as deeply troubled from an early age. Barbara Binion Fechser, at the age of twenty-two, was married but separated, and already the mother of three. As the oldest child in the Binion household, she had long fought parental authority, and especially bridled at the financial straits imposed by her father's imprisonment. Heading a gang of robbers took rebellion a bit further. Police believed she had assembled a criminal cadre of three men. The robbery of the California victim—who was an ex-boyfriend of Barbara's—served as a trial run. Next, they had planned a string of holdups that targeted the wealthy of Las Vegas. Among the planned victims: former lieutenant governor Cliff Jones and Jake Friedman, one of the owners of the Sands. Jones, sometimes known as Big Juice, was considered one of the most powerful men in the state. Friedman, a Russian immigrant by way of Houston, cut a less than threatening figure. Although he liked to dress as a cowboy, he barely cleared five feet in his western boots, and he liked to douse himself in White Shoulders women's perfume. Still, he was a confrere of Galveston crime boss Sam Maceo, and he traveled the Strip as Vegas Brahmin.

Barbara was charged with conspiring to commit robbery and burglary, and Doby Doc posted her bail. After a battle over extradition—shades of her father—she was ultimately put on probation by a California Superior Court judge, although a probation officer had urged that she receive a thirty-day jail term. Her lawyer, Tom Foley, swayed the judge with the argument that Barbara's three children would have to be in the care of Teddy Jane during her incarceration, and "that is too much to ask of any grandmother."

The federal parole board was unpersuaded by the adventures of Binion's daughter. The board even turned down a special appeal by Binion in which he pleaded to be released for the good of his family. It took the U.S. Supreme Court to spring him from prison. In early 1957, the justices agreed to consider whether Binion's sentence, and that of top New York mobster Frank Costello, had been excessive. Binion posted bond and walked out of Leavenworth on March 19, 1957, with the $776 that had been in his inmate account. He returned to Las Vegas, a free man at last, although no one could say for how long.

"I'll tell you the reason why I'm not a damn bit sorry I went to the penitentiary. I'm absolutely glad of it," Binion said years later. "When I come out of the penitentiary, my youngest daughter was walking funny, and my family couldn't see it . . . I got out in March, kept a-hollerin', 'This girl don't walk right.' So I just kept on, kept on. Finally, in October, my wife took her and had her x-rayed, and she had a cyst inside of her thighbone, right up close to that socket, that was all ready—'most ready to burst. If it'd've bursted, it'd shattered that bone and ruined her leg. They'd had to cut her leg off, right at the hip. Well, to have me recognizing this thing makes me absolutely glad I went to the penitentiary. So they say everything happens for the best. Maybe it does. This did, anyhow."

Downtown Las Vegas in the 1960s, with the Horseshoe surrounded by the Mint, the Fremont, and the Golden Nugget.

# 20

# STRIPPERS AND STOOGES

It's not your enemies you have to worry about. It's your friends.

—BB

The relief granted by the Supreme Court didn't last. Two months after agreeing to hear it, the justices turned down Binion's appeal. With that settled, the Bureau of Prisons calculated that, including good-time credits, he still had 119 days to serve, and sought to have him returned to Leavenworth. Once again, his powerful friends brought the heat. Senator Malone of Nevada phoned the chairman of the parole board to urge official forgiveness. "If this were a less well-known prisoner," Malone said, "parole would have been granted before now." He also wrote to say that Mrs. Binion had been to see him about her husband's case: "She is herself boardering [sic] on a nervous breakdown. To send an individual back to prison just for a few months . . . might do more harm than good."

Binion's lawyers filed a flurry of motions in which they argued he should not be forced to serve the remainder of his sentence. But the bureau insisted it couldn't parole someone who was not in custody. Only if Binion returned to prison could he be considered for release. He had entered a bizarre legal purgatory: the only way to secure his freedom would be to give it up. "Binion has suffered fully for his violations of the law," one of his attorneys, John J. O'Brien Jr., argued. "It would be absurd to return L. B. Binion to prison for such a short period of time . . . A failure to parole [him] would only serve to cause unnecessary and cruel hardship for the innocent members of [his] family and mark the hand of the United States Government as unduly harsh and arbitrarily unmerciful."

Such rhetoric went to waste. Bureau officials would not be moved.

All except one. In May 1957, Hubert A. Boyd, the chief U.S. probation officer for the District of Nevada, wrote to the country's top parole official in Washington, asking that Binion "be given every consideration for immediate parole." He spent three typewritten, single-spaced pages laying out Binion's virtues and exigencies. As a free man, Boyd said, Binion could take his children to the Montana ranch. "They would have a chance to enjoy outdoor life of horseback riding, playing and helping with minor chores," he wrote. "Since the father has been away, the younger children have never enjoyed this type of privilege." He added that Binion "is one of the best liked individuals I have ever known," and had been embraced by the local community. "I have never found a person in Nevada who has spoken ill of him."

This wasn't the first such letter the friendly probation officer had penned. Less than a year earlier he had written the parole board relaying the family's urgent need to have Binion home. "Mrs. Binion is an ideal mother, and devotes her entire life to her children," he stressed. "She does all her own work and is often ironing the children's clothing at midnight or later . . . This Father's guidance is essential for the well-being of the family."

It was, for a public official, an extraordinarily impassioned exhortation on behalf of a convicted felon, with expressions of empathy and admiration that far exceeded the typical federal missive. Boyd practically accused the Bureau of Prisons of cruelty to children when he wrote that fifteen-year-old Brenda was already going out on dates and "the Father is greatly needed to assist in guiding this child."

These letters omitted one important detail. Even as Boyd was serving as the number one probation officer in Nevada, he had a lucrative second job. He also drew a paycheck as the chief of security at the Horseshoe casino.

This might have seemed odd in less enlightened precincts, but not here. "This 'moonlight' employment is not condemned by the community," said Albert Wahl, chief probation officer in Northern California. "The judges were aware of it. The law enforcement agents were aware of it and do not particularly criticize the arrangements." Wahl had investigated the situation for the Bureau of Prisons and concluded that a different—and peculiar—set of legal guidelines held sway in Las Vegas. "These are difficult to understand," he explained, "for one who is not acquainted with Nevada."

Now an old nemesis dropped in: even more income tax trouble. The government claimed Binion owed an additional $467,619 for the years 1950–53, an amount that his attorneys disputed—though they lacked much of the means to do so effectively. Binion, his counsel acknowledged, had retained almost no records from the period, and his memory was less than photographic. "He can recall the necessary details of the transactions," one of his lawyers wrote, "only after repeated questioning, long discussions . . . and constant reference by him to his former employees, business associates and friends."

To the escalating alarm of his attorneys and accountants, Binion decided that dealing with taxes and seeking parole did not constitute his most urgent business in the summer of 1957. While he was in Leavenworth, the Montana ranch had endured an extended drought, and dozens of cattle had died. Some of the livestock that survived were stolen—as many as five hundred head, he later came to believe. Others had broken free from their herds and were roaming the empty hills. Now he headed to Montana with daughter Brenda and son Jack. There they passed weeks combing the Missouri Breaks on horseback, rounding up wayward livestock. For a man who had spent more than three years behind a wall, it was—despite the missing cattle—a refreshing return to his most beloved pastime.

When at last Binion had the ranch in some form of working order, he turned his attention to his tax problems. He needed several hundred thousand dollars. To get that kind of money, and to get it fast, he turned to the typical Las Vegan's lender of choice: the mob.

Across the street in Glitter Gulch a grand new hotel was being planned, the Fremont. Built with $4 million from the International Brotherhood of Teamsters, it would be even taller than the Riviera. One of its principal developers was Ed Levinson, who came to the aid of his fellow casino man with an offer to buy shares of the Horseshoe. This was no humanitarian gesture. Levinson, a Chicago native who learned the gambling business in Detroit, was "closely associated," in the FBI's words, with syndicate lawyer Sidney Korshak, and had another powerful friend in Bobby Baker, the scheming intimate of Lyndon Johnson. Levinson had come to Vegas after working for Meyer Lansky in Havana. In Glitter Gulch, he served as a front man for Lansky, Doc Stacher, and other gangsters who already had a piece of the Horseshoe. Levinson had many attributes, including coolness under pressure and an eye for talent; he gave Wayne Newton his big Vegas break. But his greatest gift may have been his ability to skim from casinos.

Binion insisted, at least for public consumption, that Levinson was buying out Joe W. Brown, who had tired of running a Vegas club. That was yet another fiction, because Brown had almost no shares to sell. Actually, the money—enough to pay his back taxes—went to Binion. In return, Levinson now had effective control of the Horseshoe, and he wasted no time in putting his stooges in key positions. All of a sudden a local bail bondsman named Harry "Spinach" Coopersmith was running the cashier's cage, at least until he got caught stealing bagfuls of coins. The new manager of slot machines was Oscar "Daddy Joey" Rubinsky, formerly a pool hall owner out of Minneapolis. And the casino manager's post now went to Louis "Paddock" Walker, once the Detroit mob's top gambling man in Toledo. This arrangement had its tensions. On one occasion, an FBI report said, Binion "had a disagreement" with Levinson and "backed Levinson into a corner and threatened to beat his head off."

Such encounters aside, Levinson was now the president of the Horseshoe. This represented, in the tight world of Vegas casinos, a major shift, but it wasn't the only one on Fremont Street in 1958. As Binion sold out to Lansky's lackeys—in essence providing a new source of cash to a worldwide criminal enterprise—he again exercised his astounding skill at working both sides of the fence.

On June 5, 1958, yet another memo from the Las Vegas office, with Benny Binion in the subject line, arrived on J. Edgar Hoover's desk. Once more, Binion's history as a "ruthless racketeer and hoodlum" got the detailed treatment. But Special Agent Leo Kuykendall added that Binion had been behaving himself since his release from Leavenworth. "Investigation up to the present time does not indicate that he has resumed his former type of racketeering tactics," he wrote. "He has become well respected and liked by many prominent people in Nevada." Not only that, but Binion had "made numerous disparaging remarks regarding convicts who were in . . . Leavenworth during the time he was there." Here came the FBI's version of the new Benny Binion, an anti-outlaw with the zeal of the convert: "He . . . has stated that persons who committed crimes will eventually find out there is no way they can possibly derive anything from their criminal operations."

As laughable as it might be to anyone who knew Binion's past, this was the public image that he had been trying to present—reformed, respected, perhaps even revered. And ready to do business with the feds. On the second page of the memo came this stunner from Kuykendall: "Bureau authority has been requested to develop Binion as a potential criminal informant."

Binion had persuaded his friends and associates that he loathed the FBI, all while he and Kuykendall discussed his becoming a secret bureau pigeon. "He has stated to Agents that the FBI is the only law enforcement agency that anyone can trust or have faith in anymore," Kuykendall wrote, and "he was very friendly." Binion, he insisted, could be developed into a "valuable informant."

He was already providing some information to agents. On the morning of February 18, Binion had called Kuykendall at his office to advise that Harold "Happy" Meltzer, a ranking member of Meyer Lansky's international narcotics cartel, had hit town. Binion spotted Meltzer half a block from the Horseshoe, visiting a chum at the Bird Cage Casino.

Hoover was intrigued. This notion of flipping Binion might help the bureau map the network of mobsters moving money in and out of Las Vegas. "You might consider developing Binion's front in order to identify others participating in the activity," he wrote to Kuykendall. "Afford this matter continuous and preferred attention."

While Binion was being courted as a government snitch, Las Vegas embarked on a brief flurry of moral indignation. The Nevada Gaming Commission came to learn in 1959 that the New Frontier Hotel employed a female impersonator as a lounge act. Thomas "T.C." Jones, a married man and U.S. Navy veteran, specialized in wigged and gowned renditions of Judy Garland, Tallulah Bankhead, and Edith Piaf. By all accounts, the act drew appreciative crowds. But the gaming commission, a law enforcement memo said, "felt that such a type of entertainment attracted an undesirable element." Under threat of license revocation, casino management hastily dropped Jones from its lineup.

At the El Rancho Vegas, these same commissioners expressed alarm over the newest headliner, exotic dancer Juanita Phillips, aka Candy Barr. A former Dallas prostitute, she was for a while engaged to marry Los Angeles mobster Mickey Cohen. Onstage she wore a skimpy fringe-and-boots costume, with cap guns in holsters, and she made $2,000 a week slowly removing this getup for paying customers. "The Commission indicated it was not proper for the morals of the community to permit Candy Barr to perform," the memo said, "and it was especially a poor example for the youth and general reputation of the community." Like the female impersonator, Barr found herself quickly out of work.

Las Vegas had now been made safe from the scourge of Edith Piaf impersonators and cowgirl strippers. Meanwhile, mobsters were skimming millions from casinos with little worry about interference from authorities. Down in Glitter Gulch, Levinson and his crew bragged that they were raking $700,000 a year off the top at the Horseshoe alone. When their skim from the Sands, the Flamingo, and the Fremont was added to that, they were taking—and this was a conservative estimate—between $3 million and $4 million tax-free annually.

The FBI believed that Levinson and former Nevada lieutenant governor Cliff Jones parked much of their share of the skim in a bank in Geneva, Switzerland, where they held numbered accounts. Periodically, Levinson had to distribute cash to other shareholders—to Doc Stacher, to Gerry

Catena, to Lansky. Vincent "Jimmy Blue Eyes" Alo and Charlie "the Blade" Tourine got theirs too. Some of the stash was shipped in the sleeves of laundered shirts. But most went the time-honored way—stuffed into suitcases and hauled by armed couriers on passenger trains. Ida Devine, wife of Irving "Niggy" Devine, whose meat company supplied Vegas casinos, was a favored cash mule. Boarding the train in Las Vegas, couriers might stop in Chicago, Detroit, and New Jersey. Others would go first to Florida, then migrate up the Eastern Seaboard. Occasionally they made a side trip to Hot Springs, Arkansas. It operated like a milk run, once every thirty days.

When Catena received his monthly payout in New Jersey, he doled out portions to his subpartners. He would hand several thousand to Angelo "Gyp" DeCarlo, one of the great East Coast entrepreneurs of loan-sharking. And on a golf course near Newark, he passed a wad of cash to Anthony "Tony Boy" Boiardo, whose father, Richie the Boot, was reputed to have a private crematorium in the back of his mansion, where he disposed of his enemies.

Through it all, Binion fed tips to the FBI. "Almost daily," a memo said, "Binion has furnished information on a confidential basis to Bureau Agents which has proven to be valuable . . . from an intelligence standpoint." That may have been an exaggeration by an agent seeking to please his supervisors. Despite his new financial links to some of the East Coast's most notorious gangsters, Binion generally provided inside scoops of little consequence—nothing on Levinson and Swiss bank accounts, nothing on Richie the Boot.

But he did help out with an interstate car theft. He also advised agents to keep a marginal ex-con named Danny Davis under watch because Davis "would not be prowling around . . . unless he intended to steal something." And, he admitted to agents—now that he no longer required the ruse—that the story about Joe W. Brown owning 97 percent of the Horseshoe had been garbage. As usual, Binion employed pragmatic charm: twice he visited the ailing Kuykendall in the hospital.

His efforts finally paid off. On March 2, 1960, Binion's FBI status officially changed. "This case is being closed as to the Anti-Racketeering, Top Hoodlum investigation," Kuykendall wrote, "and Binion is being converted to a Criminal Informant."

Binion hid his new law enforcement role from even his closest friends. Years after his death, some of his steadfast pals received the news with open-mouthed astonishment. "That's an absolute lie," said lawyer Oscar Goodman. "Benny hated the FBI."

Eddie LaRue, a Las Vegas private detective who occasionally did work for the Horseshoe, strongly doubted Binion would cooperate with the bureau. "I don't think Benny would tell them anything."

Billy Bob Barnett, a Texan who adored Binion, refused to accept the statements in FBI documents. When told about them for the first time, he stopped eating his lunch and stared out the window of a Dallas restaurant. "I'd no more believe that," he said, "than I'd believe Martians just landed in that parking lot."

Yet playing both sides functioned as a basic component of Binion's life-long strategy. He had exploited this type of arrangement since the days of his kinship with Bill Decker back in Dallas. By spoon-feeding some inside tips of questionable value to the local FBI functionary—who was, after all, under continual pressure from Washington to develop confidential informants—Binion duped his chief pursuers into believing he was now on their side. More important, he had them on his.

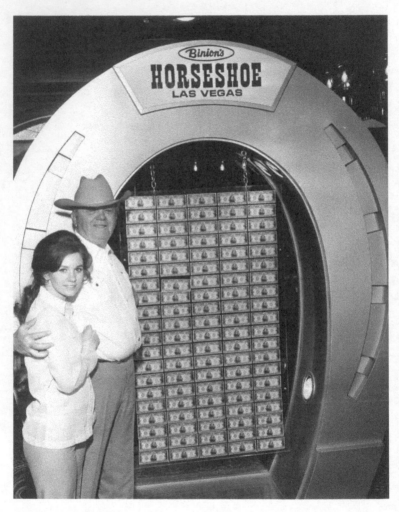

Binion and daughter Becky at the Horseshoe's famous million-dollar display, 1969.

# 21

# CHARLIE, ELVIS, AND THE REVOLUTION

Hell, all I want's four walls and crap tables, and a roof to keep the rain off, and the air condition to keep people comfortable. Got to have that, you know.

–BB

In some ways, Las Vegas experienced the sixties like other parts of the country. It struggled, for example, with civil rights, and was occasionally derided as the "Mississippi of the West." Casinos were strictly segregated. The black entertainers who headlined at Vegas clubs couldn't sleep or dine there. "In Vegas for 20 minutes, our skin had no color. Then the second we stepped off the stage, we were colored again," Sammy Davis Jr. recalled. "The other acts could gamble or sit in the lounge and have a drink, but we had to leave through the kitchen with the garbage . . . What they said was that they didn't want to offend the Texans." In a small gesture of protest, black actress and singer Dorothy Dandridge dipped her foot in the pool at the Last Frontier, and management responded by draining every drop of water. After Lena Horne spent the night in a cabana at the Flamingo, they burned the sheets. But in 1960, after a threatened march by the NAACP, club owners agreed to integrate.

This represented progress, though modest and spotty, and the Horseshoe was slow to comply. "Benny Binion being the strong man that he was in the community, the situation with his Horseshoe club was different," said Dr. James McMillan, president of the Las Vegas NAACP. McMillan's group did not press the matter at the Horseshoe because of Gold Dollar, the ex-chauffeur who had gone back to work for Binion. "This guy was six-foot-six inches tall and weighed 300 pounds. A rough, tough, bad cowboy," McMillan said of Gold Dollar. "Him being a security guard there, we felt that we just couldn't challenge Binion at that particular time. We let that alone. Binion took his own time hiring black people, and he took his own time letting black people in."

While the Horseshoe evoked a time-stands-still quality—not much about it had changed since it opened, and it showed not the slightest aspiration to trendiness—it made cameo appearances in two of the decade's great dramas. After the assassination of John F. Kennedy, and Jack Ruby's shooting of Lee Harvey Oswald two days later, the FBI began probing the old Dallas rackets scene. That included a visit to some of Binion's associates, R. D. Matthews among them. "They said Ruby had my phone number in his pocket," Matthews said. "I didn't believe it." He and Oswald's killer were hardly companions: "I knew Jack Ruby to speak to him on the street. That's all." Agents also questioned Lewis McWillie, a friend of Ruby's. McWillie had worked for Binion at Top O'Hill back in Texas, ran a casino for Meyer Lansky in Havana, and was later employed at the Horseshoe. The FBI appeared to learn little from either of these interviews.

A few years after JFK's death, the Horseshoe's second brush with sixties infamy came when Charles Manson and his "family" breezed through town, taking the time to pose for a photograph in front of Binion's million-dollar display. After this exercise in bourgeois tourism, Charlie and his deranged acolytes kicked off their wave of gruesome murders in Southern California.

Such brief and strange encounters aside, many of the celebrated countercultural events of the decade had little effect on Binion's casino or, for that matter, the beating heart of Las Vegas. Other towns could concern themselves with Woodstock or the Summer of Love. Las Vegas was busy fawning over the ghost dance of the Rat Pack and paying good money to see lounge singers in velveteen tuxes croon "Danny Boy." In much of America, 1967 will be remembered as the year when a hundred thousand

Vietnam War protesters marched on Washington, when Jimi Hendrix and Janis Joplin played the Monterey Pop Festival, when groundbreaking movies like *The Graduate* and *Bonnie and Clyde* hit the screens. In Las Vegas, it's the year that Elvis Presley married Priscilla Beaulieu at the Aladdin.

Vegas may have inhabited an insular world—light on the psychedelic, heavy on the ring-a-ding-ding—but it was about to shake and rattle from its own seismic shifts. The nation's most famously eccentric billionaire played a big role. So did a motley collection of poker players. But first, the feds took their shot.

At the U.S. Department of Justice in Washington, newly appointed attorney general Robert F. Kennedy launched a campaign against organized crime. This extended to one of its main generators of illicit cash—the casinos of Nevada. Throughout the sixties, money from Teamsters union pension funds flooded Vegas, and the Teamsters had multiple connections to numerous crime syndicates. Union loans financed the construction of Strip showcases like Caesars Palace, a Greco-Roman extravaganza of imported marble, elaborate fountains, and elegant gardens, where Victor Borge played the main room. From mob-connected Vegas operations, millions in skimmed cash flowed out of town to criminal enterprises across the globe. As far as Kennedy was concerned, it was dirty money in and dirty money out.

In 1963, FBI agents installed phone taps, approved by Kennedy, at a handful of Las Vegas's leading clubs, including the Stardust, the Sands, the Fremont, and the Desert Inn. Kennedy had proposed, then abandoned, a dramatic and headline-grabbing raid on the state's casinos. Even as plans for such a grandstanding move remained on the shelf, the Justice Department's desire for its own brand of Vegas action endured. In 1964 the FBI's Las Vegas office produced a 245-page report titled *Nevada Gambling Industry*. Via dozens of confidential informants, the bureau described in elaborate detail the secret mob ownership, hidden skimming operations, and international connections of the major Las Vegas casinos. The federal government clearly intended to mount an offensive.

Such designs worked, strangely enough, to Binion's advantage. He had been planning since his time in prison to reclaim the Horseshoe—and, by his telling, had a long-standing arrangement to do so. "I had a deal to get it back," he said.

Under different circumstances, Ed Levinson, who had been using the Horseshoe as a cash spigot for his syndicate pals, would have been in no mood to talk. But he now found himself in the crosshairs. Here was a typical passage from the FBI's gambling industry report, recounting an informant's version of a conversation between Levinson and the vice president of the Fremont: "Levinson and Edward Torres were in the office at the Fremont Hotel on January 21, 1963, and counting money and ascertaining the amount to be skimmed. Levinson stated that Meyer, believed by the source to be Meyer Lansky, was getting the New Jersey money. When Torres remarked that he thought Meyer handled only the Florida area, Levinson replied that it all goes to Florida, then to New York and New Jersey."

The FBI's hot breath was no secret in Vegas, and when Binion presented Levinson and his associates with an offer to buy back the Horseshoe, they listened. Binion mortgaged the Montana ranch, borrowed nearly $2 million from the Bank of Las Vegas, and in 1964 purchased the shares of Levinson and associates. More than ten years after his Leavenworth exile, the founder of the Horseshoe had regained it. "Through hook or crook, I got it back a hundred percent," he said. Some extra neon was soon added to the outdoor signage for all the gambling world to see: it was officially Binion's Horseshoe again.

Order, Binion-style, was then restored. He sent Levinson's puppets packing and brought his own friends and associates back into the operation. The restaurant once more served beef from his Montana ranch; a steak dinner, with potato and salad, could be had for a few bucks. And the horseshoe-shaped million-dollar showcase, which Levinson had removed, went back up near the main entrance. "That million-dollar display is, I'd say, just as good a advertising thing as they is in town," Binion said, though it took a while to locate the right kind of currency for encasement in plexiglass. "We like to never found the ten-thousand-dollar bills."

With his federal felony conviction, Binion had no hope of winning another state casino license. Instead, son Jack became the licensee, while Benny assumed a figurehead title: director of public relations. This was another sham. Not long after it was put in place, Binion described this new management setup. "My wife works here, and my daughter [Barbara]," he said. "They count the money and look after the office. And Jack is the boss. Ted's the next boss."

Still, no one doubted who was in charge. "Them boys," Binion said, "mind me like they was six years old."

Binion's lawyers had fought in court for years to keep him from serving the remainder of his Leavenworth sentence, but they finally ran out of legal room. In the fall of 1965, a judge ordered him to do the rest of his time at the Clark County Jail. This pained Binion greatly, but it was a minor interruption. He strolled out in less than two months.

Back on the job at the Horseshoe, Binion as always worked his connections. In February 1966, he walked across Second Street to the Fremont, where he met with Levinson and U.S. senator Howard Cannon, Democrat from Nevada and long a recipient of Binion's campaign contributions. They discussed the possibility of a senate subcommittee holding hearings in Las Vegas on the FBI's use of electronic surveillance. While the gamblers had no love of hidden bureau microphones, they also feared the exposure that a hearing might bring, for many of them remembered Estes Kefauver and his crusading band of self-righteous publicity hounds. Binion said he opposed the hearing in Vegas. Levinson agreed, saying, "Hell, no, we don't want them anywhere in the state of Nevada." Cannon told them not to worry, that he would take care of it.

Because he still operated as a bureau informant, Binion gave the FBI a full account of the meeting that same day. Agents used this information to depict Cannon—in confidential memos—as a conniving hypocrite. Before he told his Vegas supporters he would derail the hearing, the senator had urged the subcommittee chairman to convene it in Nevada. He had raised the possibility for one purpose: so that he could kill it. This put the senator in the position, the bureau noted, of "emerging in the eyes of gamblers as the individual who can put a stop to any hearings that might be embarrassing to their interests."

If he knew about the true nature of Cannon's machinations, Binion didn't let it bother him; he had bigger plans for the senator's influence. He had begun to think of pressing for legal action to clear his criminal record, and he wasn't talking about some judge's measly order to seal case files, or a governor's declaration. Those things he could have tomorrow, with a single phone call. Binion was going to the top. He would seek a presidential pardon. With Cannon on his side, he reasoned, he might get it.

The decade's next tectonic shift, Vegas version, occurred at 4:00 a.m. on November 27, 1966, when a private train from Boston stopped at a desolate crossing north of town. One of the world's richest men emerged—carried on a litter—from a customized Pullman car. Howard Hughes was loaded into a waiting van and taken to his new home, the top floor of the Desert Inn.

Now in the crazed-hermit period of his life—at sixty-one he was gaunt, unwashed, and addicted to narcotics—Hughes liked the Desert Inn and the secluded aerie it provided. He felt so at home that he wouldn't leave. This distressed Moe Dalitz, one of the DI's owners. Hughes had agreed to depart by Christmas, but by New Year's he was still there and showed no sign of decamping. Dalitz needed the two floors Hughes had rented—one for the man himself, one for his aides—for high rollers who would drop thousands, maybe millions, at the casino. Hughes, however, never left his quarters, and his staff, composed mostly of Mormons, didn't gamble. This arrangement therefore cost the DI plenty. Management ordered Hughes to vacate. Never one to be shoved around, Hughes made the Desert Inn's owners an irresistible counteroffer: he bought the place.

Hughes didn't stop there. He purchased a number of Strip properties, including the Frontier, the Castaways, and the legendary Sands. He bought a small airline and an airport. He bought a TV station so that it would show the late-night movies he wanted to watch. When the mirrored sign at the Silver Slipper disturbed his sleep, he bought that place too. In only one year, Hughes spent $65 million in Vegas. The town now had a new type of owner—one with his own money, and beholden to no distant clan of hoods. Hughes's buying spree ultimately helped ease the way for the Nevada legislature's passage of the Corporate Gaming Act of 1969, a revolutionary development in the history of the state. Now publicly traded companies could own casinos. Soon heavily capitalized corporations would begin buying and building ever more elaborate Strip resorts, elbowing aside the wiseguys. Hughes's arrival opened the door for this defining characteristic of today's Las Vegas.

Binion, of course, had been acquainted with Hughes as a relatively low-stakes gambler in their Dallas days. "Oh, I knew him a long time before, but I didn't see him when he was here," Binion said about seven years after Hughes's arrival in Las Vegas. "Some newspaper guys come in here ask me, say that they understand that I know Howard Hughes . . . And I kinda rared back in my chair and like—just like I was gonna tell 'em something. 'Well,' I says, 'I guess I know as much about him as anybody.' Oh, they got all thrilled and said, 'What do you know?' I said, 'Nothin'.' So I don't. I don't think nobody knows anything."

In familiar fashion, Binion looked on the bright side when considering the mysterious recluse. "Well, I don't see that he's any worse than any other corporation. Same thing, ain't it?" Binion said. "I think Howard Hughes was good for this town. He spent a lot of money here, and I don't think money hurts any damn place."

Money also helps build a reputation, which Binion knew well. As other racketeers were bought out, sent to prison, or killed—the Riviera's Gus Greenbaum got his throat slit in Phoenix—Binion continued to feather his image as a man of charity. On some afternoons, he and his grandson, Key Fechser, who was Barbara's son, would pass out free hamburgers to hungry black kids who congregated in the alley behind the club. He was forever giving cash to busted rodeo hands drifting through the Horseshoe and to penniless gamblers needing one more stake. "Just pay me back when you can," he instructed them. Some did, and some didn't. "Now, I've damaged a lot of people, lettin' them have money over the years," he said. "I've drowned some of 'em, and I learnt better'n that." Where some saw a soft heart, Binion insisted he simply considered giveaways a good business practice. "I'm kinda freewheeling," he said, "and sorta like the old saying, of bread cast upon the water comes back."

These small incidents built heaps of individual goodwill. Like others in his line of work—Moe Dalitz being a prime example—Binion also under-stood that publicly acknowledged gifts on a much larger scale could pro-vide a sure route to respectability. The city had no blue bloods. Philanthropy could vault a man, despite humble forebears and a checkered past, into the first rank of Vegas society.

Now that the Horseshoe rested safely in his family's hands, Binion had big money to spread around. He directed thousands of dollars to local, state, and national politicians. The always prudent payoffs to law enforcement stayed on schedule. Such distributions fit the very definition of quid pro quo arrangements. With grander goals, Binion went far beyond that; he became one of the most generous donors to the local Catholic diocese. Part of that arose from the religion he found in prison, and part from strategic maneuvering. "Most Nevada gamblers," a U.S. Department of Justice report observed in 1964, "support all church drives in order to curb opposition to their operations." Schools and hospitals also received major gifts, in the tens of thousands, from Binion. On a more personal level, he donated to the Las Vegas High School Rhythmettes so they could travel with the football team, and purchased cattle every year from the local 4-H show.

With these gestures, Binion was rapidly emerging as one of the city's great benefactors. At the same time, he gave aid and comfort to the feds, maintained his old friendships with the mob boys, and dabbled in the upper ranges of politics. It was, in a Vegas-skewed sort of way, the very picture of a model citizen.

Now was the time, Binion figured, to seek the presidential pardon that he wanted so badly. Twice, with Senator Howard Cannon's help, he applied. And twice he was turned down.

It couldn't have helped his application that his thug side, from all indications, never quite receded. As Binion noted a few years later, "If anybody goes to talking about doing me bodily harm, or my family bodily harm, I'm very capable of, thank God, of really taking care of them in a most artistic way."

One December day in 1967, someone came to the family with inside information about a plot to kidnap and kill Binion's son Ted. The informant had been part of the original scheme, but he now saw profit in exposing his co-conspirator. He fingered a friend of Ted's, a cabdriver and petty criminal named Marvin Shumate, as the main actor. Benny Binion did not forward this matter to the police.

Shumate was last seen at a bar, after getting off work, at Flamingo and

Paradise Roads. Days later, his body was found at the base of Sunrise Mountain. He had been shot in the chest with a shotgun and, in case that wasn't artistic enough, in the head with a .357 handgun. Though police long had their suspicions that Binion had ordered Shumate's murder, they never made an indictable case.

The money kept coming, though the Horseshoe anchored the wrong side of Vegas. Out on the Strip, one palace after another rose from the desert—grand resorts with mesmeric stage revues, tropical pools, and a tourist's fantasy of decadent indulgence. But in old Glitter Gulch, the stretch of grind joints and pawnshops made Fremont Street feel like the sad end of a bad trip. Moderately heeled visitors enjoyed a choice: endure the grit and crumble of downtown—with cigarette butts in the gutters and gray-skinned dead-enders stuffing nickels into slot machines—or live like a modern emperor at Caesars? Luxury was only a $10 cab ride away.

Binion's answer was to keep marketing the Horseshoe—which didn't even have a swimming pool—as the purest place for the stone gambler. "There's thousands of people comes on the Strip don't even know there's a downtown," he explained. "That's the reason I've got this high limit, to attract people downtown." High limits let a craps player ride a hot streak, and Binion's was the only spot in town, it was said, where a $5 bettor could become a millionaire. If you craved chorus lines and magicians, the Stardust and the Sands could give you that and more. But if you wanted to gamble like a cracker sultan, you went to the Horseshoe.

In an oft-told tale, a Texan named William Lee Bergstrom bet $777,000 at a Horseshoe craps table and won. He came back later and bet $1 million, and lost on a single roll. Not long afterward, penniless and alone, Bergstrom killed himself in a Vegas hotel room. "I knew him pretty well," Ted Binion said, "and his reasons for suicide were more romantic than financial." The Binions paid for Bergstrom's urn, with an inscription memorializing the man—so directed by Bergstrom in his suicide note—as "The Phantom Gambler."

The numbers were not made public, but many believed the Horseshoe to be the most profitable casino in Vegas. Five years after Binion regained the club, it was doing so well that Aristotle Onassis tried to buy it. "We would have sold it to him for $8 million," Ted Binion said later, "but he wouldn't give us but $6 million." This was another stroke of Binion luck: the Horseshoe was about to assume even greater status, and it didn't need help from any Greek shipping magnates.

In 1969, Tom Moore, a transplanted gambling impresario from San Antonio, hosted a Texas Gamblers Reunion—a series of high-stakes poker games—at his Holiday Hotel casino in Reno, 350 miles northwest of Vegas. Moore assembled an all-star cast from the poker underground, including Johnny Moss, Puggy Pearson, Sailor Roberts, and Doyle Brunson, also known as Texas Dolly. Here was something new. The usual run of gaming-room operators wouldn't think of showcasing a bunch of cardsharps, much less giving them prime real estate on the casino floor. Casinos that tolerated poker generally confined it to small venues to the side of the main action, because it attracted scant attention and generated little in the way of profits. Unlike, say, blackjack or craps gamblers, poker players were playing each other—not the house—for the big pots. All Las Vegas casinos together had only about fifty poker tables. But Moore figured that fast-money players could spark some public interest during a slow time of the year.

The Reno gathering, alas, did not produce much extra traffic. It did, however, mark the first time that Doyle Brunson came face-to-face with the legend that was Benny Binion, who had traveled to Reno with son Jack. "I'd heard about Benny all my life. He was just a tough old cowboy," Brunson recalled. As usual, Binion wore a western shirt with gold coins for buttons, and he moved through the room as if he owned it. "He just carried himself with an assurance that comes with self-confidence," Brunson said.

Binion loved what he found at Reno, especially one contest in particular. "I've seen a lot of poker games. This one this time was the most thrilling game I've ever seen." It featured Moss and Pearson, battling over $130,000. "Pug was down to $30,000 once. Johnny Moss was down to $30,000 once," Binion said. "Johnny Moss come back, put Pug down to $30,000."

Moss took the pot with—not uncharacteristically—a hand of nothing. "Johnny Moss bluffed, single ace," Binion said. "Johnny's a big bluffer."

After Moore announced that this gamblers' reunion would be his last, Binion and son Jack got to talking. It might be a good idea, they thought, if they had a similar tournament at the Horseshoe the next year. Gather a few of the top players, Brunson among them, and let them play for big stakes while people watched—a low-key affair that might occasion some minor publicity and bring extra people to the casino.

We could call it, Binion said, the World Series of Poker.

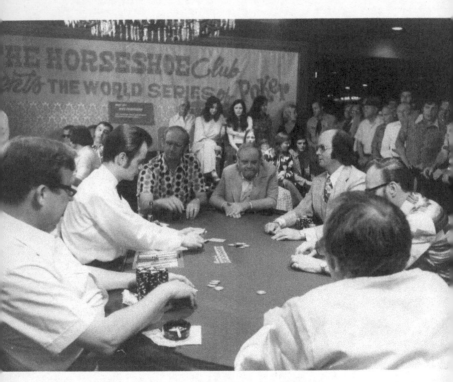

The World Series of Poker, with Binion at the center of the action.

# 22

## ANOTHER ONE BLOWS UP

Anybody had done anything to me, I was sure to do something
to them, but they might never know who did it.

—BB

s he strode through his casino—past the spinning roulette
wheel, alongside the tumbling dice, and through rows of
ringing slot machines—Binion could see at least two problems with a big-time tournament.

First, he didn't have a poker room at the Horseshoe. Second, despite
Binion's enthusiasm for the thrilling business he had witnessed in Reno,
poker contests generally didn't offer much as a spectator experience. Why
would any sane person want to watch a bunch of paunchy middle-agers
with pool-hall tans and stunted social skills, wreathed in cigar smoke, play
a slow match full of prolonged silence, crawling action, and—in the form
of folding—multiple pre-climax surrenders?

Yet such a display had its fascinations, not so much in the game itself
as in the backstory of the players.

Elsewhere in the country, poker was illegal, so high-stakes affairs took
place out of sight, in hotel rooms, social clubs, and off-the-books game
rooms. Many of the better and richer players had to hit the road. And the
best and richest of those traveled a familiar route known as the Texas

Circuit, though it included Oklahoma, Louisiana, and a few other states. The life of the gambler who rode the circuit was naturally itinerant, and it was dangerous.

Doyle Brunson spent years "fading the white line," as the players called it, from burg to city to tank town, chasing big suckers and bigger pots. "You had to worry about winning the money," he said. "You had to worry about getting cheated while trying to win it, you had to worry about getting paid after you won it and you had to worry about getting arrested before, during and after." And you had to worry about being robbed, which is why he kept a loaded shotgun in his backseat. Over the years, Brunson had been held up by thieves with guns, knives, and baseball bats. Some games operated as if under siege. "I played in a game in Oklahoma once, they had a .50-caliber machine gun sitting up on top of the house," he said. "That place I don't think ever got robbed."

Many professional poker players had come up poor and unschooled, but not Brunson. He had been a star athlete at the college level, good enough to catch the interest of the NBA's Minneapolis Lakers, but a broken leg killed his basketball dreams. He went on to earn a master's degree in business administration. Although he had played poker as a student, Brunson sought a real career. He determined quickly that he wasn't cut out for working nine to five, right after he drew his first check as a salesman of bookkeeping equipment. "I saw that I could make more money in one [poker] pot," he said, "than what was in that entire paycheck." He hit the road to play cards, though he told his parents he was a traveling insurance salesman.

In the 1950s, Brunson honed his skills in the collection of bars, hotels, and all-purpose dives near the Fort Worth Stockyards. Once a major shipping point for livestock, and later a concentration of packing plants, the stockyards began to fade and decay after World War II. Law enforcement had all but abandoned the area. "That's the toughest place I've ever been, down on Exchange Avenue," Brunson said. "It was like something out of the old West . . . I saw four people get killed on the street, right out in the open." An argument had broken out on the sidewalk, and guns were drawn. "There were four or five guys on each side. They were shooting at each other like something out of a movie. The police really didn't care."

One of those making their fortunes along Exchange Avenue was Tincy

Eggleston, a rotund hoodlum who was widely feared and loathed in Fort Worth. "Tincy was the most vicious and dangerous man on the Avenue, and that was saying something," Brunson said. Eggleston's shakedowns, threats, and general business model finally went too far. Police found his car parked near the stockyards in the summer of 1955 with blood dripping from the front seat. A week later his body was discovered stuffed in a well north of Fort Worth. He had been an associate of, among others, Benny Binion.

The first year of the World Series of Poker, 1970, drew a handful of players, but it was nonetheless—as Binion had envisioned—a collection of superstars. Among them were Moss, Brunson, and the irrepressible Amarillo Slim Preston. "The first time he comes into the Horseshoe, he tells a dirty joke," Brenda Binion Michael remembered of Slim. "Because my mother's there nobody laughs. He thinks nobody gets it so he tells it again."

Binion solved the problem of where to play by having workers move some of the other games out of the way to make room for poker tables. Before long he had a gathering of outlaws with long sideburns and polyester slacks, playing stud.

The competition that first year had been loosely organized, and at the end of it the players were asked to vote on a champion. When each one voted for himself, Jack Binion asked them to vote for who they thought was second-best. Johnny Moss won.

There were a few other difficulties, but nothing Benny Binion couldn't handle. At one point, a known poker game hijacker was spotted in the crowd. Binion sidled over to him and said, "You're makin' a lot of my customers uneasy." The man responded that it was a free country and he wasn't doing anything wrong. "Look," Binion said, "you're a young man, and you think you're tough. I'm an old man and I know I'm tough. If you think not, let's just go out in the parking garage right now."

The thief got up and left without another word.

The next year the Binions changed the series to a winner-take-all tournament. Once a player lost his chips, he was out. Johnny Moss won that one too. Over the next several years, the series picked up momentum—more money, more players, more attention.

Generating notice for the tournament outside Vegas proved easier than Binion might have thought, because Jimmy "the Greek" Snyder had been fired from his publicity job by Howard Hughes. He knocked on Binion's door seeking redemption. "He didn't charge us anything," Binion said. "He wanted to prove hisself, what he could do." Snyder, also a football odds-maker, worked his gambling and publishing connections across the country, and it didn't hurt that he was pushing a product like none that had come before. "He put it in seven thousand newspapers . . . That's pretty doggone good," Binion said. "Hell, nobody thought you could get this much publicity out of this poker game. I didn't. But he did."

Even better, network shows such as *CBS Sports Spectacular* and ABC's *Wide World of Sports* were now covering the tournament. "This poker game here gets us a lot of advertisement," Binion said. Never mind that the Horse-shoe was shopworn, low-ceilinged, lit like a Texaco station, and smelled of old Camels and last night's beer. The hotel rooms weren't much better. In later years, journalists who came to cover the series were quietly advised to stay across the street at Steve Wynn's refurbished Golden Nugget.

For tournament players the Horseshoe was home, and Binion received them as if they were showcase acts, with good food and slavish attention—the winners especially, who took home gold bracelets and were treated like heavyweight champs. After all the years of resisting performers at his place, Binion finally had some. "He understood gamblers," Doyle Brunson said. "He kind of adopted us." The friendship between Brunson and Binion blos-somed as the series grew. Brunson admired Binion's business savvy: "He was successful in Vegas because he gave the public what they wanted," and he gave his friends what they needed. "He helped everybody."

In Brunson's case, the help he required was the result of a run-in with Tony "the Ant" Spilotro, a Vegas mobster—Joe Pesci portrayed a character much like him in the film *Casino*—who famously squeezed a man's head in a vise until his eyeball popped out. Now Spilotro had a plan for a poker-room cheating scheme, and he tapped Brunson to work with him. If Brunson didn't comply, a friend advised him, Spilotro would "stick twelve ice picks in that big fat belly of yours." Brunson sought an escape route through Binion, who put the word out that he had Brunson's back, and helped negotiate his release from the scheme. "Without that protection," Brunson said, "I have no doubt that Spilotro would have killed me."

It was, he said, another example of the Binion way. "He was the wisest man I've ever known. He understood people better than anyone I've ever known. He was just really a great guy," Brunson said, then added, "But if anybody bothered his business or his family, he was a dangerous guy."

William Coulthard, a fifty-six-year-old former FBI agent and state assemblyman in Las Vegas, had carved out a successful career as a lawyer. His real estate interests included a 37 percent stake in the property on which the Horseshoe stood. In the summer of 1972, Coulthard and Binion entered negotiations for a new lease. Coulthard rejected Binion's offers, and Binion rejected his. Their talks turned difficult if not acrimonious. Herbert Noble's survivors might have predicted how this would play out.

On the afternoon of July 25, another searing Las Vegas day, Coulthard walked out of his office in the Bank of Nevada building downtown—he was the bank's general counsel—and onto the third level of the adjacent parking garage. He got into his four-year-old Cadillac. The car had been parked in its space for six hours, during which someone had placed, directly beneath the steering column, four sticks of dynamite. As soon as Coulthard settled into the driver's seat, they blew. The blast destroyed the Cadillac, ripped a hole in the reinforced concrete, and caused five other cars to explode. It killed Coulthard, a father of four, instantly. "He was," the *Review-Journal* reported, "blasted apart, burned and not facially identifiable."

Homicide investigators, who were well aware of the Horseshoe lease dispute—and prior car bombings in Texas—questioned Binion, but came away with nothing but twangy denials. "Oh, he was tough," Binion said regarding Coulthard's demands. "That doesn't make a goddamn bit of difference. We was not mad at him. Never was mad at him." He suggested that other parties in the property ownership structure had reasons to kill the man. "He had control and he's making a lease the other side didn't like, his partners didn't like . . . His brother-in-laws were mad at him." Then this: "I ain't saying who blowed him up. I know I didn't."

Las Vegas police failed to solve the murder, though investigators claimed they worked hard to pin it on Binion. "If I felt that Benny Binion had done it," homicide detective Beecher Avants said, "and there was some way to prove it, I would have picked him up and put him in jail."

One Las Vegas detective told the local office of the FBI that the bomber was probably a Texan named James Henry Dolan, a career criminal who had been on the bureau's radar for more than ten years. He was known as Doc, perhaps because he had attended college briefly, perhaps because he picked up extra cash performing back-alley abortions. A former boxer, Dolan lived in Dallas, where he had run a talent agency for strippers, magicians, and ventriloquists. In this capacity he became acquainted with Jack Ruby. After Ruby shot Oswald, agents descended on Dolan's house and searched every room, but found nothing of investigative value and accomplished little beyond frightening his wife and child.

Dolan's police record included arrests for robbery, burglary, and gambling. He had also worked, the FBI believed, as a "muscle man" for Florida mobster Santo Trafficante. But Dolan was at heart a traveling con man. One of his favorite swindles involved a counterfeiting machine that produced perfect hundred-dollar bills. It was, naturally, a fake—a counterfeit counterfeiter—but by the time the machine's purchasers figured that out, Dolan had skipped town. Another scam involved having a partner set up big-stakes poker with civic luminaries in small communities. Once lots of cash was on the table, Dolan would enter the room, claim to be an IRS agent, and seize all the money. That hustle got him convicted for impersonating a federal agent. A subsequent probation violation put him in Leavenworth at the same time Binion was serving time there. At some point he also got to know one of Binion's favorite sidekicks, R. D. Matthews.

Now the FBI was being told that Vegas police believed "that Binion owns a 1,000 acre ranch in Mexico on which he is hiding two subjects, one of which is possibly . . . Dolan." Though the bureau devoted many hours to probing Dolan, the investigation made no progress and finally ran out of steam.

Dolan died in 1984, shot to death in San Antonio, Texas, the apparent consequence of selling fake drugs. The Coulthard case, despite occasional talk of breakthroughs, and the offer of a $75,000 reward, stayed unsolved. "It was . . . believed by law enforcement officials investigating this matter that the Binions were behind this bombing," an FBI report said years later, referring to Benny and son Ted. "Unfortunately, the beliefs . . . were never substantiated." Benny Binion maintained his innocence for the rest of his life, and it remains one of Las Vegas's enduring mysteries.

Las Vegas private detective Eddie LaRue, who often worked for Binion, said he never believed his boss had ordered the hit. "Do I think Benny would kill Coulthard?" LaRue said. "Sure. But Benny was not sophisticated like that. He'd have somebody shoot him between the eyes with a .45."

One big winner emerged out of Coulthard's murder: Binion ultimately got a new lease at much more favorable terms.

Clark County sheriff Ralph Lamb, who presided over some of the Coulthard investigation, was tall, handsome, and rough-hewn; like Binion, he had grown up riding horses and roping cattle. By common reckoning, he was the most powerful law enforcement official in the state of Nevada. He was also one of Binion's closest friends.

Like many in Vegas, Lamb appeared to live beyond his means. This attracted the attention of federal authorities, and he was indicted for income tax evasion. "In how many other cities," the *Valley Times* of Las Vegas wondered, "does the sheriff, who earns a relatively modest salary, walk around peeling off $100 bills, paying cash for his $100,000-plus house, and developing a net worth in excess of $250,000?" And in how many other cities would Benny Binion be a star prosecution witness?

Binion readily admitted he had passed stacks of cash to Lamb, although he rebuffed federal agents when they asked to see proof on paper. "I didn't keep no records," Binion told them. "The last time I kept records, you assholes put me in Leavenworth."

The feds called him to the stand anyway, and Binion crossed the courtroom in his custom-made boots. Holding his white cowboy hat at his side, he swore to tell the truth and nothing but, and commenced to destroy the government's case. Under questioning, he disclosed that he had indeed given Sheriff Lamb $30,000. This made for bombshell testimony—until he added that he had simply advanced the funds to Lamb as a loan. He had not been repaid, had imposed no repayment schedule, had executed no lending agreement, and had charged no interest, Binion said, but it was a still a loan.

And the law did not require the payment of income taxes on borrowed money.

U.S. district court judge Roger D. Foley, whose brother, Tom, had represented Binion in his own tax matters, dismissed the case against Lamb before defense lawyers called a single witness. "Many fringe benefits come to a public official which may be accepted along the honest discharge of duty," the judge reasoned. Spectators in the courtroom erupted in applause.

Upon his acquittal, Lamb had some harsh words for the federal government, and not solely because of the way he had been handled. He objected mightily to prosecutors' treatment of his pal Binion when the Cowboy wouldn't give them the testimony they wanted. "That was silly for them to imply Benny was a liar," Lamb said after walking victorious from the courtroom. "They know Benny and I have been friends for 30 years, very personal friends. His family, his kids, his grandkids. It is more than an ordinary friendship. I could go to him for anything."

And Binion could likewise go to Lamb, having paid hard cash for such favors. "Oh, yeah, always give ol' Ralph a little money," Binion later explained. "I done it for influence. They asked me what I did this for. I said so he'd do something for me if I needed it."

In such push and pull, he proved himself a master. Leo Kuykendall, the FBI agent who had enlisted Binion as a confidential informant, later became chief of the Las Vegas police. But he lost his job after a dispute with the mayor. Binion promptly hired him as a security manager at the Horseshoe.

Binion never lost the talent for making and keeping such friends, many of whom he did not have to pay off. Moe Dalitz was one. "Me and him puts on a party every December at the Las Vegas Country Club," Binion said in 1973. "And it's the best party they have around here, everybody says."

Meyer Lansky was another. Las Vegas publicist Dick Odessky was having lunch at the Horseshoe when Binion got a phone call at his table, picked up the receiver, and said, "Hello, Meyer. How you feeling? Won your election, I see." Lansky was calling after voter approval of casino gambling in Atlantic City. He offered Binion a chance for his own casino on the Boardwalk, but the opportunity was politely declined.

There were many others. "Colonel" Tom Parker, Elvis Presley's manager, often had dinner with Binion while in Vegas, then played roulette at the Horseshoe. Country star Merle Haggard would have his tour bus parked on Second Street, right outside the Horseshoe, and come inside for an evening or more of gambling. He became so close to the casino's patriarch that he named one of his sons Binion. The film director Sam Peckinpah gave Binion a special cut of the director's 1969 western, *The Wild Bunch,* for viewing at the Montana ranch. Visitors at the ranch included Steve Wynn, well into his emergence as one of the greatest hotel and casino builders in Vegas history, and Dalitz, who had assumed his own status as a Las Vegas benefactor and elder statesman. Wynn knew his way around a horse, while Dalitz looked like a lost retiree who had wandered onto a movie set.

Actor and cowboy Chill Wills, a companion from Binion's early Dallas days, made the Horseshoe a frequent stop. Wills's manager, Bob Hinkle, found himself at Binion's table one afternoon during the World Series of Poker. Binion turned to Hinkle and said, "You ought to do a movie on Titanic." He was referring to Titanic Thompson, the great gambler and golf hustler who had been the inspiration for Damon Runyon's character Sky Masterson in the musical *Guys and Dolls.* Pool player Minnesota Fats had called him "the greatest action man of all time." Beyond his gambling exploits, Thompson kept the excitement coming; he had married five times and killed five men.

Thompson himself walked into the Horseshoe about half an hour later, and joined Hinkle and Binion at the table. "Who owns the rights to your story?" Binion asked him.

"I do," Thompson said.

"What'll you take for those rights?"

"Twenty-five thousand dollars," Thompson said.

Binion went to the cashier's cage, got $25,000 in hundred-dollar bills, and gave the money to Thompson. Then he said to Hinkle, "Bob, you're gonna do this for me." But Hinkle never could get the movie produced, making it one of the few business enterprises of Binion's that didn't work.

The poker series was hitting its stride, and with that came new and wide exposure for the game of No Limit Texas Hold'em. Among the attractions of this variant of seven-card stud were big-money pots and—by poker standards anyway—watchability.

In Hold'em, each player receives two cards facedown. Bets are placed. Then three "community cards" are dealt faceup. This is known as the flop, after which a round of betting occurs. The next community card, known as the turn, is dealt, followed by another round of betting. The last card, "fifth street," or "the river," precedes more betting. From seven cards—two facedown, five faceup—each player makes a five-card hand.

With no limits, the big bettor—who may hold a promising hand or may be bluffing—can run many of the players out of the round before the last card is played.

Psychology, aggression, body language, and intuition assume as much importance as math and probability. "Limit poker is a science," player Crandell Addington has said. "But no-limit is an art. In limit you're shooting at a target. In no-limit the target comes alive and shoots back at you."

Poker lore has it that Hold'em originated in Texas, hence the name, although its provenance is impossible to prove. That didn't stop the Texas legislature from officially declaring that the game, which had "taken the world by storm," originated in the charming South Texas burg of Robstown. "Texas Hold'em takes a minute to learn and a lifetime to master," the legislature noted in its resolution, and—this being Texas—added some self-serving bluster. "A successful hold 'em player relies on reason, intuition and bravado, and these same qualities have served many notable Texans well throughout the proud history of the Lone Star State."

Amarillo Slim Preston wasn't born a Texan, but he played one to the hilt, with a rattlesnake band on his cowboy hat and a constant stream of High Plains wisecracks. He liked to say of various opponents, "They had as good a chance of beating me as getting a French kiss from the Statue of Liberty." And he described himself as "so skinny I look like the advance man for a famine." After winning the 1972 world series at the Horseshoe, Slim made the first of his eleven appearances on Johnny Carson's *Tonight Show*, a priceless run of publicity for the poker tourney. For years, rumors swirled that Binion had fixed the '72 series so that the telegenic and attention-seeking Slim could serve as his promotional front man.

Binion himself appeared on Merv Griffin's nationally broadcast TV talk show, and on Tom Snyder's late-night NBC show, a siren song to insomniacs. Snyder asked Binion why the hotels on the Strip had $500 betting limits, while he had none. "Well," Binion drawled, "they got great big hotels and little bitty bankrolls. I got a little bitty hotel and a great big bankroll." The show, Amarillo Slim said, was "an hour's commercial for the Horseshoe."

The poker tournament gave tired, tattered downtown Vegas new life in the form of a spectacle unmatched anywhere in the world. Out on the Strip, the resort operators turned to extravaganza and silliness to rope in tourists: the shiny new Circus Circus had trapeze artists flying above the casino floor. But at the Horseshoe—the funky, smelly old-school Horseshoe—Benny Binion had done nothing less than create a new dimension in the world of gambling.

It was drawing packs of spectators. They stood ten deep on the worn carpet and crowded the velvet ropes that separated them from the action by only a few feet. Many of them would stick around later to lose at the Horseshoe craps and blackjack tables. That, after all, was Binion's grand plan, to lure them inside and take their money. His bait—the kings of the poker, chasing fantastic pots—was irresistible: Slim, Brunson, Moss, and the rest, plying their once-secret trade for anyone to watch, almost close enough to touch. For the average Vegas visitor who might ordinarily venture no further than a game of penny-ante stud in the rumpus room, this tableau generated excitement and awe. And there was no more fitting place for it than a casino with its own ready-made aura of danger.

Benny Binion didn't know frisson from fried chicken, but he was selling it now.

Binion with his brilliant but deeply troubled son Ted.

# 23

# HEROIN AND THE HIT MAN

My other son, Ted, he's sorta like I am.

—BB

I f you wanted to mix with some of the heavy hitters of Las Vegas, you went to lunch at Binion's place. So on a sunny day in 1979, a recently crowned mob lawyer walked six blocks from his office on South Fourth Street, making his way to the Horseshoe. Oscar Goodman was a tall, slightly hunched, bearded man who wore a dark pin-striped suit, modish tinted glasses, and alligator-skin cowboy boots. Over the previous few years he had built a reputation as legal counsel to some of the stars of organized crime. Meyer Lansky had been a client. Tony the Ant was one too. The boots he wore were an expression of gratitude from Jimmy Chagra, a Texas drug dealer who had recently blessed Goodman with a million-dollar fee. On behalf of such defendants, Goodman treated prosecutors the way a mongoose treated cobras.

At Second Street, Goodman entered the Horseshoe's side door and stopped in at the club's newsstand, staying just long enough to scan the headlines on the local and out-of-town papers. From there he strode toward the sound of laughter coming from the Horseshoe's restaurant, where he found his friend Benny Binion at his customary booth, with a bowl of squirrel stew in front of him. The squirrel's black glassy eyes stared up at the man who was eating it.

Goodman took a chair and ordered a salad, as he was a man who watched his weight. He liked looking slim, or something close to it, in the numerous front-page photographs in which he appeared escorting notorious clients under indictment to and from courthouses. Around him now in the Horseshoe restaurant had gathered the regular collection of lawyers, politicians, police officers, and a state supreme court justice.

The food was cheap and filling, but this crowd wasn't here for the cuisine. This was where gossip was exchanged and business transacted, and where loyalties were forged.

Harry Claiborne sat next to Binion, as he did almost every day. Binion and Claiborne had remained the closest of friends since Binion hired him as his lawyer three decades before. Claiborne treated Binion's club as a combination frat house, dating service, and bank. He had married a Horseshoe waitress in 1978, divorced her after two months, then remarried her in 1979, which made her his fourth and fifth wife. He cashed his checks at the Horseshoe and kept a $100,000 stash in the casino's vault, withdrawing money whenever he needed it. He regarded the Horseshoe almost as a second home.

Claiborne was also a federal judge, having been appointed to the bench in 1978 after a recommendation by Binion's friend Senator Howard Cannon. As such, he reigned as one of the most powerful legal figures in the state.

Like Binion, Claiborne hailed from a rural backwater—he grew up on an Arkansas cotton farm—and rose to the upper reaches of his profession. Both men still wore the perpetual demeanor of sharp operators from the sticks. Both of them rode and owned horses. And both loved swapping stories. "It was like two great personalities got together," Jack Binion said. "They enjoyed each other's company so much."

At lunch, the U.S. district court judge and the former federal prisoner talked and guffawed, a couple of old cowboys telling tales. As Binion and Claiborne carried on, two men in suits watched from the casino floor—FBI agents. Binion had fallen away from his status as a confidential informant with a change in local bureau administration. Now he was back to being a bureau target. He and Claiborne had that in common too.

———

More than ever, running the Horseshoe had become a family affair. Binion and his wife had departed their Bonanza Road house—simply walked away, leaving behind furniture, keepsakes, and kitchenware, with clothes still hanging in closets. "Everything's in there like they'd gone on a trip, but they just never came back," Jack Binion said. The couple then moved into separate quarters at the Horseshoe. In part, this was because Binion spent great stretches of time in Montana, and he didn't like having Teddy Jane alone at the Bonanza spread. He also couldn't stand his wife's four-pack-a-day cigarette habit.

"She don't think they hurt you, but she's just hooked so damn bad that she doesn't want to fool with [quitting]," Binion said. He recalled one night in his Horseshoe room: "She had a little old dog. The door's closed between us there. She was in there working the books all night. She opened that door. That little old dog ran in there and he was sneezing and rubbing his nose on the carpet and raising hell. I said, 'Goddamn it, you're killing your goddamn dog.' That sonbitch about 10 days later died with a heart attack. Them cigarettes killed that little old dog." Perhaps the living arrangements also had something to do with the weariness of a long marriage between strong characters. Sometimes, in place of arguing, Benny and Teddy Jane would glare at each other and make rat-a-tat machine-gun noises.

Teddy Jane was a common, and arresting, sight on Fremont Street—a tiny, wiry woman with hair dyed bright red, walking her Chihuahua and her poodle, wearing high heels while puffing on a cigarette, shadowed by a stocky Horseshoe security guard. She still worked the cashier's cage, and for a while slept in an office above it, before moving into the hotel. The rooms were small, and Teddy Jane accumulated clutter. As she filled the space with her various possessions, she would simply move to the room next door. When she packed that one full, she would move again. Over the years, she filled up nine rooms.

Binion's habit of happily giving away money enraged his frugal wife; this included his comping of meals for Horseshoe customers. "He'd pick up this check, pick up that check," R. D. Matthews remembered. "Teddy Jane said, 'Every time he walks through the restaurant it cost us a hundred dollars.'" She found the actual presence of currency comforting. When she couldn't sleep at night, which was often, she would take the elevator down to the casino's counting room, grab a bag of silver dollars, and go through the coins one by one, sorting and stacking them by date.

The Binions' older son had inherited a lot of his mother's business savvy. Thin and bald, Jack Binion had the abstemious mien of a bookkeeper and the work ethic of a monk. "There ain't nobody works harder than Jack," his father said. "Long hour man." Over the years, Jack gradually assumed management of the Horseshoe with all the cool of a supremely talented executive.

The younger son, Ted Binion, often ran the night crew at the Horseshoe. Far more expansive than his brother, not to mention flashy, Ted boasted in the mid-1970s that his father's club made more than any downtown casino, and "Binion's Horseshoe has $15 million in the bank right now."

Ted appeared to have inherited the old man's freewheeling traits without the mitigating pragmatism. He often spent much of the night shift smoking dope, keeping watch on the casino floor from the Horseshoe's eye-in-the-ceiling vantage point. Rakish and engaging, he burned through money and good times. Ted wore his hair shaggy but dressed in cowboy clothes. He was highly intelligent yet completely undisciplined—a self-educated history buff and math whiz who also enjoyed gambling and strippers. "He was a cross between Larry Flynt and a bum," said his nephew, Benny Behnen. "He'd leave home with $30,000 in his pocket, but he'd be wearing ratty denim, and he cut his own hair. He wouldn't go home until the money was gone." Once, when a woman wouldn't sleep with Ted, he set fire to a succession of hundred-dollar bills to soothe his wounded ego. "Ted was brilliant. He had phenomenal insight into what life was about," Oscar Goodman said. "But he had demons."

Chief among them was an addiction to black tar heroin. Ted rolled the heroin into a ball, put it on aluminum foil, lit it, and inhaled the smoke. "I'd find these little foil bowls all over the place," a Horseshoe worker said. So it was no surprise to anyone that Ted Binion began to associate with Jimmy Chagra. Another émigré from Texas, Chagra had made his fortune by smuggling marijuana from Colombia on an oceangoing freighter, at which point he decamped for Vegas, where his heavy wagers on craps gained him instant fame. "In five minutes," a friend said, "he might bet a million dollars."

Such heavy-stakes gamblers naturally gravitated to the Horseshoe, and

Chagra's frequent presence at the Binions' place was hardly a secret, especially after he tipped a cocktail waitress $10,000 for bringing him a bottle of water. The "Gambling Gambit" column in the *Las Vegas Sun* reported in May 1979 that he had "created a sizable stir at the Horseshoe only about two weeks ago when he walked away with about $490,000 after an evening of craps and blackjack." A haul like that was unusual for Chagra. Usually he lost—and lost big—which made him a welcome customer at the Horseshoe. Federal agents suspected he had other reasons for visiting the casino. Benny and Ted Binion "allegedly assisted major drug trafficker Jimmy Chagra in laundering money through the Horseshoe," an FBI report said. "Additionally, investigation linked Ted Binion to Chagra's illegal narcotics network."

The Binions were not charged with drug smuggling. Chagra was indicted in 1979 by a federal grand jury in Midland, Texas, for conspiracy to import marijuana and cocaine. The judge presiding over his case was John Wood, known as Maximum John for his harsh treatment of traffickers. Chagra was in enough trouble without having a black-robed avenger staring down at him, itching to order hard time. He now faced the very real possibility that Wood would put him away for life without parole. When a reporter in Vegas asked Chagra to reckon his chances of acquittal, Chagra answered that with Wood presiding, about fifty-fifty. But without Wood, he said, "much, much better."

Chagra's odds improved when he met yet another Texan inside the Horseshoe. Charles Voyde Harrelson, the father of actor Woody Harrelson, had been a door-to-door encyclopedia salesman before finding bigger paydays as a coolheaded, cold-blooded killer for hire. One time, after receiving a fifteen-year sentence for murder, he responded, "That's not so bad." At the moment, he was between prison stretches. Harrelson and Chagra got to talking about the drug case and the tough ways of Judge Wood. One month later, the judge was dead, gunned down outside his San Antonio town house.

Chagra was ultimately charged with conspiracy in Wood's death. Enter Oscar Goodman, who destroyed the prosecution's case, much of which had been based on the testimony of a jailhouse snitch. Although Chagra was convicted of drug crimes, he was acquitted of murder. "Thank God for Oscar Goodman," he proclaimed as he walked from the courthouse.

Harrelson did not fare nearly so well. In a separate trial—he was not represented by Goodman—he was convicted of killing the judge and sentenced to life in prison.

A few weeks before Judge Wood's murder, Ted Binion had his own brush with a homicide case. Oscar Goodman was involved in that one too.

It started with a man named Rance Blevins, who had grown up in Kermit, Texas, where he had been a pretty good high school football player. After a stretch in the army, he drifted for a while—through Austin and finally to Las Vegas, where he found a job on a drilling rig at the Nevada Test Site. Eventually he bought a trailer and married, and he and his wife had two children. But the marriage fell apart. Blevins, now thirty-eight, began to stay out all night, an easy thing to do in Las Vegas.

One Monday in May 1979, a few minutes before 5:00 a.m., he found himself playing poker at the Horseshoe. After some losing hands, Blevins concluded that the dealer and another player were cheating him, and he started a loud argument. Horseshoe security guards hustled him from the place, but on his way out, Blevins managed a parting shot. He kicked a pane of plate glass, and it shattered. Then he committed what may have been his worst error. He ran.

Blevins made his escape down Fremont Street as at least three men—a Horseshoe guard, a pit boss named Walt Rozanski, and Ted Binion—pursued him. From his parked car, a Las Vegas taxi driver named John Koval watched the chase, telling himself, "Oh, they're going to fuck this guy up." It took about twenty seconds for him to be proved correct.

After one block, and at Third and Fremont, Blevins stumbled and fell. His pursuers surrounded him in the light of the flashing Horseshoe neon. One of the three men took a 9-mm handgun from the security guard's holster and pressed the barrel against the top of Blevins's skull.

"He just pulls a gun out," Koval recalled, "and shoots him in the head."

Without a pause, the guard, Rozanski, and Ted Binion turned and walked back into the casino, calmly leaving Blevins dead on the sidewalk for the crime of breaking glass.

Now it was time for the Vegas version of criminal justice to swing into action. As soon as the first uniformed police officers made the scene, Koval offered to provide a positive ID of the shooter. He had once been a police officer in New Jersey, so he had a pretty good idea of how these things worked. "Let's go in the casino and I'll point the guy out," he said. That's when one of the Vegas cops looked toward the Horseshoe, frowned, and shook his head. "We can't go in there," he said. "We're not allowed."

Others did make the effort, with predictable results. About an hour later, assistant district attorney Dan Bowman arrived at his downtown office to find police detectives waiting for him. They said their attempts to enter the Horseshoe for a search had been rebuffed by none other than Oscar Goodman. "He told the cops that he represented all employees of the Horseshoe, and he was not giving them permission to go in," Bowman recalled. It took Bowman about five hours to find a judge to sign a warrant. By that time, the gun that had been used to shoot Blevins had disappeared from the Horseshoe forever.

Investigators had no weapon to dust for prints. Nor did they conduct a timely test for the presence of gunpowder residue on the hands of any of the three men who had been surrounding Blevins when he was shot. Jerry Blevins, brother of the dead man, phoned a detective to ask why such a test had not been done. "He said, 'That's not something we normally do,'" Jerry Blevins remembered.

Koval, the cabbie, had no doubt that Walt Rozanski shot Blevins. Rozanski, the Horseshoe pit boss, was a twenty-four-year-old former linebacker for the University of Nevada, Las Vegas, varsity football team. He stood six foot three and weighed 225 pounds. "It was the big guy who did it," Koval said. But prosecutor Bowman had three eyewitnesses who would positively identify Ted Binion as the shooter. They were, in fact, unwavering in their identification of him.

Taking on one of the most powerful families in Las Vegas, Bowman prepared his case against Ted Binion—and then watched it collapse. "All three witnesses mysteriously changed their story," Bowman said. Now the three were saying that Rozanski had pulled the trigger. "I was just screwed," Bowman said. "There was no way I could prosecute that case and win."

With Goodman at his side, Rozanski told the court the gun had discharged accidentally. He pleaded guilty to manslaughter and received probation. He never served a day in prison for the death of Rance Blevins.

"And," Bowman said, "Ted Binion walked."

More than three decades later, it is no struggle to find people in Vegas—the ex-prosecutor among them—who believe Benny Binion fixed the case for his son. Bowman, now retired, relaxed on a stool in a Henderson, Nevada, bar and shook his head over the old riddle, still baffled. "I can't understand," he said, "how three witnesses would change their stories overnight." His best guess: bribes. "Benny Binion had a lot of juice, and a lot of money to spread around. He took care of his own problems . . . In my personal opinion, I think money changed hands."

One man who might be able to clear everything up—Rozanski—has stayed silent. Book publishers and movie producers have offered good money for his story, he said, but he has turned all of them away. From a distance of years, he recalled the shooting's aftermath obliquely. "I'm 58 years old now," he said in a note, "and I often look back with sadness, heartache and dismay over what happened, what was lost and how it was spun."

He endured hard times after the shooting, Rozanski said, but he put himself back together. He does not blame Binion for his difficulties. "To this day," he wrote, "I am proud to say I am grateful to have met and worked for Benny Binion! He was a great man!"

On an autumn afternoon thirty-three years later, sipping coffee in a near-deserted diner in Florida, Rozanski laughed ruefully at the notion that Binion bribed him to take the rap. "Everybody said I got paid," he said, "but I was sitting there living in poverty . . . I never got a penny." He would not, however, give his account of what happened on Fremont Street on that morning so long ago. Rozanski glanced outside, toward a busy street, and hinted darkly of unnamed forces and possible murderous revenge against himself and others.

"Each man's destiny has their side of the story. Some never tell it! Some don't get the chance," he wrote in a note. "Some just wait till the time is right and some don't tell because of who it would hurt! Believe it or not, Benny taught me that."

Promoting the World Series of Poker in 1976, Binion does *The Merv Griffin Show* with actor Jack Klu
man (far left) and poker player Jack Straus (far right). Ironically, Griffin is the one dressed like a mobs

# 24

# U-TURN AT THE
# GATES OF HEAVEN

Used to really live dangerously. And I was dangerous . . . Well, I
don't do that no more.

–BB

The early and mid-1980s brought Binion his greatest promi-
nence and moments of deepest pain and disappointment.

The poker world series was growing every year, but Jack
Binion sought more national and international exposure. He hired a Los
Angeles public relations specialist named Henri Bollinger, who spent a few
weeks hanging around the Horseshoe. Bollinger found colorful poker players, such as Perry Green, an Orthodox Jew and fur trader from Alaska, and
Mickey Appleman, a New Yorker with master's degrees in education, sta-
tistics, and business administration. John Jenkins III, a Texan known as
Austin Squatty for his cross-legged poker position, spent his non-gambling
hours as a distinguished historian and rare book dealer. None of them
quite fit Bollinger's plans.

Series entrant Stu Ungar had an irresistible story that could have been
publicity catnip for Bollinger. He was a scrawny waif and gin rummy
genius who had learned to gamble as a schoolboy in his father's bar on
New York's Lower East Side. By the time he hit Vegas, many considered
him the world's greatest poker player. As a public face, Ungar had his

drawbacks. He responded to reporters' questions with either a mumble or a snarl, refused to bathe regularly, and indulged a cocaine habit that later killed him.

Bollinger kept looking for a marketable star. After spending time with the tournament's top man, inspiration hit him. Bollinger told Jack Binion, "Benny Binion is your brand."

Under Bollinger's direction, the World Series of Poker began producing a steady stream of press releases that made the Cowboy the face of the event. Binion is "a folk hero," said one dispatch. "A throw-back to the Old West," proclaimed another. And: "He is a member of an elite group of men whose personal lives parallel the development of the American frontier." It was pure public relations mythologizing.

Before the 1981 series, Bollinger got a call from a British writer, Al Alvarez, who was proposing a piece for the *New Yorker*, which meant Bollinger had drawn the publicist's equivalent of a royal flush. Alvarez, a distinguished poet and critic, came to downtown Vegas for the first time and discovered an alien but perversely fascinating landscape. The grimy sidewalks of Fremont Street, he observed, were thick with "the humped, the bent, the skeleton thin, and the obese, cashing in their Social Security checks, disability allowances, and pensions, waiting out their time in the hope of a miracle jackpot to transform their last pinched days." For them, "Glitter Gulch is the absurd last stop on the slow train to the grave." Yet inside the Horseshoe—"shabby, ill-lit and crowded at all hours"—Alvarez found the mecca of single-minded, hard-core gambling. He came away enchanted.

Alvarez titled his account "Welcome to Dreamland," and in it he depicted Binion as a peaceful lion-in-winter. "Benny Binion is now seventy-seven years old," he wrote, "a genial, round-faced, round-bellied man, like a beardless Santa Claus in a Stetson, benign and smiling." He waved at Binion's bloody past, but left it there. "Tough times may make tough people," he observed, "but age, reputation and great wealth turn tough people into lovable old characters."

The *New Yorker* piece, later published in book form as *The Biggest Game in Town*, vaulted Binion and his poker series into the ranks of the lower highbrow. Before long, *Harper's* magazine, *Le Monde*, and the *Times* of London would send their erudite essayists to the Horseshoe too.

Such attention solidified Binion's role as one of the Horseshoe's—if not Las Vegas's—leading attractions. This phenomenon had begun some years before, thanks to the criminal headlines and Binion's television appearances. Binion's friend R. D. Matthews dealt with it as the Horseshoe's casino manager. "I didn't have a floor show I could comp people to," Matthews said. "So people would just want to come back to see Benny. Someone would say, 'I want to see Mr. Binion. He's one of my closest friends.' I'd tell Benny who it was, and he'd say, 'I never heard of that person in my life.'" But Binion would meet with these customers anyway, and treat them like boon companions. He would put on his cowboy hat, and maybe his buffalo hide coat, and pose for round after round of pictures. If they were from Texas, plenty of talk about home would ensue. "He knew how to treat people," Matthews said.

Yet it was more than that. Binion was the approachable racketeer, the affable killer, the conversational kingpin. For certain tourists and other gawkers, this was like Disney's Pirates of the Caribbean ride. Only in this case, the pirate—however genial—was real.

Joseph Yablonsky had dropped into this strange place in 1980. FBI director William Webster—J. Edgar Hoover, Binion's nemesis, was long gone—personally asked Yablonsky to take charge of the bureau's Vegas office. Yablonsky was a tall New Jersey guy who wore aviator glasses and smoked big cigars, and who had a gift for bluntness. He described one New York City criminal encounter this way: "Five Puerto Ricans sideswiped me. I chased them up the East River Drive to the Bronx. They got out of the car, and one of them came at me with a rum bottle. I shot him right through the dick."

Yablonsky's talent for, and success at, FBI undercover bait operations had gained him the nickname the King of Sting. Now the bureau was depositing him in a city that could be considered one of the worst assignments it could offer—or the best, depending on the point of view. Previous federal agents in Las Vegas received free meals and show tickets from casinos, and could count on landing well-paying security jobs at the resorts when they retired from the FBI. As always, the town had its own ways of coopting, corrupting, and conniving. "I thought I knew it all," Yablonsky said, "until I got there."

Never short of provocative quips, Yablonsky proclaimed that he had come to "plant the American flag" in Las Vegas. "We were working to turn it into a normal America." To Yablonsky, Vegas featured more than a few odd circumstances and pairings. One of the oddest was Judge Harry Claiborne's friendship, and frequent lunches, with Binion. "What would a man learned in legal terms have in common with an illiterate such as Binion?" Yablonsky wondered. After some study, he found what he believed to be the answer: corruption. "Binion," he said, "would be the guy to go to if you wanted to put a fix in."

He instructed his agents to reinvestigate the 1972 bombing death of William Coulthard, because he had no doubt that Binion bought it. "Oh, absolutely. There's no question in my mind that Binion was behind that," Yablonsky said years afterward. "He [Coulthard] wanted more money, and with Binion that would be enough." The FBI nibbled around it for years, but never mounted a prosecutable case. "We just never could put it together," Yablonsky said. Agents also looked into the shooting of Rance Blevins, hoping to find evidence of bribes and Ted Binion's complicity, but came away empty there too.

Yablonsky had better luck with Claiborne, whom he accused of soliciting protection payments from a Reno-area brothel owner. Binion leaped to his best friend's defense, in a Benny-like way: "Since I've known him, I don't know of anything he's done that was a violation of anyone's law—other than maybe getting drunk. While he was under the whiskey, he may have said a thing or two he regretted. The point is, as a lawyer and a judge, he is absolutely honest. I don't know a more honorable man."

As Binion unwittingly hinted, Claiborne didn't project the ideal image of a federal judge, at least as citizens outside Nevada understood the position. In addition to his near-constant presence at the Horseshoe, Claiborne had, as a *Las Vegas Review-Journal* columnist noted, "a taste for strong whiskey, frisky women and trim horses." The *Valley Times* of Las Vegas struck a similar chord. "Claiborne doesn't happen to look very judicial," the paper said in an editorial. That understated the matter: with narrow eyes and a flicking tongue, Claiborne could have been dipped in snake oil. "Indeed," the editorial continued, "a Hollywood director would be more likely to make him a two-bit hood in a 1938 Jimmy Cagney crime movie than a distinguished jurist."

Many Las Vegans regarded such characteristics as typical if not admirable, and they viewed Yablonsky as an overzealous, overreaching outsider pursuing a local—and misunderstood—hero. Claiborne "socializes with women who happen to be attractive," Oscar Goodman said. "And that, in Yablonsky's perception, is part of a federal crime." The same *Valley Times* editorial that described Claiborne's gangsterish deportment also declared him to be innocent of any wrongdoing because he said so—no further evidence required. "The feds . . . should simply ask Claiborne the facts," the editorial reasoned. "He'd tell them the truth, and that should be that." The *Las Vegas Sun,* published by Binion loyalist Hank Greenspun, beat this drum relentlessly. The paper's strategy consisted not so much of defending Claiborne as attacking Yablonsky. "The Nevada FBI chief came to Las Vegas with a preconceived notion that everyone in Nevada is evil," Greenspun wrote. He later added, "We're inviting . . . Yablonsky to sue us, because we charge him with an arrogant abuse of power and criminal misconduct."

The FBI's investigation of Claiborne dragged on for years, with multiple fits and starts, but finally resulted in the judge's conviction on tax evasion charges and a sentence of two years in prison. Though Yablonsky regarded taking down Claiborne as a career capstone, it made him a pariah in influential Vegas circles. He had hoped to stay in the region after he left the FBI—perhaps picking up a lucrative consulting job at one of the casinos—but soon abandoned those plans. "He was run out of town," Oscar Goodman said decades later with a smile.

The thought of his Vegas repudiation still causes Yablonsky to gaze at the wall in bewilderment. "In most cities, if you were nailing crooked politicians, you'd become a hero," Yablonsky said almost thirty years later from the comfort of his Florida home. "In that place you were messing things up for them."

Binion had escaped another attempt by the feds to hammer him, but now he faced bigger concerns. His younger son's heroin addiction and erratic actions had become hard to ignore. It wasn't just that Ted liked to cruise Vegas in a limo, firing a .45 at the sky from the moonroof. The FBI suspected that he was part of a drug-smuggling ring operating from Bermuda through Florida to Las Vegas. "Teddy Binion is believed to be one of the main suppliers of cocaine in the Southern Nevada area, and is also a heavy cocaine user," an agent wrote. Another agent said, "[Ted] Binion uses the casino cage at the Horseshoe Hotel and Casino to launder the drug money." Though no charges were filed, it was clear to his father that Ted had fallen deep into troublesome associations and bad behavior. "Ted broke Daddy's heart," daughter Brenda said.

Binion had already been through a wrenching ordeal with his oldest daughter, Barbara. Although she had abandoned her early plans for an armed-robbery ring, she—like brother Ted—had her demons. "Used dope," her father said.

Barbara had struggled for years with deep emotional problems, and with a heroin addiction of her own. She had been married and divorced three times. "She had a lot of Benny's young blood in her," a friend of Binion's said. At one point she tried to commit suicide with a shotgun. She put the barrel in her mouth and shot off part of her cheek and jaw, but lived. "They did all sorts of reconstructive surgery, but it was still a horrible mess," said a family acquaintance. As a result of the wound she couldn't see well and was in near-constant pain. She spent much of her time in bed, and a lot of the rest with the wrong crowd.

Binion responded to his daughter's addiction by threatening to declare a bounty on Las Vegas drug dealers. Ted Binion may have made it more than a threat. An FBI memo said Ted ordered the ejection of one of Barbara's boyfriends from the Horseshoe because he thought the man had supplied his sister with drugs. "I'm going to waste that fucker," Ted was reported to have boasted. The next day, the FBI said, "the boyfriend was found dead in the desert with half his head blown off."

In the summer of 1983, with Binion in Montana, other family members planned a trip to Disneyland. "Well, they come down here to meet," Binion said, referring to the Horseshoe, "and Barbara come down here and she's kind of lit up." The others left for California, and Barbara stayed behind. That night, she was seen at the Horseshoe about four in the morning, talking to a friend. Then she went to her modest Las Vegas house, less than two miles from the casino. She was found there hours later, dead of an overdose.

Family members refused to believe Barbara had committed suicide. She only wanted to dull her facial pain, they said, and had swallowed too much codeine. "She got it accidentally, I'm sure," Binion said. He took some solace in one of her final acts. Days before she died, Barbara had asked her father for money, and vowed to go straight. "I said, 'All right,' and I give her $5,000," Binion said. "Now what I feel good about, she got on this jag, but she still had $4,800" when she died. "She didn't piss it off. Her intentions were still good. She might have spent some of that $200, but she still was just shooting around a little. She wasn't really getting down at it like they do."

Among those comforting Binion in the days after Barbara's death was Doyle Brunson, whose own daughter, Doyla, eighteen, had died the year before of heart problems aggravated by bulimia. Brunson said Binion, though deep in grief, maintained a stoic front in public. "He took all the phone calls from people giving him condolences," Brunson said. "He handled it very well. But that was his first-born. So it was very tough."

While Binion mourned with public poise, Barbara's mother remained bereft. "By God, she can't get over it," Binion said of Teddy Jane. "She thinks she's the cause." In the aftermath, daughter Brenda said, Teddy Jane "spent months walking around with Barbara's baby pictures, crying."

Through it all, Binion seemed to be a one-man tourism engine. Most of his fellow rackets kings who had pioneered Vegas decades before were long gone now. But he kept at it—promoting the town and writing big checks. In 1984, he helped pay for the National Finals Rodeo to move from Oklahoma City to Vegas. This would bring tens of thousands of visitors to town every December, which had always been the slowest month for casinos, when resorts would paint the rooms and replace the carpet.

His philanthropic efforts were generous and broad, with big donations for a number of Las Vegas hospitals and private schools. Little League teams got money too. When Binion learned of the plight of Clifford Henry Bowen, a Texas bank robber turned poker player who had been framed for murder in Oklahoma, he helped pay Bowen's substantial legal fees. Bowen was freed on appeal, and took up semipermanent residence at the Horseshoe.

Binion seemed to be riding a crest of wild commercial success, effusive publicity, and general public acclaim. Then he almost died.

He was at least twenty pounds overweight, having long favored a diet that ranged from fatty to fried. He had smoked much of his life. All of it was catching up with him in the form of congestive heart failure. Twice in 1984, while he was hospitalized, his heart stopped, and he was revived with a defibrillator. A new heart drug called amiodarone worked well, and helped get him up and out of the hospital bed.

The health problems slowed Binion down some, but softened him not much at all. Although a nurse now accompanied him when he traveled, he still kept a .22 handgun in his pocket. As was his custom, the hammer of the pistol had been filed down so it wouldn't catch on the fabric if he had to draw in a hurry, because no one knew when an eighty-year-old man with a nurse at his side might encounter a gunfight. "He said that [a .22] is the best gun for shooting someone," friend Bob Hinkle remembered. "He said, 'That'll tear somebody up.'"

A few years after the near-death episodes, Binion told a Las Vegas journalist that during one of his heart failures he had briefly encountered Jesus. "He had long hair, like you see in the pictures, and I don't believe he was a very old man," he said. "You have to remember, I wasn't there long enough to see much. You die longer than a second, you stay." Jesus said only one thing to him, Binion recalled. He said, "Benny?" Binion didn't say if this indicated that the Savior was uncertain of his identity or just surprised to see him.

The interviewer allowed that Binion might meet Jesus again. "From what I've been told," Binion said, "I'm supposed to go the other way." Not if you repent, the writer said. "That's the problem," Binion said. "There's some of it I can't repent. I've tried, and I just can't."

Maybe he couldn't obtain divine forgiveness, but governmental absolution in the form of a presidential pardon remained possible. He had already been turned down four times, including twice by Jimmy Carter, in 1978 and 1980. That second chance with Carter had been looking good until Binion popped off about a Mafia stool pigeon named Jimmy "the Weasel" Fratianno. In court testimony, and later in a best-selling tell-all book, *The Last Mafioso*, Fratianno said that Russian Louie Strauss, Binion's former bodyguard, had tried to blackmail Binion. Fratianno claimed he helped strangle Strauss, and Binion paid him $60,000.

"Which is bullshit," Binion said. He was outraged at the allegation—not that he was accused of ordering the killing of Strauss, but that he had hired a sniveling rat like Fratianno to do it. "Now some reporter called me," Binion said, "and he was putting it on me pretty strong, and I said, 'Listen go back and tell them FBIs I'm still able to do my own damn killings.'" This might have been industry-standard bravado in Vegas, but it attracted immediate, and unfavorable, notice in Washington. "Goddamn, I made a mistake," Binion said. "It did set 'em off." Soon afterward, he claimed, the Carter administration used his statement "as an excuse for not giving me no pardon."

It wasn't only the old man who had been indiscreet. Yablonsky, the former FBI special agent, remembered having lunch with a couple of colleagues at the Horseshoe shortly after Fratianno's book was published. "Ted [Binion] came running up to the table and said, 'That book is a piece of shit,'" Yablonsky recalled. "He said, 'My father never gave a contract to kill that son of a bitch. If he'd wanted him killed, he would have done it himself.'"

But that was a different time. Now, with Ronald Reagan in the White House, Binion's hope for a pardon sprang anew. "When ol' Reagan went in there," he said, "I just thought he was going to do wonders." In 1984, with help from his friends, he launched one more campaign. "I want to be free. I want my rights restored," Binion wrote in a pardon application. "It has been almost 40 years since I under reported my income and I have been law abiding since." Covering his bets as usual, he also made a campaign contribution to the president. "I knew my pardon was coming through there and would be on his desk. I sent him $15,000," Binion said. "Don't look like to me he'd take my money and turn it down now, does it?"

His effort drew support from some of the most powerful people in Nevada. "He is a man of his word," John Code Mowbray, a justice in the state supreme court, said in a letter to the U.S. Justice Department. "He has integrity. He is a loyal American." Harry Reid, a congressman from Nevada destined to become Senate majority leader, wrote to say that Binion deserved a pardon because, in part, he had donated to the Las Vegas public TV station so his granddaughter could watch *Sesame Street*. Binion "is a tradition in this state," Reid said. U.S. senator Paul Laxalt, a close friend and adviser of Reagan's, told the pardon office it should grant one last wish to a deserving—and dying—man. "During his many years of poor health, which at times has put him at death's door, he has maintained a strong wish to be pardoned," Laxalt wrote. "He has the support of many respected Nevadans."

The pleas on Binion's behalf did not come solely from well-funded brokers of influence. A thirteen-year-old boy sent the president a handwritten letter in which he recounted his visit to the Horseshoe. "Mr. Binion was very nice and showed us his coin collection and his hotel," the boy said. "He is a real nice man." A fourteen-year-old boy who had been present on the same visit had this to add about Binion in his own letter to Reagan: "You would like him if you met him."

It was up to the Justice Department's pardon office to make a recommendation to the president, and such deliberations on these matters were kept confidential. But the department's thinking was made plain in a 1985 memo from an assistant attorney general to the chief pardon attorney. "The Criminal Division last expressed its opposition to Mr. Binion's pardon in 1978," the assistant AG wrote. "Since then, all information which has come to the attention of this Division and to the public concerning Mr. Binion has been of a negative nature."

The memo went on to warn that Binion's Las Vegas operations offered all manner of reasons for concern. The Horseshoe "has figured prominently in recent prosecutions and investigations of . . . Judge Harry Claiborne and others as a repository and cleansing facility for illegal or unreported funds," it said. "Current investigations will almost certainly result in additional public disclosures of this nature, making Mr. Binion an inappropriate subject for executive clemency." It probably didn't help Binion's case that Reagan's pal Laxalt had been accused in 1983 of having connections to a Nevada casino from which great portions of skim allegedly went to organized crime. No one in the administration wanted that dredged up again.

In the spring of 1986, Reagan denied Binion's application. Back in Vegas, Binion received the word from a newspaper reporter. "I said, 'Well, I swear, I hate that,'" he recalled. He began to tell friends that the refusal had given him a new reason to live. "I'm going to outlive that sumbitch," he said of Reagan, "and piss on his grave."

It was a pretty good laugh line, and he repeated it often. But the pardon refusal had deeply disappointed Binion. He had exhausted his last chance, and he would die a convicted felon. He explained it in familiar terms. "Everything to me is like you throwed three. When you throw three on the dice, you've lost your money and you've crapped out. Anytime anything happens, I just say the dice throwed three. Crapped out."

A roundup at Binion's Montana ranch with, from left to right, casino mogul Steve Wynn, Ted Binion, Benny, Moe Dalitz, and Dalitz's driver.

# 25

# "THEY DO THINGS LIKE THAT"

Fear will not keep 'em from stealing. I've caught 'em, seen 'em, have 'em lay down on the floor, say, "Kill me! I'm a dog. I'm no good." Damn near killed some of 'em, too.

—BB

eople journeyed to Las Vegas to have fun and win money, and sometimes these seekers of pleasure and cash became overexuberant, or turned larcenous. If a customer caused an extraordinary disturbance, or if a gambler was caught cheating, casino security routinely called the cops. Several times a week, on average, managers filed criminal paperwork with the Clark County district attorney's office, seeking prosecution of customers who cheated or stole. The Binions almost never lodged such complaints. That's because the Horseshoe took care of its own problems. This approach made perfect sense if one were operating, say, an illicit dice room in Depression-era Texas, but perhaps less so for a legal enterprise in a tourist town. Yet such was Binion's legacy.

Even after Rance Blevins was shot in the head for kicking in some glass, Horseshoe managers—the children and grandchildren of Binion, along with their functionaries—showed little tolerance for what they defined as misbehavior. That hardness extended to the ragged and the homeless, especially those who were black. Security men, who carried handguns and billy clubs, swept them from the casino and hustled them to the back alley—the same alley where Binion had given away hamburgers to poor kids—and made sure they knew never to return. Sometimes the guards knocked them around first. A Horseshoe waitress said she watched as security handcuffed a black man, used his head as a battering ram to open the back door, and threw him outside. In 1983, one woman had the audacity to enter the Horseshoe coffee shop as the white half of a biracial couple. A guard cuffed her, called her a "fucking nigger-lover," kneed her in the tailbone, and tossed her into the street, where a cab nearly hit her. On other occasions, if the guards were in a gentler mood, they might simply escort the reject outside, hose him down, and steal his shoes. For some, this served only to humiliate. On a winter's night, though, for a street dweller with only one suit of clothes and a single pair of shoes, it constituted brutal if not deadly treatment.

Those were mere preliminaries. The real punishment was reserved for those who tried to steal money from the casino. "You didn't cheat at the Horseshoe," Oscar Goodman said.

On occasion, the Binions made deals with known scammers—those who slid shims into slot machines, for example, or counted cards at the blackjack tables. Pull your schemes at other casinos, they were told, and you're still welcome here. But, they were warned, don't try any of these stunts at the Horseshoe. Those cheaters who were caught paid dearly, the Horseshoe way. "They run their house," one prosecutor said, "like it's the Wild West."

Binion didn't bother denying it. In fact, he bragged about it. "The most contemptible-looking human beings I've ever seen," he said. "Well, we used to just beat the goddamn shit out of them." He claimed he was talking about handbag thieves. "One day . . . they's whipping a guy back in there," he said. "[An] old woman come through there, and she heard 'em a-whipping him and a-hollering and taking on and said, 'What are they doing to that man?' The guy said, 'That man stole a lady's purse.' She said, 'Kill that son of a bitch.'"

Either the Horseshoe endured a continuing epidemic of purse snatchers, or—as usual—Binion was shading the facts. In a 1985 interview with the *Wall Street Journal,* he cast the Horseshoe's tactics as part of a long-running comic bit. As the *Journal* described the plight of one gambler:

> The customer had suffered an unlucky streak at the craps tables on money he had borrowed from the casino. The trouble began when he brazenly informed a pit boss that he wasn't paying it back. Benny Binion, the casino's crusty, plain-speaking founder, walked over and questioned the man. "He tells me he ain't got no money," Mr. Binion remembers. "I says, 'Well, then you don't need them damn clothes.'" Out went the naked customer, who quickly managed to don new attire and return with enough money to retrieve his confiscated clothes.

While the story recounted that situation with a certain wry detachment, in truth suspected cheaters were beaten by the dozens under Binion's reign. The lucky ones left the Horseshoe with a couple of broken fingers. Others departed with fractured arms. A Horseshoe bartender said the incidents were so common he didn't even notice them anymore. One guard admitted to an investigator that over the course of about ten years roughly a hundred patrons were beaten by security.

Even if a battered gambler called police, officers often didn't respond. Police ate for free at the Horseshoe. Some even lived there. When narcotics officers needed a wad of bills to flash for a drug buy, the Binions provided it from their cashier's cage. That might explain the treatment of an Arkansas man who in 1983 was pummeled and robbed by Horseshoe security. They apparently believed he had rigged a slot machine. After his punishment, he phoned the Las Vegas police and spoke to an officer, who said, "This is happening quite often down there." The victim could file a complaint, police advised, but unless he had witnesses, nothing would come of it.

The man, a used-furniture dealer, said he then called the Horseshoe and talked to Ted Binion. "Look, I'm going to tell you how it is, brother," Ted warned him. "You've got three choices. You can die and be buried in the desert, spend the rest of your life in an insane asylum or you can forget about it and be happy." He added an advisory: "Quit bothering me. I know where you're at."

Speaking later to a private investigator, the Arkansan said he had decided to drop the matter. "I ain't gonna be wanting to die," he said. "I know they do things like that."

So it went for years. Those who bothered to complain were bought off, frightened away, or simply ignored. But once in a while the Horseshoe would go too far—security guards might stomp the wrong person, or progress from serious punishment to savage. Then the authorities would be forced to act. And they would learn all over again that Benny Binion, though ailing and old, still had the juice.

About 10:00 a.m. on November 22, 1985, two friends, Barry Finn and Allan Brown, had a blackjack game going at a table in the Horseshoe. Brown was an engineer from California. Finn, a thirty-one-year-old airplane pilot, lived in the Las Vegas area. It had been a decent morning for them, as they were up a few thousand bucks. What they didn't know was that Horseshoe security had been watching them the entire time, and believed the pair were cheating.

Managers had been on high alert at the Horseshoe, because word had leaked that it was a casino where blackjack players could use a scheme known as hole carding. It worked this way: After each player has been dealt two cards, the dealer checks his facedown card to see if his is blackjack, or 21. Sometimes the less-than-rigorous dealer might expose this hole card to the player to his left. When that player sees the dealer's card, he signals its value to his partner, who adjusts his play accordingly.

Many gamblers found Binion's place to be fertile ground for this tactic. "For some time now," noted a gaming newsletter, "graveyard shift at the Horseshoe has had a reputation as being the best place in town to find sloppy dealers." Such a scheme was not illegal, or even considered actual cheating—the Nevada Supreme Court so ruled in 1984—but those who were caught generally faced expulsion from casinos. The Horseshoe's unofficial policy exceeded this standard.

After their dealer went on break, Finn and Brown picked up their chips and left the table. Plainclothes guards flanked them both and said, "Come with us." Finn resisted, and the guards dragged him from the casino. "Big, beefy guys," recalled Finn, who then weighed about 130 pounds.

As Finn later recounted it to a grand jury, the guards took him and Brown out the back door of the Horseshoe to a small building in the parking garage—the security office. Four or five guards pushed the two gamblers into a ten-by-ten windowless room with cinder-block walls. One of the guards was Steve Fechser, Binion's grandson, who, at thirty, bore a striking resemblance to his grandfather at the same age. There was a desk in the room, along with a couple of chairs and file cabinets, and in one corner stood a wastebasket full of walking canes left behind by Horseshoe gamblers, the lost-and-found for the halt and lame. Someone slammed the steel door shut. That, Finn said, is when Fechser ordered, "Beat the hell out of them."

A guard grabbed one of the canes, raised it, and began to strike Brown. Other guards used their fists and boots on both men. "They beat the crap out of us," Finn remembered. "At least two of them were wearing cowboy boots. They kicked us with the points of the boots and stomped on us with the heels."

Finn saw one of the guards pull a handgun. Then, Finn recalled, Fechser said, "Why are we wasting our time with these two? Let's just take them out to the desert and kill them." Fechser told one of the men to back the casino van up to the back door and added, "Don't forget the shovels."

The punches and kicks kept coming. "I thought they were going to kill us," Finn said. One of the men grabbed Finn and slammed his head into the wall. Finally it stopped, the guards gasping for breath, and Finn and Brown curled on the floor, bleeding and moaning. Fechser said, "I don't think they've had enough." And it started again. When at last it was over, Finn said, they opened the door and told the two gamblers, "Get out and never come back."

A friend met the two next door at the Mint and called an ambulance. Finn spent nine hours in the emergency room at a Vegas hospital, where he learned that he had several broken ribs and a concussion. Brown suffered even more, with nine broken ribs and a lacerated spleen. He spent five days recovering at Sunrise Hospital. Without medical treatment, a doctor said later, he would have died.

These beatings of Finn and Brown were so severe, so outrageous, and generated such headlines that authorities realized they might have to do something, which created its own dilemma. A police detective tried to take Finn and Brown on a "walk-through line-up" at the Horseshoe, but another set of security guards ordered all of them to leave, which they did. Ned Day, a columnist for the *Review-Journal,* surveyed this legal scene: "The prickly hair is up on the back of the Binion clan's collective neck," he wrote. "And when it turns up, the affable, unfailingly courteous Binions become a group that no sane man in Las Vegas wants to cross. They can turn deadly serious faster than a startled West Texas rattlesnake."

District Attorney Bob Miller, in whose lap this case had now landed, was one such sane man, as well as an ambitious one who envisioned a political future grander than the unceremonious office he now held. A run for lieutenant governor loomed on the immediate horizon. Beyond that, Miller—the son of a gambler with mob connections—harbored plans to be governor. To accomplish that, he had assembled a long list of campaign contributors, including the Binions, who had given him $30,000.

When an investigator wanted a search warrant for the Horseshoe— seeking security camera tapes and guard work schedules—Miller balked. "He said, 'We do not execute search warrants at hotels,'" a prosecutor recalled. No one in the DA's office had heard of such a policy before. Miller suggested that someone call the Horseshoe instead, and kindly ask that management voluntarily surrender any evidence as a matter of civic duty. To no one's surprise, the Binions refused this request.

Some days later, a warrant was secured and a detective was able to enter the Horseshoe. The surveillance videotape for the date of the beating, November 22, had vanished, although the tapes for November 21 and November 23 somehow remained. A Horseshoe employee said she last saw the missing tape when she gave it to Fechser. The cane used to beat Brown had been spirited from the premises and destroyed by another guard.

Even with missing evidence, the case appeared stout enough that it could not be dropped. Miller then declared a conflict of interest: The family of the wife of one of his deputies leased property to the Binions. Therefore, the DA argued, his office could be disqualified from prosecuting the case, and a judge agreed. "Ingenious," columnist Day observed of the tactic. "The Binions are a very wealthy and powerful family. They've been in town for a long time. They're active politically. They have clout. Bob Miller, on the other hand, is a young man with high political ambitions . . . Well, he won't have to take any heat now."

The state attorney general's office took over the prosecution in his stead. Three Horseshoe employees, including Fechser, were indicted for kidnapping, battery, and robbery. (The robbery charges had been lodged because the guards were accused of seizing, and not returning, Finn's and Brown's initial stakes and their winnings.) The case went to trial in state district court in Las Vegas before Judge Tom Foley, and that's where the dark farce really began.

This was the same Tom Foley who, as a private attorney, had represented Binion in his tax case—for a fee of $200,000, according to the FBI—and whose brother had dismissed the tax charges against Sheriff Ralph Lamb. Tom Foley had also represented Barbara Binion Fechser when she was arrested as part of her armed-robbery cabal. Now he had Barbara's son before him as a criminal defendant, and he seemed disposed early on to mercy. "He fixed it in his mind that the two victims were the bad guys," said the prosecutor, assistant attorney general John Redlein. "Tom Foley did not want the Binion family put through this . . . He would have known Benny Binion for 40 years at that point and thought he was a jolly good guy."

From the first, Redlein said, Foley expressed doubt that the defendants had committed a serious crime. "He came right out and said early on in the trial that they had all been overcharged . . . He tried to strong-arm me into reducing it to something not as serious, to a misdemeanor." Redlein would not do that, and the case proceeded.

Oscar Goodman represented Fechser, of course. Also sitting at the defense table was Harry Claiborne, still Binion's closest pal. The former federal judge had served his sentence for tax evasion, doing time in an Alabama prison. He had also been impeached by the U.S. Senate, the first sitting federal judge to be removed from the bench in fifty years. As a result, the Nevada Bar asked the state supreme court to suspend Claiborne's law license. The court refused. Ex-con Claiborne, attorney-at-law, was back in business. He represented the third guard, Emory Cofield, and this trial was his first after five months in a North Las Vegas halfway house. The judge issued a hearty welcome. "Isn't it wonderful," Foley said from the bench, "that Harry Claiborne is back in the courtroom?" Jack Binion also had a seat at the defense table, and Foley took the time to praise him as a good friend and a man of fine character.

Despite such remarks, and the legal talent arrayed against him, Redlein believed he had a good chance to win. For one thing, the victims would be able to make solid identifications of the men who beat them. But when Finn and Brown took the stand, their certitude wavered. Fechser "looked like" one of the men who had punched and kicked them, Finn testified. Brown could do no more than say he believed Fechser was among those who had assaulted him.

Finn later explained: "The day before the trial started we got a warning, from a friend of a friend. We were told it would be in our best interest not to positively identify the people involved." Thus their haziness under oath. "We gave them what they wanted," Finn said. "We thought they would kill us."

The trial took three weeks. The jury apparently overlooked Foley's statements and the star witnesses' spotty memories, and found two of the Horseshoe's men—Steven Dale Witten and Fechser—guilty of robbery, battery, and conspiracy. Cofield was acquitted. Finally, it seemed, the Binions would have to pay for the way they operated. The two defendants now faced as much as thirty years in prison.

But Judge Foley had not finished. Several weeks after the jury's findings, he announced that he believed law enforcement officials—including Redlein—had acted improperly. "The trial atmosphere was so tainted" that it prejudiced the jury, Foley angrily and loudly declared from the bench. "I am disappointed and hurt deeply by the conduct of some counsel in the case." With that, the judge overturned the jury's verdict and ordered a new trial. Said Finn, "I didn't even know he could do that."

He could, though this seemed to push the bounds of suitable judicial behavior. "The good-old-boy network in Las Vegas told me there was no way they let the convictions stand, so I wasn't surprised," Nevada attorney general Brian McKay said. Letter writers to the *Review-Journal* expressed outrage. "After Judge Foley's decision," one said, "I walked by his courtroom and smelled the most awful odor." Wrote another, "With his decision in the Horseshoe Casino trial it appears that Judge Thomas Foley has covered his markers with the Binion family." And Jackie Jackson, a trial juror who had voted to convict the pair, wrote, "I am not proud of what our court system let happen with the Binion trial."

Yet all was not lost for the prosecution. With the attorney general's backing, Redlein planned to appeal Foley's judgment to the state supreme court, and he reasoned he had solid grounds. To file his appeal, however, he required the official transcript of the trial. But the court reporter had taken her tape—the mechanically produced shorthand record of the proceedings—and moved to Utah. She had not produced a transcript, she said, because she had been ill. Months went by, and still no transcript. Finally, "after years of waiting for her," Redlein said, he arranged with the state court reporters board to have someone else do the transcription. That's when the original court reporter told him the tape had been lost.

Redlein suspected the defendants might have played a nefarious role in the loss of the tape. "The Binions wouldn't have been beyond saying, 'It would be helpful to us if this transcript is not made.'" He had no proof of this, but it made perfect sense to a prosecutor who believed he had been swindled out of a verdict by the Binions' cash and sway.

Finn and Brown did not walk away empty-handed; they filed suit against the Horseshoe and settled the case for $675,000, though much of that went for medical and legal bills. Fechser found work with another Vegas casino where, Binion said, the owner "just whips the shit out him" if he is seen drinking. This, Binion said, improved his behavior.

One man did emerge wholly triumphant. That was Bob Miller, the district attorney and Binion beneficiary who was reluctant to pursue the case against the Horseshoe. As predicted, Miller did indeed seek and win higher office. He was elected lieutenant governor the next year, then went on to serve for ten years as governor of Nevada.

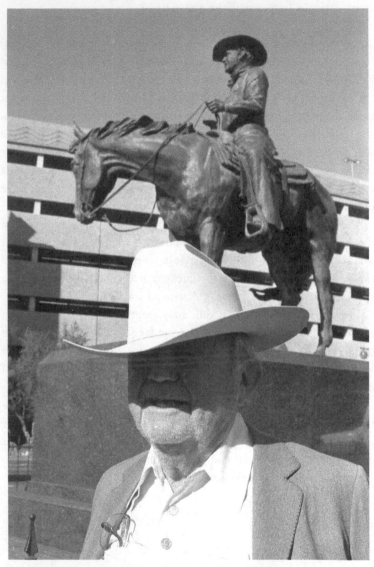

Benny and his statue in downtown Vegas, before it moved yet again.

# 26

# HAPPY BIRTHDAY, DEAR BENNY

I don't worry about but one thing. That's sickness. Sickness, you got trouble. Other things will go right away.

—BB

**B**inion was now an old man—and a rich one. In 1987 the Horseshoe had a net profit of more than $60 million. Under the direction of Jack Binion, the company bought the adjacent Mint Hotel for $27 million. That added twenty-five stories and three hundred rooms to the Horseshoe, and allowed for a major expansion of the casino. When his health would permit it, Binion spent time at the Montana ranch, which had now grown to 85,000 acres. He traveled there from Las Vegas in a chauffeured, customized bus. Other trips were made in a limo, such as one visit to the old homestead in North Texas. Binion took a reflective walk around the property and showed his driver where everything had once been. "That old house was right over there," he said, "and the old well was out there." Then he smiled. "I left here with two mules and a wagon," he said, "and come back in a Rolls-Royce."

There were frequent tributes befitting a man of many years and much public generosity. He was named Man of the Year by the National Jewish Health hospital, as it showed institutional gratitude for big donations. A video produced for the ceremony featured testimonials from a number of

Vegas luminaries, including another old racketeer in his dotage, Moe Dalitz. "He's a very quiet man until he's aroused," Dalitz said of Binion. "But he's never aroused unjustly." Steve Wynn called Binion "the most unforgettable character I've ever met in my entire life," and added, "He's a perfectly honest man." Others attested to the affection of Binion's lifelong customers and compadres. "All the poker players love you," said Bobby Baldwin, a former poker series champion. "You're the greatest guy in the world."

For some time there was a statue of only one man on horseback in Las Vegas, that of Rafael Rivera, believed to be the first non–Native American to ride into the valley almost two centuries earlier. In 1988, a second one was added—of Binion. Atop a massive granite pedestal, Binion rose an additional twelve feet in bronze as he sat heroically astride one of his daughter's favorite horses. With one hand on the reins and another gripping his lariat—and a little more svelte than most might remember—he now dominated the corner of Second Street and Ogden downtown. Like the man himself, the statue was a Texas refugee. It had originally stood outside a Fort Worth honky-tonk owned by Binion's friend Billy Bob Barnett. But when Barnett went broke, the three-thousand-pound bronze Binion was unbolted in the dead of night and trucked to Las Vegas. Now it offered one more indicator of the city's affection for the Cowboy. The governor of Nevada sent a proclamation, and the mayor of Las Vegas came and posed for pictures. "He's the best damn human being I ever knew," Harry Claiborne said shortly after the statue was unveiled. "He's a credit to the whole human race."

Maybe so. But a few blocks away at the federal courthouse, the government was mounting one more attempt to take Binion down.

In 1989, after a three-year investigation, federal authorities in Las Vegas assembled a special—and secret—strike force, including officers from the metro police and the Nevada Gaming Control Board. Its mission was to infiltrate the Horseshoe. The Vegas feds proclaimed it to be "the top priority within their office," a confidential memo said. Like many such undercover endeavors, this one had a name: Operation Benny Binion.

Finally, authorities believed, they would nab him. To justify Operation

Benny, they summoned years' worth of bad behavior at the Horseshoe, most of which had already been aired. Customers had been beaten, they noted, and robbed, which constituted civil rights violations. One unsubstantiated report said a blackjack dealer who had been caught cheating the Horseshoe was handcuffed to a stream pipe in the basement for three days. Prosecutors also cataloged the family's assorted relationships with mobsters, including Tony the Ant and Moe Dalitz, both of whom were, at this point, dead. One FBI telex even mentioned Jimmy "the Weasel" Fratianno's account of having killed Russian Louie Strauss on Binion's behalf. Strauss had been murdered more than thirty-five years before.

Federal investigators also reinterviewed witnesses to the ten-year-old shooting of Rance Blevins, hoping once more to pin it on Ted Binion. John Koval, the cabdriver who had witnessed the sidewalk killing, said FBI agents showed up at his house one day and took him downtown for a special interrogation. "They hypnotized me," Koval said, but nothing in his story changed. "Everything I said was the way I said it in the first place. They thought I got paid off by the Binions." Agents also tried to pry a new version of events out of the man who had been convicted of the shooting. Strike force officials promised Walt Rozanski a spot in the federal Witness Protection Program if he would testify that Ted Binion had actually killed Blevins. He refused.

Those running Operation Benny also hoped to prove that the Horseshoe was an absolute hive of criminal money laundering, especially under the auspices of Ted Binion. But first, they needed a Horseshoe insider, and here they bumped up against the Binions' standard way of doing business, which was to depend on family and a close circle of devoted friends. "The Binions are very cautious of who they conduct business with," an FBI report observed, "and it is practically impossible for someone unacquainted with the Binions to get close to them." The only real inside informant the bureau had ever developed at the Horseshoe was Benny himself.

The strike force decided to set up a sting operation. The plan: Rent three hotel rooms at the Horseshoe. Then, a "cooperating witness," someone with knowledge of the Binions, was to be furnished with more than $100,000 in government money. As agents covertly watched and taped the witness, who would be wearing a wire, he would try to engage the Binions in a laundering scheme.

If this was successful, authorities could seize the Horseshoe under the federal racketeering statute. Strike force officers reasoned that shutting the Horseshoe would be "a singular opportunity to strike at organized crime in the Las Vegas division." And it carried, potentially, a tremendous public relations value. Nailing the Binions, said a memo to FBI director William Sessions, could "send a clear message to casino operators that the FBI is cracking down on [money laundering] activity." Sessions was familiar with at least one of the characters who had been accused of laundering money at the Horseshoe; he had been the presiding judge when Jimmy Chagra was acquitted of murdering Judge John Wood.

Now, near the end of 1989, the sting was approved by senior Justice Department officials and set to go. But the feds' intricate plans were derailed by a funeral.

He hadn't felt good for a long time, mainly because of his persistent heart trouble. "Breathing's hard, walking's hard, and I can't do nothing," Binion complained one day as he sat at his table in the Horseshoe restaurant. As he became increasingly infirm, he lived with his daughter Becky. He turned eighty-five, and soon he couldn't walk at all, and the breathing seemed about to stop. A few days before Christmas 1989, he entered Valley Hospital in Las Vegas, and this time his chances looked worse than ever. "I'd asked the doctors in gambler's terms what were his odds," son Jack said, "and they told me six or eight to one against him." As Benny would know, that was a sucker's bet. Someone called a priest for last rites. Binion wanted to go that way, for as he once said, "Religion is too strong a mystery to doubt." He died on Christmas Day.

This was front-page news in Nevada, and the instant eulogists went quickly to work. One of the most perceptive summations came from columnist John L. Smith in the *Review-Journal*. "Revisionist historians will paint Binion as a sweet old man with a few minor blemishes in his youth," he wrote. "You know, like a bare-knuckle-era boxer with a broken nose. That picture is not only a lie, but it does Binion a disservice. He was not simply a good old boy with a few scars; he was a living legend who crafted his image with muscles, blood and a keen eye for action."

Several years before, Binion had attended the Las Vegas funeral of an old and broke prospector, and observed the light attendance. "One thing I've noticed in this town," he said then. "A man dies here and he ain't got no money, he don't draw worth a damn."

That wouldn't be a problem now for the Cowboy. The memorial service at Christ the King Catholic—where Binion had been the first and largest contributor to build the church—drew about a thousand mourners. Some wore funeral finery, while others came in rodeo wear. Former mayors, ex-senators, and retired judges arrived, along with enough professional poker players to fill a couple of Strip card rooms. Mourners remembered him as a dedicated family man, generous philanthropist, and Vegas original. Steve Wynn, now the king of casinos in Las Vegas, addressed the gathering. "He was a man who never showed one shred of pretense . . . We will never see the likes of Benny Binion in our lifetime again," Wynn said. "He was either the toughest gentleman I ever knew or the gentlest tough man I ever met." Atop Binion's coffin sat his cowboy hat.

The procession to the cemetery was led by the Horseshoe stagecoach, pulled by six black horses. Binion made his last trip through Vegas the modern cowboy way. It was also the Benny Binion way. He had used the stagecoach to advertise the Horseshoe at rodeos and livestock shows for years. Binion was promoting his business until the very end, and then some.

He also took a victory to the grave, as Operation Benny Binion had lost its biggest target. With his death, he beat the FBI one last time.

Most of the great organized crime chieftains—those who lived long enough anyway—saw their toughness squeezed from them. They went to prison and came out broken, like syphilitic Al Capone. Or they were reduced to shuffling through the streets in a bathrobe to feign insanity and avoid prosecution, like Vincent "the Chin" Gigante. Or, in the manner of Meyer Lansky, they walked their dogs in gelded, dwindling retirement. Few of them emerged from thugdom with an enhanced and celebrated glory, but Binion did so. He didn't renounce his past, or overcome it. He made it a crucial ingredient of his triumph, inseparable from the man, and it stayed with him until the end.

Binion's funeral had its share of tributes and tears, but like many such memorial services, it was a sanitized and grieving affair that couldn't capture his essence, or the breadth of his accomplishment, or the regard in which he was held. To understand that would require traveling back from the funeral a couple of years, to his eighty-third birthday.

His family decided to hold a big party, and rented the Thomas & Mack Center, the basketball arena of the University of Nevada, Las Vegas. Admission to the event was free. So was the beer. Willie Nelson performed, and the place was packed. Only a mile from the highway on which Binion had first rolled into town, with tommy guns and a trunk full of cash, they all gathered to honor the boss. Gene Autry, the original singing cowboy, was there. So was Hollywood star Dale Robertson. Moe Dalitz, by now deaf and two years from the mausoleum, came as well. One-eyed R. D. Matthews, who had been with Binion on that first trip from Dallas to Vegas, took a seat on the stage with the guest of honor. "Thank you for coming," Binion told the crowd. "I never dreamed it'd be anything like this. I'll do it again someday. God bless you all."

After Willie Nelson played, Hank Williams Jr. and his band turned the volume up so loud that Binion and his family got up and left. Late in the evening the beer ran low, and a few fights broke out. Maybe more than a few. But the real celebration had occurred earlier that night, after a mammoth, four-tier birthday cake appeared, and the crowd sang "Happy Birthday" in beery unison. Some eighteen thousand people were on their feet, clapping and shouting. Then they began to chant, "Benny! Benny! Benny!"

All the mayhem, all the bodies, all the car bombs, and all those who had tried to take him out had slipped to the hazy past, but none of it was forgotten. It had instead distilled into legend. Binion had outshot his rivals, outspent them, outmaneuvered them, and outlived them. Now, in the place to which he had fled forty-one years before—where his cunning and his vision coursed through the city's veins—the adulation rose to the rooftop. "Benny! Benny! Benny!" they cried, and the noise filled the arena. "Benny! Benny! Benny!" The old man in the cowboy hat smiled and waved. "Benny! Benny! Benny!"

He had become the most beloved gangster of them all.

Benny near the end, still keeping his eyes on the play.

# Epilogue
## BACK IN THE SADDLE

The sky's my home. I can go anywhere. I never did see no place
that I just thought I couldn't leave. I was raised in a wagon too
much, moved around too much. I don't miss nothing after I
leave it.

                                                              —BB

t took a few years, but the authorities finally abandoned Operation Benny Binion. Eight Horseshoe employees had been
indicted. But the charges were dropped, the head of the strike
force said, because "the evidence we obtained didn't stand up." The Binions
didn't need the federal government to damage the family and its business.
They could handle that task themselves.

Ted Binion slipped deeper into his addictions, and lost his gaming
license because of drug problems and associations with mobsters. "Ted had
three loves in life," said friend Michael Gaughan. "Ted loved pussy. Ted
loved dope. Ted loved to fish. His first two loves killed him." He died in
1998, at the age of fifty-five, of an overdose of heroin and Xanax. His girlfriend, a former topless dancer, and another man—with whom she was
consorting—were convicted of murder in one of Las Vegas's more spectacular trials. They were later granted a new trial. In 2004, the two were
acquitted of murder but convicted of lesser charges related to the theft of

about $7 million in silver that Ted Binion had buried in the desert. Like his parents, Ted enjoyed silver.

Teddy Jane Binion died in 1994, and a family struggle for control of the Horseshoe followed. After a particularly nasty lawsuit, Becky Binion Behnen—Benny and Teddy Jane's daughter—bought out her siblings and took over, after which the Horseshoe suffered a short but rapid decline. In 2004 the IRS seized $1 million from the Horseshoe to satisfy unpaid union benefits, which forced a sale to Harrah's Entertainment. What had been strictly a family operation was now a small cog in the world's largest gaming company. It opened seven new Horseshoes in such non-Vegas locales as Cleveland, Ohio, and Tunica, Mississippi.

The Fremont Street original was sold, and as of 2013, it was called Binion's, though no family members have a role. Except for the missing electric horseshoes, the red-and-blue lighting out front looks much the same as always. The club's bar is named Benny's Bullpen, and the steakhouse has been christened Binion's Ranch. There's even a Binion's Hall of Fame Poker Room.

But the casino floor is Benny blasphemy, with only four dice tables and most of the space given over to about eight hundred slot and video poker machines. Tourists fill the place now, as the legendary high rollers have moved on to other tables in other rooms. Parked out back is one vestige of the glory days: the Cowboy's old white Cadillac Fleetwood, with the horns of a longhorn steer attached to the hood.

Binion's original house on Bonanza Road still stands, but barely. In 2004 the Las Vegas planning department proposed taking possession of the home and converting it into a cultural and historical center. Those plans fell through after the family refused to deed the property to the city. By 2013 it was a sad hulk in an empty landscape—abandoned, boarded-up, and gutted by fire. A locked gate and No Trespassing signs kept vagrants and curiosity seekers away. The lush grove of trees died long ago, and the surrounding blocks are an expanse of battered apartments, homeless camps, and industrial sites.

In bright contrast, the World Series of Poker has soared to success beyond anyone's expectations. Harrah's bought the tournament when it purchased the Horseshoe, and in 2005 relocated it to the Rio, a massive hotel and casino just off the Strip. No longer would the players and railbirds be seen in Glitter Gulch. The game moved from the intimate, if decrepit, confines of the Horseshoe's casino to sprawling, cavernous meeting rooms with the charm and atmosphere of a warehouse.

The Horseshoe version of the series had been a cozy gathering, where a spectator could imagine he was watching Dolly, Slim, and Titanic reading faces and working the odds at a backroom game off a hidden side street. But the Rio rendition featured a great sea of tables and players stretching anonymously to the distant wall, with the constant sound of shuffling poker chips like plasticized crickets. The Horseshoe tournament was loaded with characters. They wore top hats and smoked cigars. The Rio series has a bunch of guys in hoodies and Ray-Bans, sipping Red Bull. But they come by the thousands to play.

Binion had once expressed his devout hope that the poker series might grow to fifty participants. In 2013, its main event competition—the No Limit Hold'em World Championship—had 6,352 players, and awarded a total of $59 million in prize money. Harrah's became known as Caesars Entertainment, and its World Series of Poker reaches eighty-four countries on five continents via ESPN. Every year, the final tournament is held in Las Vegas. It is, the press release minions at Caesars have claimed, "the longest-running, largest, richest and most prestigious gaming event in the world."

That by itself is not a bad legacy for a cowboy with a second-grade education, hailing from the Texas hinterlands.

Binion's statue could stay in one place no more than could Binion the man, and in 2008 the sculpture was moved again. This time it left Vegas on the bed of a pickup truck, the real-deal cowboy rolling past the fake Venice, the ersatz Paris, and the phony New York of the Strip. Binion's likeness had a new spot in a new casino, South Point, on the outer reaches of the city's suburban sprawl, twelve miles south of downtown. South Point's owner, Michael Gaughan, had bought it from the proprietors of the former Horseshoe for one dollar. "It's a great piece of artwork," Gaughan said. "The birds had crapped on it for four or five years."

To show his respect for a man he considered one of the great figures of Vegas, Gaughan had the statue cleaned and placed at the entry to his

4,600-seat equestrian center. Benny's bronze likeness now anchors a broad, carpeted hallway inside the resort, a few paces from the casino coffee shop, and a plaque fittingly identifies him as "one of the city's founding fathers." He's out of the weather and away from the birds, with good sight lines to the gambling floor. The look on his face says he might be enjoying it.

These were, after all, two of Binion's favorite places: on horseback, yet with a clear and commanding view of the action. Always, the action.

# Acknowledgments

Over the past three years, I have asked many friends, and even more strangers, for favors. The list of those who extended to me their time, knowledge, and forbearance is a long one.

Scott Parks, Gregg Jones, and Brent Williams were gracious enough to read parts of the manuscript and offer good, helpful advice. Mike Cochran arrived at the very beginning as a guiding force. Gary Sleeper, whose book *I'll Do My Own Damn Killin'* is a wonderful treatment of Binion's early years, provided valuable tips on tracking down records. Sam Gwynne was a source of counsel, encouragement, and inspiration throughout.

A number of kind people in distant places assisted in the pursuit of facts and photos. Kevin Ingram at the Nevada Department of Corrections and Chuck Williams at the Notre Dame law school helped me mine some important but deeply buried material. Researchers at the Las Vegas–Clark County Library were immensely helpful. Bridget Pappas of the FBI's Las Vegas Division was a textbook example of a diligent, responsive, and courteous public affairs officer. The staff at the Nevada State Archives found documents I had not even known to ask for. The Center for Gaming Research at the University of Nevada, Las Vegas, is a priceless asset for researchers. I'm especially indebted to UNLV's Delores Brownlee for her courtesy and professionalism.

Closer to home, John Slate, archivist for the city of Dallas, was of great help. Brian Collins and his associates at the Dallas Public Library's Texas/

Dallas history collection responded to my requests with amiable alacrity. Vickie Bryant spent an afternoon giving me a lively tour of what remains of Top O'Hill Terrace. Willetta Stellmacher, a delightful woman, was generous with her time and memories. She died in 2013.

Fred Merrill Jr., a man of elegance and refinement, furnished remembrances, photos, and good cheer. I now count him as a friend. R. D. Matthews, who died in 2013 at the age of ninety-two, was the purest of gentlemen as he recollected the old days for me. Thanks also to Mickey Bickers, Bob Compton, Jim Ewell, Carlton Stowers, Jim Dolan, Billy Bob Barnett, Bill Alexander, Jerry Blevins, Eddie LaRue, Bob Hinkle, Oscar Goodman, Joe Yablonsky, Doyle Brunson, Dan Bowman, John Redlein, Barry Finn, and Vernon McGuyer for their insights and assistance. Robert Wilonsky and Jerome Sims of the *Dallas Morning News* were there when I needed them.

To my disappointment, two of Binion's three surviving children chose not to talk to me for this book. But Brenda Binion Michael, Benny's middle daughter, spent many hours with me. She was unfailingly cheerful and helpful, and gave me insight into her father—whom she loved deeply—that I could have gained nowhere else. Brenda opened up her Amarillo home to me, and took no end of follow-up phone calls. When I needed to know the name of Benny Binion's favorite song, I phoned Brenda. I'm deeply grateful for her cooperation and lovely spirit.

Agent David Patterson was a crucially important adviser and advocate, and editor Melanie Tortoroli rode to the rescue with enthusiasm, intelligence, and a keen eye. David and Melanie are a couple of consummate pros who represent the best of the book business.

My wife, Susan, endured summertime trips to Nevada with patience and love, and never complained about my MIA status as husband and parent. My late father-in-law, Bob Rogers, introduced me to Las Vegas as only he could. Miss you, Bob.

Finally, I owe a great debt to George Getschow. This book was born at the Mayborn Literary Nonfiction Conference, the annual North Texas gathering of which George is director, guiding force, and tribal chief. He and his editing pencil stayed with this project from beginning to end, and it's no exaggeration to say it never would have happened without him. George has changed the lives of many writers much for the better. I'm one of them.

# Notes

There are no "Benny Binion Papers" at any university library. Binion did not write many letters and did not, as far as is known, keep a journal. Nor did he pen—or dictate—his life story. "No books, no nuthin'," he once told Las Vegas publicist and author Dick Odessky, who urged him to commit his adventures to print. "What I know, I know, and it's goin' to the graveyard with me." Many journalists and authors, and a few historians, interviewed Binion over the decades, but most of them came away with little of true substance. Binion engaged his questioners with well-worn anecdotes, practiced set pieces, and twangy observations. He might throw in a couple of tall tales as well. Sometimes his children would admonish him with, "You know that's not the way it happened." And Binion would respond, "But that's the way I like to tell it." To outsiders who sought to understand him, Binion was often accessible but seldom truly revealing.

Three exceptions stand out. Historian Mary Ellen Glass conducted two days of taped interviews with Binion in 1973 for the Oral History Program at the University of Nevada, Reno. While the meandering ninety-page transcript is a masterful collection of deceptions, circumlocutions, and evasions by Binion, it is nonetheless his only auto-biography, and provides many insights and recollections of value. Second, Las Vegas writer A. D. Hopkins succeeded in coaxing from Binion ruminations on his poor prospects for a happy afterlife that I've not seen matched elsewhere. Last, and far from least, Steven R. Reed of the *Houston Chronicle* engineered a remarkable series of interviews with Binion for a lengthy profile in 1989, less than a year before Binion's death. Reed got more out of Binion on a variety of uncomfortable topics than any other journalist, and provided a critical addition to the historical record.

Much of this book relies on law enforcement files, principally those of the Dallas Police Department, the FBI, and the federal Bureau of Prisons. This carries certain obvious hazards, because such documents are often self-serving, biased, and full of errors. Great portions of them may be redacted by government censors, and they are, by their nature, one-sided. Still, the men who filed these reports functioned as on-the-scene recorders whose job it was to investigate Binion and his cronies, and who wrote down what they saw or learned, frequently at great length. They produced, as they watched and chased Binion and his cohort, tens of thousands of type-written pages. In particular, Lieutenant George Butler of the Dallas police spent years on the trail of Binion and his associates, and was a prodigious, and often colorful, memo writer. Many of his investigative reports have been collected at the Texas Ranger Museum in Waco, Texas.

I have attempted wherever possible to corroborate facts in these law enforcement papers, or at the very least to cross-reference them with other sources, and have endeavored to weed out the patently false and misleading portions, or to point them out as such.

No conversations have been imaginatively re-created. Every spoken quotation comes from a written source, from the memory of a participant, or from my inter-view with an individual.

### Abbreviations

DMN: *Dallas Morning News*
DPD: Dallas Police Department
DTH: *Daily Times Herald*, later changed to the *Dallas Times Herald*
HC: *Houston Chronicle*
LAT: *Los Angeles Times*
LVRJ: *Las Vegas Review-Journal*
LVS: *Las Vegas Sun*
NSJ: *Nevada State Journal*
OH: Oral History Program, University of Nevada, Reno
OHUC: Oral History, University of California, Berkeley
REG: *Reno Evening Gazette*
SAE: *San Antonio Express*
VT: *Valley Times*
WSJ: *Wall Street Journal*

## PROLOGUE: THE HAPPY RACKETEER

1 "Do your enemies before they do you": Multiple sources, including www.pbs
.org/wgbh/amex/lasvegas/peopleevents/p_binion.html.

1 A weak sliver of moon hung low: U.S. Naval Observatory Astronomical Applications Department.

2 one of the hidden men gripped the insulated copper wire: *DTH*, Aug. 8, 1951.

2 "A big, beefy, jovial sort": *DMN*, Feb. 13, 1951.

2 "You couldn't keep from liking him": Interview, R. D. Matthews.

3 "No one in his right mind": Brunson, *The Godfather of Poker*, 132.

3 "There's been a lot of them": OH, Glass, *Lester Ben "Benny" Binion*, 30.

## Part One: The Roll of the Dice

### 1. SNIDES AND DINKS: AN EDUCATION

7 "We was all grifters": Vinson, *Las Vegas*, 123.

7 family took in boarders: U.S. Federal Census, 1910.

8 lightning bolt struck Sloan's: *DMN*, May 7, 1909.

9 "That's the best farmer I know": OH, Glass, 3. Unless otherwise noted, "OH, Glass" refers to the oral historian's interview with Binion.

9 "Kind of a wild man": OH, Glass, 2.

9 "There's more than one kind of education": Sheehan, *The Players*, 51.

10 "I was real good at it": OH, Glass, 4.

10 "They had heaves": OH, Glass, 5.

11 Wads of cotton: Welsch, *Mister, You Got Yourself a Horse*, 111.

11 "The Horse Trader's Song": Ibid., 12.

11 "Get a horse up on a kind of a high place": OH, Glass, 5.

11 "He was an adult his whole life": Interview, Brenda Binion Michael.

12 "I kind of got in": OH, Glass, 4.

13 "The brains of Texas Rangers": *United News*, April 9, 1922.

14 "Descending upon the rum-runners in speeding automobiles": *DMN*, July 24, 1929.

14 "He had a gravel wagon": Sheehan, *The Players*, 52.

14 "My dad was a happy, jolly man": Interview, Brenda Binion Michael.

14 "I didn't need a bodyguard": *HC*, March 12, 1989.

### 2. THE BUMPER BEATER

17 "I try to keep anybody": *HC*, March 12, 1989.

17 "one of the best towns that I ever seen": OH, Glass, 13.

18 Dallas had impaneled its first grand jury: Greene, *Dallas: The Deciding Years*, 10.

18 "a city of skyscrapers": Payne, *Big D*, 3.

19 One successful brothel: Dallas Historical Society, *Legacies*, Spring 2006.

19 founded the Berachah Rescue Home: *DMN*, March 14, 1912.

19 "Some hundreds of girls": Payne, 50.

20 "What about the men": *DMN,* March 13, 1911.

20 Chief among the brothel property owners: Payne, 52.

21 "Regardless of its registered attitude": Ibid., 262.

21 "a long blue blaze": *DMN,* July 14, 1929.

22 A 1925 study: Payne, 112.

22 "I never did make no money": OH, Glass, 9.

23 "They had more money": Interview with Vernon McGuyer, a relative of the Youngs.

23 "But the Oklahoma whiskey didn't seem to be as good": OH, Glass, 10.

23 "Binion began to muscle": DPD, Butler.

23 "Me and a guy": OH, Glass, 9.

23 "I got 60 days one time": OH, Glass, 10.

24 "Me and him was sitting": *HC,* March 12, 1989. Some contemporaneous newspaper accounts refer to Binion's victim as Frank Bolden.

25 "The guy hadn't pulled the knife yet": Sheehan, 53.

25 "Bill McCraw was the district attorney": *HC,* March 12, 1989. McCraw did indeed run for governor some years later. He lost to W. Lee "Pappy" O'Daniel. Among the votes McCraw failed to receive, according to historian Rose-Mary Rumbley, was that of his own mother. "I have been an O'Daniel fan for years," she explained to him. "He's a good man."

## 3. PANCHO AND THE KLAN

27 "Tough times make tough people": Brunson, *The Godfather of Poker,* 126, and multiple other sources.

27 "I opened up what they call a 'policy'": OH, Glass, 6.

28 "I started with fifty-six dollars": Ibid.

28 "'Cullud folks jus' gotta gamble'": *DTH,* Sept. 15, 1936.

29 "somebody had to hang": Greene, *Dallas: The Deciding Years,* 17.

29 Fully one-fourth . . . were "unfit for human habitation": Payne, *Big D,* 83.

29 Klan's fifty-member drum corps: Prince, *A History of Dallas,* 73.

30 "As I understand the case": Payne, 85.

30 Firemen blasted the rioters: *DMN,* May 21, 1925.

30 "I don't believe . . . in hanging": Sleeper, *I'll Do My Own Damn Killin',* 16.

31 "Down on 'Deep Ellum'": Holmes, *WPA Dallas Guide,* 294.

31 "Under the veneer of civilization and custom": Ibid.

31 "It's not his way": *DMN,* Oct. 2, 1929.

31 "Urban was . . . generally regarded": FBI, Feb. 28, 1958.

32 putting a pencil through the man's eye: *Texas Monthly,* "Benny and the Boys," Oct. 1991.

32 "I remember the pride": *DTH*, Jan. 29, 1990.

33 "Warren Diamond was as fine a man": OH, Glass, 8.

33 "I admired him very much": Ibid.

34 "I don't miss nothing": OH, Glass, 84.

34 "his little brother could whip him": Interview, Brenda Binion Michael.

34 he and a like-minded criminal stormed an East Dallas house: *DMN,* July 22, 1932.

35 "Dad never spoke to her again": Interview, Brenda Binion Michael.

36 pulled his handgun: Interview, Bob Hinkle.

37 "All them oil men had money": OH, Glass 16.

37 Binion loved the movie: Interview, Brenda Binion Michael.

## 4. GOOD FRIENDS AND A DEAD RIVAL

39 "I had a lot of . . . friends": OH, Glass, 30.

39 On a gentle North Texas afternoon: Interview, Willetta Stellmacher. Most of the details about Top O'Hill come from Miss Stellmacher, who performed regularly at the club, and from Vickie Bryant, who has done exceptional work as the historian of the casino. Mrs. Bryant is the wife of the former president of Arlington Baptist College, the latest incarnation of Top O'Hill. Most newspaper accounts don't place Binion at the club until the 1940s. But Miss Stellmacher, one of the few living witnesses to Top O'Hill's glory days, said she saw Binion there a number of times in the early 1930s.

42 "They need the money": Interview, Stellmacher.

43 During the service: *Texas Monthly,* "The Whole Shootin' Match," Feb. 2001.

43 "You'd have to know somebody": OH, Glass, 14.

44 His previous dealings with criminals: Sleeper, *I'll Do My Own Damn Killing,* 81.

44 "Because he's a big fellow": *DMN,* July 26, 1942.

44 "Every living human in Dallas": *HC,* March 12, 1989.

45 Then one of them spotted Ben Freiden's car: The description of the shooting of Freiden is drawn from extensive contemporary accounts by the *Dallas Morning News* and the *Daily Times Herald.* In some stories, the victim's name is spelled Frieden.

47 "Well, I don't know": *HC,* March 12, 1989.

## 5. THE THUG CLUB

49 "I ain't never killed a man who didn't deserve it": Interview, R. D. Matthews.

49 His partner, Bennie Bickers: Interview, Michael G. "Mickey" Bickers, son of Bennie.

49 "Whitaker foresaw the violence": FBI, Nov. 25, 1953.

50 Decker trusted . . . Merrill: Interview, Fred Merrill Jr., son of Fred Merrill.

50 "a world's exhibition Texanic": *DMN,* March 16, 1936.

51 "We've got to open up": Payne, *Big D*, 194.

51 "brought in quite a substantial sum": FBI, July 9, 1957.

52 "They just let the town": *HC*, March 12, 1989.

53 One of Binion's men: The description of the Southland dice room and its operations is drawn from my interviews with R. D. Matthews. He died in 2013.

53 "We'd just have a big suite": OH, Glass, 16.

53 Marshall took up a criminal career: *DMN*, Feb. 11, 1932.

53 An ex-con, Dorough: *DMN*, Nov. 20, 1936.

54 The East Side functioned: Sleeper, *I'll Do My Own Damn Killin'*, 51.

54 "There will be . . . no solution": DPD, Butler.

54 "He wasn't a high player": *HC*, March 12, 1989.

54 "He shot the craps": Ibid.

55 "Benny didn't want truck drivers": Interview, R. D. Matthews.

55 "There was a group": OH, Glass, 13.

55 Millions of his dollars: DPD, Butler.

55 "It is believed": FBI, Crime Survey, Dallas Division, April 1947.

56 "Business was *real* good": OH, Glass, 16.

56 "We all got along": Ibid.

56 "played an important part": DPD, Butler.

56 calls to mobster Carlos Marcello's brother: Ibid.

57 "They proudly boasted": *DMN*, Dec. 25, 1949.

57 "I'll show you how tough": FBI, Dec. 9, 1946.

58 "Shoot the s.o.b. in the guts": DPD, Butler.

58 "Green and Grisaffi were . . . loaned": Ibid.

## 6. SHOOT-OUTS AND PAYOFFS

61 "You had to have political help": OH, Glass, 14.

62 "a colorful and near-legendary figure": *DTH*, June 18, 1940.

62 "had a part in maintaining": Ibid.

63 "Don't move or I'll shoot": Ibid.

63 "Sam threatened me": Ibid.

63 "had differences regarding livestock": Ibid.

64 "in broad daylight": *DMN*, July 5, 1940.

64 "I had a crap game": OH, Glass, 15.

64 "The problem would be simple": *DMN*, Dec. 28, 1946.

65 One of the brass . . . held a press conference: *DMN*, Aug. 11, 1937.

65 "They had a real good city administration": OH, Glass, 16.

66 "All gambling establishments": FBI, Crime Survey, Dallas Division, 1944.

66 "I want everything closed": *DMN*, Oct. 25, 1940.

66 "They're on their way": Sleeper, *I'll Do My Own Damn Killin'*, 78.

67  "Gambling is presently operated": FBI, Crime Survey, Dallas, 1944.

67  "Loudermilk had developed an antagonism": FBI, Feb. 28, 1958.

67  He married Sam Murray's widow: The account of Loudermilk's life and of his shooting is drawn from contemporary stories in the *Dallas Morning News* and the *Daily Times Herald*.

69  "The grand jury lost no time": *DMN*, April 3, 1943.

## 7. THE MOB WAR IS JOINED

71  "I wasn't to be fucked with": *HC*, March 12, 1989.

71  "Binion's interests had complete control": FBI, Nov. 25, 1953.

71  "Used to call him up": *HC*, March 12, 1989.

71  gambling business had exercised an "evil influence": City of Dallas, Vollmer.

72  "A lot of people from other parts": Sheehan, *The Players*, 53.

72  such a raid was doomed to failure: FBI, Aug. 6, 1946.

73  she sat for hours chain-smoking and sketching: Interview, Brenda Binion Michael.

73  "Pay me back when you can": *Amarillo Globe-Times*, Jan. 13, 1960.

74  "I turned to gambling": *DTH*, Aug. 8, 1951.

74  "I operated a little place": Ibid.

75  "were making so much money": DPD, Butler.

75  "We have received some complaints": *DTH*, Aug. 8, 1951.

75  "Benny had a bunch of thugs": Ibid.

75  "collected a bunch of hoodlums": DPD, Butler.

76  Noble headed for his ranch: The account of this incident is drawn from stories in the *Dallas Morning News* and the *Daily Times Herald*, as well as Dallas Police Department reports.

76  "You're carrying a lot of heat": DPD, Butler.

78  "Informed underworld sources": Ibid.

## 8. "LIT OUT RUNNING"

81  "Hell, you can stub your toe": OH, Glass, 86.

81  "I have given you law enforcement": *DMN*, July 14, 1946.

82  "My sheriff just sat on his ass": Sleeper, *I'll Do My Own Damn Killin'*, 84.

83  "I will wear out the . . . Jail": *DMN*, Dec. 10, 1946.

83  "Guthrie and Noble . . . had an extremely close personal relationship": FBI, July 9, 1957.

84  "survey this area": FBI, Jan. 29, 1947.

84  "their suitcases had a lot of money": *DMN*, March 23, 1954.

84  "as hard a crew": *DMN*, June 18, 1947.

85  "they just didn't come there": OH, Glass, 17.

86 "I don't have to tell you who Benny Binion is": The account of this meeting is taken from Texas Ranger transcripts reproduced in FBI files, and later collected by the House Select Committee on Assassinations. They can be accessed via www.maryferrell.org/mffweb/archive/docset/getList.do?docSetId=1516.

88 "This arrangement . . . had done played out": *HC*, March 12, 1989.

88 he'll either be dead or in prison: Interview, Fred Merrill Jr.

88 "I depend on the dice": OH, Glass, 33.

89 He recruited two of the best: Interview, R. D. Matthews.

89 "burglar, armed robber, narcotics pusher, gambler, murderer": FBI, Oct. 10, 1958.

89 "Everybody was afraid of R.D.": Interview, Mickey Bickers.

## Part Two: Death and Taxes

### 9. MOBBED-UP PILGRIMS

93 "There's nothing on earth": OH, Glass, 21.

94 It was a broad desert basin: This short account of Las Vegas's beginnings is drawn from a number of sources. Among them are Moehring and Green, *Las Vegas: A Centennial History*, and Ferrari and Ives, *Las Vegas: An Unconventional History*.

97 "There is precious little humor": *New York Times*, March 20, 1941.

98 "a sunny place for shady people": Berman, *Lady Las Vegas*, 49.

98 "They weren't . . . Sunday school teachers": Kefauver committee transcripts.

99 "It was in sorry shape": Lacey, *Little Man*, 152.

100 "You may say for me": Ibid., 151. Much of the background on Siegel comes from Lacey's biography of Meyer Lansky.

101 "That was the biggest whoop-de-do": OH, Glass, 21.

101 "most accommodating, most likable fellow": OH, Glass, 48.

101 "I don't believe all that stuff": Ibid.

101 "With his glowing personality": Caldwell, *With All My Might*, 241.

102 "On your hands and knees": Reid, *The Green Felt Jungle*, 23.

102 "A heck of a good man": OH, Glass, 48.

103 "another high-class guy": Ibid.

103 "Very fine man": OH, Glass, 66.

103 "During periods of stress": Berman, *Easy Street*, 26.

### 10. TEXAS VS. VEGAS

105 "My friends can do no wrong": Interview, Doyle Brunson.

105 "How's your mammy?": Interview, Brenda Binion Michael.

106 "wasn't but something like 18,000 people": OH, Glass, 19.

106 It had previously served as an apartment house: Interview, Brenda Binion Michael.

106 "This Las Vegas Club wasn't the most beautiful place": OH, Glass, 22.

107 "The guy played so long": OH, Glass, 39.

107 "And he says, 'That doesn't worry me'": OH, Glass (Cahill), 508.

107 "I didn't pay no attention": OH, Glass, 22.

108 "as honorable and honest as any man": OH, Glass, 27.

108 "A cold-blooded, vicious son-of-a-bitch": Alverson, *Country Lawyer in a Maverick Boom Town,* 46.

108 "You know how you can tell": DPD, Butler.

109 "Sit down and shut up": Ibid.

109 "He almost got on his knees": Ibid.

110 "He was crazy": OH, Glass, 36.

110 He drew his Colt automatic pistol: FBI lab report, May 17, 1947.

111 "You've got to kill him sometime": OH, Glass, 27.

111 "a bunch of stupid cowboys": Vernetti, *Lies Within Lies,* 15.

111 "because all my goddamned friends are drunks": Alverson, 25.

111 "We have a problem": Ibid., 47. This rendering of the encounter with Houssels is drawn from Claiborne's recollections, in which he gives himself a rather heroic role.

112 "brutal gangland killing": Letter from Jones to J. Edgar Hoover, May 13, 1947.

112 "District attorney Jones stated today": FBI telex, April 3, 1947.

113 "these two splendid agents": Letter from Jones to Hoover, Oct. 2, 1947.

113 "I did everything I could for him": OH, Glass, 27.

113 "He used to take my kids riding": OH, Coles, 201.

114 "How in the hell did you convict": OH, Coles, 200.

114 Cupit unloaded his story: OH, Coles, 201.

115 "I want to hire you": Alverson, 102.

115 "Me and Claiborne is the best friends": OH, Glass, 28.

116 "I just kinda kept a-rollin'": OH, Glass, 29.

## 11. "A KILL-CRAZY MAN"

119 "It lasts a long time": *HC,* March 12, 1989.

119 "He snuck in a lot": Interview, Brenda Binion Michael.

120 "The Las Vegas Club was a damn good operation": OH, Glass, 39.

121 "kinda got in there with partners": Ibid.

121 "They just weren't the type of people": OH, Glass, 35.

121 "Maybe I put up something like $3,500": *HC,* March 12, 1989.

122 "This attempt was made": DPD, Butler.

123 "A nicer ride": The account of this episode and Noble's reaction is drawn from contemporary stories and photographs in the *Dallas Morning News* and the *Daily Times Herald*.

125 "29-year-old underworld member": *DTH*, Nov. 30, 1949.

125 "very strong reaction": DPD, Butler.

125 "I told him those tests": Interview, R. D. Matthews.

126 "He shot me in the head": Ibid.

127 The Sky Vu was a cavernous dance hall: The account of events at the Sky Vu is drawn from coverage in the *Dallas Morning News* and the *Daily Times Herald*, as well as Dallas police reports penned by Butler. A side note: In 1954 Sky Vu owner Joe Bonds was convicted of sodomy and sentenced to eight years in prison. While the case was on appeal, Bonds and Dale Belmont fled Texas. He was found four years later in Washington, DC, where he was operating another nightclub under a different alias. Though he claimed he was insane, Bonds was returned to Texas to serve his sentence.

128 "He was loved and respected": *DTH*, Dec. 28, 1949.

128 About a week after the funeral: *DMN*, Jan. 6, 1950.

129 "I left the state of Texas three years ago": *NSJ*, Jan. 14, 1950. The account of the police raid is taken from contemporary news coverage and Dallas police files.

130 "I am a gambler": *REG*, Jan. 3, 1950.

131 "It sounded like a cannon": *DTH*, Feb. 7, 1950.

131 "a person with wanton disregard": Ibid.

## 12. "TEARS ROLLING DOWN THE MAN'S EYES"

135 "Courage is a fine thing": Brunson, *The Godfather of Poker*, 129.

135 "This devil's stew": *DMN*, Feb. 19, 1950.

136 "The people of Nevada were made to look like a bunch of miscreants": *NSJ*, March 12, 1950.

136 "This . . . is the beginning of the final stage": *DMN*, Jan. 8, 1950.

136 "I think it's a political frame": *DMN*, Feb. 11, 1950.

136 "It's Noble who's doing all the hollering": Ibid.

136 "I don't think I ever in my life": *HC*, March 13, 1989.

137 "Eventually . . . we'll get him": *REG*, March 2, 1950.

137 "Wasn't . . . none of them guys tough": Sheehan, *The Players*, 56.

138 "I was in the counting room": Berman, *Lady Las Vegas*, 93.

138 "stupid and devious": DPD, Butler.

138 "I've been all over the country": Butler's transcript of this meeting was entered as part of the record of the Kefauver committee.

140 "dressed in the western style": *DMN*, March 14, 1950.

141 "What the hell are you doing?" Sleeper, *I'll Do My Own Damn Killin'*, 159.
142 "They had warned Daddy": Interview, Brenda Binion Michael.
143 "Yeah . . . They're all over me": *DMN*, Jan. 24, 1951.
144 "scorpion-tongued vixen": Russo, *The Outfit*, 266.
144 "He's got a great, big black brush": OH, Glass (Cahill), 764.

## 13. THE BENNY BRAND GOES NATIONAL

147 "The only people I don't like": Vinson, *Las Vegas Behind the Tables!*, 129.
147 "and don't bother to come back": *DMN*, July 7, 1950.
147 "mild-looking middle-aged man": *DMN*, Feb. 21, 1951.
148 "They didn't even leave me the trash cans": *DMN*, May 16, 1952.
148 "This is the big one": FBI, memo to Hoover, Aug. 23, 1952.
149 Caudle was convicted of conspiracy: Dunar, *The Truman Scandals*, 151. Caudle served five months in prison, and received a full pardon from President Lyndon Johnson in 1965, after which he ran for Congress from North Carolina, but lost. Newspaper columnist Drew Pearson once wrote in his diary that he believed Caudle was not guilty, but merely dumb.
149 "Noble has often made the statement": DPD, Butler.
150 the judge's bench . . . was conveniently bulletproof: The old federal building now houses Las Vegas's Mob Museum, and the second-floor courtroom has been faithfully restored to its 1950s condition.
150 "So many flashbulbs popped in his face": *LVRJ*, Nov. 15, 1950.
151 "Privately, my father and his friends had joked": Berman, *Lady Las Vegas*, 104.
151 "The top brass of the underworld": Ferrari, *Las Vegas: An Unconventional History*, 111.
151 "Well . . . it depends on how you describe 'high integrity'": Kefauver committee transcripts.
152 "What I have seen here today": Denton, *The Money and the Power*, 111.
153 "Hoodlums, racketeers and the other inevitable parasites": Kefauver, *Crime in America*, 230.
154 "Benny never did like me too much": *DMN*, April 4, 1951.
154 "We've got nothing to hide": *DMN*, Aug. 30, 1950.
154 "What will happen if the gangsters get into the oil business?": *DMN*, March 31, 1951.
155 "I would be foolish to pay my way down there": *DMN*, March 30, 1951.
155 "It would be a fine state of affairs": *DMN*, Dec. 7, 1950.
155 "I told him I didn't want any part": *DTH*, Aug. 8, 1951.
156 The contract included a special clause: *DMN*, Aug. 9, 1951.
156 "me and my son . . . went out to the Desert Inn": *HC*, March 13, 1989.
156 "I was getting some pressure put on me": OH, Glass, 37.

157  "I've bribed many a man": Ibid.

157  "And that's always been your way?": *HC*, March 14, 1989.

## 14. THE CAT'S LAST DAYS

159  "They said he had nine lives": Interview, Billy Bob Barnett.

160  "There was nothing good enough for her": *DMN*, July 10, 1952. The account of Noble's death is taken from contemporary reports and photographs in the *Dallas Morning News* and the *Daily Times Herald*, as well as internal memos written by Lieutenant George Butler.

160  "I always get a lot": *DTH*, Aug. 9, 1951.

160  "Boisterous, buxomy Ginny Hill": *LVRJ*, Aug. 14, 1951.

161  "I put the first carpet on the floor": OH, Glass, 53.

161  "He was the type of man that didn't understand gambling": OH, Glass, 59.

164  "The first night . . . me and my wife went home": OH, Glass, 55.

165  "The carpet cost $18,000": OH, Glass, 53.

165  "The law enforcing here . . . honest and tops": OH, Glass, 42.

166  Binion bought the publisher . . . a brand-new car: Reid, *The Green Felt Jungle*, 155.

167  "had been propositioned to kill or attempted to kill": Butler, DPD.

168  "You left yourself open to the argument": OH, Glass (Cahill), 270.

168  "Most of the prolonged applause . . . came from the other big time gamblers": DPD, Butler, and Texas Rangers, Crowder.

169  "No one . . . has ever come to me": *NSJ*, Nov. 22, 1951.

169  "see hundreds of them stacked up in the lot": OH, Glass (Cahill), 742.

169  "McCarran never quit trying": OH, Glass (Cahill), 1134.

170  He was "cool and collected": The account of this meeting is taken from the extensive written report jointly filed by Butler and Crowder after they returned to Dallas, now archived in the Texas Ranger Museum.

172  "A good man, Glen Jones": OH, Glass, 68.

## 15. "THEY WAS ON THE TAKE"

175  "Them dice just run in cycles": OH, Glass, 41.

175  "one of the best things that has happened to us": *NSJ*, Nov. 29, 1951.

176  Miss Atomic Blast . . . "radiating loveliness": U.S. Department of Energy, "Nevada National Security Site History."

176  "low-use segment of the population": Gallagher, *American Ground Zero*, 110.

177  "Binion had this very engaging style": Johnston, *Temples of Chance*, 31.

177  "Just a nigger I caught stealing": Ibid.

177  "Binion is a man you can believe in": *REG*, Dec. 1, 1951.

178 "They was on the take": OH, Glass, 37.

178 "Reports were received from reliable Informants": FBI, Nov. 25, 1953.

178 "A wealthy Texan named Blondy Turner": NSJ, Jan. 1, 1952.

179 "We could talk about anything": Details on Binion's family life and the house on Bonanza Road are drawn from interviews with Brenda Binion Michael and Fred Merrill Jr., and from a visit to the property.

180 "I'm just a gambler": OH, Glass, 39.

180 "Their money management system is simple": Johnston, 35.

181 "He come in here in 1906": OH, Glass, 49.

182 From this realm comes the story of the great Horseshoe battle: Poker scholars continue to debate whether this event actually occurred. It's certainly curious that in his extensive 1973 interview with Mary Ellen Glass, Binion does not even mention a contest that would have been a significant milestone in his and the Horseshoe's history. When Nick the Greek died in 1966, obituaries in the Las Vegas newspapers made no references to any monumental face-off with Moss. Moss's self-published biography describes the battle with the Greek in great detail, but says it happened at the Horseshoe in 1949. The Horseshoe didn't open until 1951. James McManus, in Cowboys Full, his exhaustive history of poker, takes the middle road: it probably happened, but has been enhanced in the retelling. "Accounts of the hand-to-hand combat of historical figures have always been embellished somewhat," McManus writes. "But it's safe to say that Dandalos and Moss were exceptional high-stakes players who engaged in a midcentury showdown that Dandalos lost. It was apparently something of a spectacle. And the spectacle was hosted by the impresario who would launch the World Series of Poker two decades later." It may be too much to expect a definitive answer. Poker is, after all, a game of secrets and deception.

182 "I would rather fall from a mountaintop": Grotenstein, All In, 15.

182 "He made Omar Sharif look like a truck driver": Ibid.

182 "Well, Nick the Greek, he was the strangest character": OH, Glass, 45. The snake-in-the-pocket quip was not original to Binion nor unique to Nick the Greek. It's a common gambler's encomium to convey cunning.

183 "recite by heart any poem in the English language": Campbell, My Friend Nick the Greek, 25.

183 "What good is money": Jenkins, Champion of Champions, 173.

183 "I learned how to gamble": Sports Illustrated, Jan. 25, 1971.

183 "Sorry, you looked too long": Jenkins, 133.

184 "little Al from Princeton": This is a great Las Vegas tale that has never been sufficiently confirmed or debunked.

185 "Moss went over to the dice table": Brunson, The Godfather of Poker, 132.

## 16. "NO WAY TO DUCK"

187 "Believe in justice": Brunson, *The Godfather of Poker*, 129.

187 Henry Wade had been elected district attorney: Wade ultimately spent thirty-six years as Dallas County DA. In 1964, he prosecuted Jack Ruby, the killer of Lee Harvey Oswald. And his name was part of the landmark Supreme Court decision on abortion, *Roe v. Wade*.

188 "Get him": Interview, William Alexander.

189 "rather slim and doubtful": Potter memo to Office of the Attorney General, July 21, 1952.

190 "As you can readily see": *DMN*, June 20, 1952.

190 "Oh, the heat just built up on me": OH, Glass, 55.

190 "must be given preferred and continuous attention": FBI, Hoover memo, Aug. 11, 1952.

191 "Well, I guess nobody will have any trouble": *DMN*, Aug. 23, 1952.

191 "And there's two little ol' girls": OH, Glass, 44.

191 "Now don't that beat all": *DMN*, Sept. 4, 1952.

192 "This is positively untrue": FBI, Aug. 23, 1952.

192 "The whole outfit was stalking me": OH, Glass, 56.

193 "The attorney general then commented on Nixon": The account of these meetings is drawn from FBI memos written by Nichols—and, on one occasion, Hoover—from Aug. 25, 1952, to Oct. 13, 1952.

194 "get publicity to keep the smoke screen": OH, Glass, 57.

195 "No one could hire me": This scene—including quotations—is described in detail in an Aug. 16, 1952, office memorandum written by the FBI agent listening secretly from an adjacent room. That same agent, Arthur Cornelius Jr., would later encounter many problems as he attempted to monitor Binion's movements in Las Vegas.

## 17. THE GREAT BONANZA STAKEOUT

197 "Never follow an empty wagon": Brunson, *The Godfather of Poker*, 129.

198 "Greenbaum said, 'We gonna bust him'": OH, Glass, 85.

198 "Send copy to A.G.": FBI, Oct. 21, 1952.

198 "I do not believe it is the policy": Potter memo to Office of the Attorney General, July 21, 1952.

199 "blown to pieces at his mailbox": U.S. Supreme Court, Case No. 623, October Term, 1952.

199 "I don't see how they could have done it": *NSJ*, Oct. 4, 1952.

199 "I don't fear the federal government": *NSJ*, Nov. 14, 1952.

199 "an abuse of federal process in aid of state court prosecution": U.S. Supreme Court, Case No. 623, October Term, 1952.

200 "a private cemetary [sic] equipped with a lime pit": DPD, Butler, as contained in an FBI memo to Hoover, Aug. 23, 1952.

200 "The attorney general . . . was most appreciative": FBI, Hoover memo, Jan. 13, 1953.

200 "If we didn't have anything to do": Interview, Brenda Binion Michael.

201 Later that morning the phone rang: FBI, Jan. 17, 1953. The details of the catastrophic surveillance are taken from a series of contemporary bureau memos attempting to explain and justify the missteps.

203 As Brownell told his freshly hired staff: OHUC, Olney.

203 "The original request apparently came from the Attorney General": FBI, April 7, 1953.

203 "While I would like to bring Binion to justice": Hoover addendum to FBI memo, Feb. 11, 1953.

204 "A quote screwball end quote": FBI, Feb. 4, 1953.

204 Binion was "very worried" about whether he had reported income: FBI, May 5, 1953.

205 "There was some aura of embarrassment": FBI, June 4, 1953.

205 "I think we should do it": Ibid.

205 "Arrangements were made . . . for a privately owned airplane": FBI, agent's report, June 12, 1953.

206 "Agents were driving at risk of their lives": FBI, agent's report, June 7, 1953. This story of Binion's toying with agents, and the details of the chase, are taken from voluminous bureau reports filed as the pursuit unfolded. Hoover's comments are from his handwritten notes in response to these memos. It should be noted that Agent Cornelius, despite his difficulties here, later went on to a brief but distinguished term as superintendent of the New York State Police.

209 "I ain't talking": DMN, June 7, 1953.

209 "They sure gave us a run, those government men": DTH, June 7, 1953.

209 "nattily dressed in a coral green suit": DMN, June 9, 1953.

## 18. "WHACKED AROUND PRETTY GOOD"

213 "The damn government's been getting bad": OH, Glass, 56.

213 Cash and real estate had a market value of $2.4 million: DMN, Sept. 5, 1953.

214 "He had $200 million": OH, Glass, 57.

214 Brown's true stake fell closer to 25 percent: FBI, Nevada Gambling Industry, Nov. 16, 1964.

214 "Don't ever tell a lie, unless you have to": Brunson, The Godfather of Poker, 129.

214 "Just me, Mrs. Brown and Christ": NSJ, Dec. 12, 1953.

214 "He was a very, very straightforward man": OH, Glass (Cahill), 903.

215 "I'm getting the rest together": *DMN*, Dec. 3, 1953.

215 Meyer Lansky bought in: FBI, *Nevada Gambling Industry.*

216 "I gambled and I lost": *SAE*, Dec. 14, 1953.

216 "I'm kinda ignorant": *DMN*, Dec. 15, 1953.

216 "Investigation has disclosed that defendant kept": U.S. Bureau of Prisons, Binion file.

217 "He thought he was going to get out of it": Interview, Brenda Binion Michael.

217 "Get a good one, boys": *SAE*, Dec. 15, 1953.

218 "I don't intend to go back": *DMN*, Dec. 18, 1953.

218 "some type of minor heart attack": U.S. Bureau of Prisons, Binion file.

218 "He will find prison life far different": *NSJ*, Dec. 22, 1953.

218 U.S. Attorney General Brownell had ordered that he go to Leavenworth: U.S. Bureau of Prisons, Binion file.

218 "I got whacked around pretty good": OH, Glass, 55.

218 "I don't know," Braggins said: DPD, Butler.

219 "I could've beat this damn case": OH, Glass, 55.

220 "There ain't no such thing as luck": *HC*, March 13, 1989.

## Part Three: The Ride Back Home

### 19. THE FIREMAN GETS RELIGION

223 "When you quit learning": OH, Glass, 52.

223 "A giant mausoleum . . . adrift in a great sea": Earley, *The Hot House*, 30.

223 "Leavenworth is hell": LaMaster, *U.S. Penitentiary Leavenworth*, 27.

224 The prison doctor reported that he had flat feet: U.S. Bureau of Prisons. Personal information, medical reports, related correspondence, official memos, and other records from Binion's prison time are taken from his Leavenworth inmate file.

225 "This is a fabulous, extraordinary madhouse": Payn, *The Noël Coward Diaries*, 246.

226 operating a power mower while wearing a large diamond ring: Interview, Brenda Binion Michael.

226 "They'd frisk him in front of us": Ibid.

226 "Dear Brenda . . . my favorite [*sic*] cowgirl": Files of Brenda Binion Michael.

227 he sometimes used an empty fire extinguisher: Interview, Brenda Binion Michael.

227 "My family's all religious": *HC*, March 13, 1989.

227 "A book wrote by a monk in 1500": OH, Glass, 85.

227 When Teddy Jane visited Leavenworth: Interview, Brenda Binion Michael.

228 "Were I in a position to make a decision": U.S. Bureau of Prisons, Binion file. Other letters pleading Binion's case come from this same file.

230 Next, they had planned a string of holdups: *LVRJ*, Nov. 16, 1957.
231 he liked to douse himself in White Shoulders: Odessky, *Fly on the Wall*, 151.
231 "that is too much to ask of any grandmother": *NSJ*, May 30, 1957.
231 "I'll tell you the reason why": OH, Glass, 57.

## 20. STRIPPERS AND STOOGES

233 "It's not your enemies you have to worry about": Interview, R. D. Matthews.
233 "If this were a less well-known prisoner": U.S. Bureau of Prisons, Binion file.
234 "Binion has suffered fully": Ibid.
235 "This 'moonlight' employment is not condemned": Ibid.
235 "He can recall the necessary details": Ibid.
236 In Glitter Gulch, he served as a front man: FBI, *Nevada Gambling Industry*.
236 Brown had almost no shares to sell: Ibid.
236 "backed Levinson into a corner": FBI, Jan. 29, 1960.
237 "You might consider developing Binion's front": FBI, memo from Hoover, May 22, 1959.
238 "felt that such a type of entertainment": FBI, Dec. 3, 1959.
238 Levinson and his crew bragged that they were raking $700,000: FBI, *Nevada Gambling Industry*.
239 Some of the stash was shipped in the sleeves: Ibid.
240 "That's an absolute lie": Interview, Oscar Goodman.
240 "I don't think Benny would tell them anything": Interview, Eddie LaRue.
240 "I'd no more believe that . . . than I'd believe Martians": Interview, Bill Bob Barnett.

## 21. CHARLIE, ELVIS, AND THE REVOLUTION

243 "Hell, all I want's four walls": OH, Glass, 54.
243 "In Vegas for 20 minutes": Ferrari, *Las Vegas*, 169.
243 "Benny Binion being the strong man": OH, King.
244 "They said Ruby had my phone number": Interview, R. D. Matthews.
246 "I had a deal to get it back": *HC*, March 13, 1989.
246 "Levinson and Edward Torres were in the office": Levinson pleaded no contest to skimming in 1968 and was fined $5,000. He had sued the FBI for bugging his offices at the Fremont, but dropped the suit.
246 "Through hook or crook, I got it back": OH, Glass, 54.
246 "That million-dollar display": OH, Glass, 79.
247 "My wife works here, and my daughter": OH, Glass, 88.
247 "Hell, no, we don't want them anywhere": FBI, Feb. 14, 1966.
249 "Oh, I knew him a long time before": OH, Glass, 83.
249 "Now, I've damaged a lot of people": OH, Glass, 31.
250 "If anybody goes to talking about doing me bodily harm": OH, Glass, 30.

251 "There's thousands of people comes on the Strip": OH, Glass, 78.

251 "I knew him pretty well": Sheehan, *The Players,* 58.

251 "We would have sold it to him for $8 million": *VT,* Oct. 8, 1975.

252 "I'd heard about Benny all my life": Interview, Doyle Brunson.

252 "I've seen a lot of poker games": OH, Glass, 81.

## 22. ANOTHER ONE BLOWS UP

255 "Anybody had done anything to me": *HC,* March 12, 1989.

256 "You had to worry about winning the money": The account of Brunson's life on the poker circuit is drawn from my interview with Brunson, from his book *The Godfather of Poker* (written with the great journalist Mike Cochran), and from an interview Brunson gave to Nolan Dalla that is posted at www.pokerpages .com/articles/interviews/interviews-brunson01.htm.

257 "The first time he comes into the Horseshoe": Interview, Brenda Binion Michael.

257 "You're makin' a lot of my customers uneasy": Brunson, 133.

258 "He didn't charge us anything": OH, Glass, 82.

258 "This poker game here gets us a lot of advertisement": OH, Glass, 81.

258 "He understood gamblers": Interview, Doyle Brunson.

259 "He was the wisest man I've ever known": Ibid.

259 "Oh, he was tough": *HC,* March 12, 1989.

260 "If I felt that Benny Binion had done it": *LVS,* April 3, 2001.

260 He was known as Doc: Information on Dolan comes from Coulthard's FBI file and from an interview with the suspect's son, Jim Dolan.

261 "It was . . . believed by law enforcement": FBI, Ted Binion file, May 7, 1987.

261 "Do I think Benny would kill Coulthard?": Interview, Eddie LaRue.

261 "I didn't keep no records": Ibid.

262 "Many fringe benefits come to a public official": *LVRJ,* Sept. 12, 1999.

262 "That was silly for them to imply Benny was a liar": *NSJ,* Aug. 5, 1977.

262 "Oh, yeah, always give ol' Ralph a little money": *HC,* March 14, 1989.

262 "Me and him puts on a party every December": OH, Glass, 66.

262 "Hello, Meyer. How you feeling?": Odessky, *Fly on the Wall,* 158.

263 "Colonel" Tom Parker . . . often had dinner with Binion: Interview, Ken Lambert Jr.

263 "You ought to do a movie on Titanic": Interview, Bob Hinkle.

264 "Limit poker is a science": Grotenstein, *All In,* 20.

264 "Texas Hold'em takes a minute to learn": House Concurrent Resolution 109, 80th Legislature of the State of Texas.

264 rumors swirled that Binion had fixed the '72 series: Greg Dinkin, "Remembering Amarillo Slim Whichever Way We Wish," *Grantland,* May 1, 2012." Preston died in 2012.

## 23. HEROIN AND THE HIT MAN

267 "My other son Ted, he's sorta like I am": OH, Glass, 74.

267 a recently crowned mob lawyer walked six blocks: Interview, Oscar Goodman.

268 The squirrel's black glassy eyes: Ibid.

268 kept a $100,000 stash in the casino's vault: Vernetti, *Lies Within Lies,* 127.

268 "It was like two great personalities got together": Ibid., 29.

268 two men in suits watched from the casino floor: Interviews, multiple sources.

269 "Everything's in there like they'd gone on a trip": *HC,* March 13, 1989.

269 "She don't think they hurt you": Ibid.

269 Teddy Jane accumulated clutter: Interview, Brenda Binion Michael.

269 "He'd pick up this check": Interview, R. D. Matthews.

270 she would . . . grab a bag of silver dollars: Interview, Eddie LaRue.

270 "There ain't nobody works harder than Jack": OH, Glass, 89.

270 "Binion's Horseshoe has $15 million in the bank": *VT,* Oct. 8, 1975.

270 "He was a cross between Larry Flynt and a bum": Stephen Rodrick, "Snake Eyes," *GQ,* Dec. 1999.

270 "Ted was brilliant": Interview, Oscar Goodman.

270 "I'd find these little foil bowls": Interview, confidential source.

270 "In five minutes . . . he might bet a million dollars": Cartwright, *Dirty Dealing,* 70.

271 Benny and Ted Binion "allegedly assisted major drug trafficker Jimmy Chagra": FBI, Oct. 13, 1989.

271 But without Wood, he said, "much, much better": Cartwright, 187.

271 "That's not so bad": *DMN,* Aug. 12, 1973.

271 "Thank God for Oscar Goodman": Smith, *Of Rats and Men,* 127.

272 It started with a man named Rance Blevins: Background on Rance Blevins comes from an interview with his brother, Jerry Blevins.

272 "Oh, they're going to fuck this guy up": Interview, John Koval.

273 "Let's go in the casino": Ibid.

273 "He told the cops that he represented all employees": Interview, Dan Bowman.

273 "He said, 'That's not something we normally do'": Ibid.

274 "Benny Binion had a lot of juice": Ibid.

274 "I'm 58 years old now": E-mail to me from Walt Rozanski.

## 24. U-TURN AT THE GATES OF HEAVEN

277 "Used to really live dangerously": *HC,* March 12, 1989.

278 "Benny Binion is your brand": Interview, Henri Bollinger.

278 "the humped, the bent, the skeleton thin": Alvarez, *The Biggest Game in Town,* 14.

279 "I didn't have a floor show": Interview, R. D. Matthews.

279 "Five Puerto Ricans sideswiped me": Interview, Joseph Yablonsky.

280 "We were working to turn it into a normal America": Ibid.

280 "I don't know of anything he's done that was a violation": *LVS,* May 10, 1983.

280 "a taste for strong whiskey, frisky women and trim horses": *LVRJ,* Dec. 11, 1983.

280 "Claiborne doesn't happen to look very judicial": *VT,* Sept. 17, 1982.

281 Claiborne "socializes with women who happen to be attractive": *LAT,* Jan. 15, 1984.

281 "The Nevada FBI chief came to Las Vegas": *LVS,* Nov. 4, 1982, and June 26, 1983.

281 "He was run out of town": Interview, Oscar Goodman.

281 "In most cities, if you were nailing crooked politicians": Interview, Joseph Yablonsky.

282 "Teddy Binion is believed to be one of the main suppliers": *LVRJ,* June 24, 2001.

282 "[Ted] Binion uses the casino cage . . . to launder the drug money": Ibid.

282 "Ted broke Daddy's heart": Interview, Brenda Binion Michael.

282 "Used dope": *HC,* March 13, 1989.

282 "She had a lot of Benny's young blood": Interview, Bob Hinkle.

282 "They did all sorts of reconstructive surgery": Interview, confidential source.

282 "I'm going to waste": FBI, Ted Binion file, May 7, 1987.

282 "Well, they come down here to meet": *HC,* March 13, 1989.

283 "She got it accidentally, I'm sure": Ibid.

283 "He took all the phone calls": Interview, Doyle Brunson.

283 "spent months walking around with Barbara's baby pictures": Interview, Brenda Binion Michael.

284 A new heart drug called amiodarone worked well: According to Binion family lore, amiodarone was not yet approved by the Food and Drug Administration and therefore was not available to Binion. Merle Haggard's road manager—so the story goes—hired a member of the Hells Angels named Foo to break into a California doctor's lab and steal the drug. Then, the story continues, one of Binion's muscle men coerced a doctor into administering the treatment. Binion was so grateful that he gave a Rolls-Royce once owned by the British royal family to Haggard's manager. It's quite a tale, but Binion's physician at the time said in a 2011 e-mail, in response to my query, that the reality was far more prosaic: "I used to see Benny Binion as a patient. He required amiodarone for ventricular arrhythmia," Dr. Kanu Chatterjee wrote. "I gave him amiodarone with the permission of the FDA as it was still an investigative drug."

284 "He said that . . . is the best gun": Interview, Bob Hinkle.

284 "He had long hair, like you see in the pictures": Sheehan, *The Players,* 66.

285 "Which is bullshit": *HC,* March 15, 1989.

285 "Ted [Binion] came running up to the table": Interview, Joseph Yablonsky.

285 "When ol' Reagan went in there": *HC,* March 15, 1989.

285 "He is a man of his word": U.S. Department of Justice, Binion pardon file.

286  "During his many years of poor health": Ibid.

286  "Mr. Binion was very nice": Ibid.

286  "I'm going to outlive that sumbitch": *HC*, March 15, 1989.

287  "Everything to me is like you throwed three": Ibid.

## 25. "THEY DO THINGS LIKE THAT"

289  "Fear will not keep 'em from stealing": OH, Glass, 34.

289  The Binions almost never lodged such complaints: Interviews, multiple sources.

290  A Horseshoe waitress said she watched: *LAT*, Sept. 30, 1990.

290  A guard cuffed her: This account and some others are taken from interviews conducted by private investigators working for attorneys contemplating legal action against the Horseshoe.

290  "You didn't cheat at the Horseshoe": Interview, Oscar Goodman.

290  "They run their house": Interview, confidential source.

290  "The most contemptible-looking human beings I've ever seen": *HC*, March 14, 1989.

291  "The customer had suffered an unlucky streak": *WSJ*, July 3, 1985.

291  A Horseshoe bartender said the incidents were so common: *LAT*, Sept. 30, 1990.

291  over the course of about ten years roughly a hundred patrons: *LVRJ*, Oct. 28, 1987.

291  "This is happening quite often down there": Private investigator research from files of attorneys preparing legal action against the Horseshoe.

292  two friends, Barry Finn and Allan Brown, had a blackjack game: The account of the beating of Finn and Brown is drawn from contemporary press reports, a transcript of grand jury testimony, court pleadings, and a 2012 interview that I conducted with Finn. Steve Fechser, who still lives in Las Vegas, told me in 2013 that he would not talk about the case.

292  "For some time now . . . graveyard shift at the Horseshoe": *Winning Gamer*.

294  "The prickly hair is up on the back": *LVRJ*, Jan. 29, 1986.

294  including the Binions, who had given him $30,000: *LVRJ*, Oct. 22, 1986.

294  "He said, 'We do not execute search warrants at hotels'": Interview, John Redlein.

294  "Ingenious," columnist Day observed: *LVRJ*, Feb. 2, 1986. Bob Miller, now a consultant in Las Vegas, told me in 2013 that he did not involve himself in the day-to-day operations of the case, but that his office conducted itself properly. It was up to the judge to decide if his office should prosecute the case, Miller said, adding, "We would have pursued it had we not been disqualified."

295  "He fixed it in his mind": Interview, John Redlein.

295  "Isn't it wonderful," Foley said from the bench: Quoted by Redlein.

296  "The day before the trial started": Interview, Barry Finn.

296 "The trial atmosphere was so tainted": *LVS*, March 2, 1988.

296 "The good-old-boy network in Las Vegas told me": *LVRJ*, March 3, 1988.

296 "I walked by his courtroom and smelled the most awful odor": *LVRJ*, March 13, 1988.

297 Finally, "after years of waiting for her": Interview, John Redlein.

297 the owner "just whips the shit out of him": *HC*, March 13, 1989. Witten and Fechser were never retried on state charges. Cofield, Witten, Fechser, Ted Binion, and several other Horseshoe employees were later indicted for racketeering by a federal grand jury. Those charges were dropped in 1992.

## 26. HAPPY BIRTHDAY, DEAR BENNY

299 "I don't worry about but one thing": OH, Glass, 36.

299 In 1987 the Horseshoe had a net profit of more than $60 million: Johnston, *Temples of Chance*, 34.

299 "That old house was right over there": Interview, Ronnie Campbell.

299 A video produced for the ceremony: From the collection of Brenda Binion Michael.

300 "He's the best damn human being I ever knew": *HC*, March 12, 1989.

300 Vegas feds proclaimed it to be "the top priority": FBI, Oct. 22, 1989.

301 "They hypnotized me": Interview, John Koval.

301 "The Binions are very cautious": FBI, Oct. 13, 1989.

302 "a singular opportunity to strike at organized crime": Ibid.

302 "Breathing's hard, walking's hard": Vinson, *Las Vegas Behind the Tables!*, 131.

302 "I'd asked the doctors in gambler's terms": *LVRJ*, Dec. 26, 1989.

302 "Religion is too strong a mystery to doubt": *Texas Monthly*, Oct. 1991.

302 "Revisionist historians will paint Binion as a sweet old man": *LVRJ*, Dec. 28, 1989.

303 "One thing I've noticed in this town": OH, Glass, 84.

303 "He was a man who never showed one shred of pretense": *LVRJ*, Dec. 29, 1989.

304 "Thank you for coming": Vinson, 133.

## EPILOGUE: BACK IN THE SADDLE

307 "The sky's my home": OH, Glass, 84.

307 "the evidence we obtained didn't stand up": *LVRJ*, June 24, 2001.

307 "Ted had three loves in life": Interview, Michael Gaughan.

309 "It's a great piece of artwork": Ibid.

# Selected Bibliography

## Books

Alvarez, Al. *The Biggest Game in Town*. New York: Picador, 2009.

Barlett, Donald L., and James B. Steele. *Howard Hughes: His Life and Madness*. New York: Norton, 2004.

Berman, Susan. *Easy Street: The True Story of a Gangster's Daughter*. New York: Bantam Books, 1983.

———. *Lady Las Vegas: The Inside Story Behind America's Neon Oasis*. New York: A&E Network and TV Books, 1996.

Binkley, Christina. *Winner Takes All: Steve Wynn, Kirk Kerkorian, Gary Loveman, and the Race to Own Las Vegas*. New York: Hyperion, 2008.

Bradshaw, Jon. *Fast Company: How Six Master Gamblers Defy the Odds—And Always Win*. London: High Stakes, 2003.

Brunson, Doyle, and Mike Cochran. *The Godfather of Poker*. Las Vegas: Cardoza, 2009.

Bryant, Vickie, and Camille Hess. *Top O'Hill Terrace*. Charleston, SC: Arcadia, 2012.

Burbank, Jeff. *Historic Photos of Las Vegas*. Nashville: Turner, 2007.

Caldwell, Erskine. *With All My Might: An Autobiography*. Atlanta: Peachtree, 1987.

Campbell, Elaine. *My Friend Nick the Greek: Life in Las Vegas in the '50s*. Livermore, CA: WingSpan Press, 2010.

Cartwright, Gary. *Dirty Dealing: A True Story of Smuggling, Murder, and the FBI's Biggest Investigation*. New York: Atheneum, 1984.

Crumpler, Jeanette Howeth. *Street of Dreams: A History of Dallas' Theatre Row*. Dallas: Crumpler, 2003.

Dalla, Nolan, and Peter Alson. *One of a Kind: The Rise and Fall of Stuey "the Kid" Ungar, the World's Greatest Poker Player.* New York: Atria Books, 2005.

Demaris, Ovid. *The Last Mafioso: The Treacherous World of Jimmy Fratianno.* New York: Bantam Books, 1981.

Denton, Sally, and Roger Morris. *The Money and the Power: The Making of Las Vegas and Its Hold on America.* New York: Vintage Books, 2002.

Dickensheets, Scott, ed. *Fade, Sag, Crumble: Ten Las Vegas Writers Confront Decay.* Las Vegas: CityLife Books, 2011.

Dunar, Andrew J. *The Truman Scandals and the Politics of Morality.* Columbia: University of Missouri Press, 1984.

Dunne, John Gregory. *Vegas: A Memoir of a Dark Season.* New York: Random House, 1974.

Earley, Pete. *The Hot House: Life Inside Leavenworth Prison.* New York: Bantam Books, 1992.

———. *Super Casino: Inside the "New" Las Vegas.* New York: Bantam Books, 2001.

Egan, Timothy. *The Worst Hard Time: The Untold Story of Those Who Survived the Great American Dust Bowl.* New York: Houghton Mifflin, 2006.

Eig, Jonathan. *Get Capone: The Secret Plot That Captured America's Most Wanted Gangster.* New York: Simon & Schuster, 2011.

Fehrenbach, T. R. *Lone Star: A History of Texas and the Texans.* New York: Collier Books, 1980.

Ferrari, Michelle, and Stephen Ives. *Las Vegas: An Unconventional History.* New York: Bulfinch Press, 2005.

Gallagher, Carole. *American Ground Zero: The Secret Nuclear War.* Cambridge: MIT Press, 1993.

German, Jeff. *Murder in Sin City.* New York: Avon Books, 2001.

Greene, A. C. *Dallas: The Deciding Years—A Historical Portrait.* Austin: Encino Press, 1973.

Greenspun, Hank, and Alex Pelle. *Where I Stand: The Record of a Reckless Man.* New York: David McKay, 1966.

Grotenstein, Jonathan, and Storms Reback. *All In: The (Almost) Entirely True Story of the World Series of Poker.* New York: Thomas Dunne Books, 2006.

Guinn, Jeff. *Go Down Together: The True, Untold Story of Bonnie and Clyde.* New York: Simon & Schuster, 2010.

Gwynne, S. C. *Empire of the Summer Moon: Quanah Parker and the Rise and Fall of the Comanches, the Most Powerful Indian Tribe in American History.* New York: Scribner, 2010.

Holmes, Maxine, and Gerald D. Saxon, eds. *The WPA Dallas Guide and History.* Dallas: Dallas Public Library, Texas Center for the Book, University of North Texas Press, 1992.

Jenkins, Don. *Champion of Champions: The Authorized Biography of Johnny Moss.* Odessa, TX: JM, 1981.

Johnston, David. *Temples of Chance: How America Inc. Bought Out Murder Inc. to Win Control of the Casino Business.* New York: Doubleday, 1992.

Kefauver, Estes. *Crime in America.* Garden City, NY: Doubleday, 1951.

King, Gary C. *An Early Grave.* New York: St. Martin's, 2001.

Lacey, Robert. *Little Man: Meyer Lansky and the Gangster Life.* Boston: Little, Brown, 1991.

LaMaster, Kenneth M. *U.S. Penitentiary Leavenworth (Images of America).* Charleston, SC: Arcadia, 2008.

Leslie, Warren. *Dallas, Public and Private.* New York: Grossman, 1964.

Levy, Shawn. *Rat Pack Confidential.* New York: Broadway Books, 2001.

Malsch, Brownson. *"Lone Wolf" Gonzaullas, Texas Ranger.* Norman: University of Oklahoma Press, 1998.

McCracken, Robert D. *Las Vegas: The Great American Playground.* Reno: University of Nevada Press, 1997.

McKay, Seth S., and Odie B. Faulk. *Texas After Spindletop.* Austin: Steck-Vaughn, 1965.

McManus, James. *Cowboys Full: The Story of Poker.* New York: Farrar, Straus and Giroux, 2009.

———. *Positively Fifth Street.* New York: Picador, 2004.

Miller, Bob. *Son of a Gambling Man: My Journey from a Casino Family to the Governor's Mansion.* New York: Thomas Dunne Books, 2013.

Moehring, Eugene P., and Michael S. Green. *Las Vegas: A Centennial History.* Reno and Las Vegas: University of Nevada Press, 2005.

Odessky, Dick. *Fly on the Wall: Recollections of Las Vegas' Good Old, Bad Old Days.* Las Vegas: Huntington Press, 2000.

Payn, Graham, and Sheridan Morley, eds. *The Noël Coward Diaries.* Boston: Little, Brown, 1982.

Payne, Darwin. *Big D: Triumphs and Troubles of an American Supercity in the 20th Century.* Dallas: Three Forks Press, 1994.

Powell, William S., ed. *Dictionary of North Carolina Biography,* Vol. 2. Chapel Hill: University of North Carolina Press, 1979.

Prince, Robert. *A History of Dallas: From a Different Perspective.* Dallas: Nortex Press, 1993.

Reid, Ed, and Ovid Demaris. *The Green Felt Jungle.* New York: Pocket Books, 1974.

Rumbley, Rose-Mary. *The Unauthorized History of Dallas, Texas.* Austin: Eakin Press, 1991.

Russo, Gus. *The Outfit: The Role of Chicago's Underworld in the Shaping of Modern America.* New York: Bloomsbury, 2003.

Scheim, David E. *Contract on America: The Mafia Murder of President John F. Kennedy*. New York: Shapolsky, 1988.

Scoblete, Frank. *Forever Craps: The Five-Step Advantage-Play Method*. Chicago: Bonus Books, 2000.

Sheehan, Jack, ed. *The Players: The Men Who Made Las Vegas*. Reno: University of Nevada Press, 1997.

Sleeper, Gary W. *I'll Do My Own Damn Killin': Benny Binion, Herbert Noble, and the Texas Gambling War*. Fort Lee, NJ: Barricade Books, 2006.

Smith, John L. *Of Rats and Men: Oscar Goodman's Life from Mob Mouthpiece to Mayor of Las Vegas*. Las Vegas: Huntington Press, 2003.

Sonnichsen, C. L. *I'll Die Before I'll Run: The Story of the Great Feuds of Texas*. New York: Devin-Adair, 1962.

Tereba, Tere. *Mickey Cohen: The Life and Crimes of L.A.'s Notorious Mobster*. Toronto: ECW Press, 2012.

Tronnes, Mike, ed. *Literary Las Vegas*. New York: Henry Holt, 1995.

Vernetti, Michael. *Lies Within Lies: The Betrayal of Nevada Judge Harry Claiborne*. Las Vegas: Stephens Press, 2011.

Vinson, Barney. *Las Vegas Behind the Tables!* Part 2. Grand Rapids, MI: Gollehon Press, 1991.

Welsch, Roger L., ed. *Mister, You Got Yourself a Horse: Tales of Old-Time Horse Trading*. Lincoln: University of Nebraska Press, 1987.

## Oral Histories

Coles, Kathleen M. *Arthur Bernard: Nevada Mine Inspector and Prison Warden*. University of Nevada, Reno, 2003.

Glass, Mary Ellen. *Lester Ben "Benny" Binion: Some Recollections of a Texas and Las Vegas Gaming Operator*. University of Nevada, Reno, 1976.

———. *Robbins E. Cahill: Recollections of Work in State Politics, Government, Taxation, Gaming Control, Clark County Administration, and the Nevada Resort Association*. University of Nevada, Reno, 1977.

King, R. T. *Fighting Back: A Life in the Struggle for Civil Rights*. University of Nevada, Reno, 1997.

Olney, Warren III. *Law Enforcement and Judicial Administration in the Earl Warren Era*. University of California, Berkeley, 1981.

## Academic Papers

Alverson, J. Bruce. *Country Lawyer in a Maverick Boom Town: The Legal Career of Harry Claiborne*. Graduate College, University of Nevada, Las Vegas, 2008.

Gragg, Larry. *The Powerful Mythology Surrounding Bugsy Siegel*. University of Nevada, Las Vegas, Center for Gaming Research, 2010.

Hannum, Robert C. *A Guide to Casino Mathematics.* University of Nevada, Las Vegas, Center for Gaming Research, 2003.

Kenna, Laura Cook. *The Promise of Gangster Glamour: Sinatra, Vegas and Alluring, Ethnicized Excess.* University of Nevada, Las Vegas, Center for Gaming Research, 2010.

## Online Resources

www.maryferrell.org

*The Handbook of Texas Online.* www.tshaonline.org/handbook/online

*The Nevada Observer.* www.nevadaobserver.com

*Online Nevada Encyclopedia.* www.onlinenevada.org

www.pokerpages.com

## Newspapers

*Amarillo Globe-Times*

*Dallas Morning News*

*Dallas Times Herald* (originally the *Daily Times Herald*)

*Fort Worth Star-Telegram*

*Houston Chronicle*

*Las Vegas Review-Journal*

*Las Vegas Sun*

*Los Angeles Times*

*Nevada State Journal*

*New York Times*

*Reno Evening Gazette*

*San Antonio Express*

*Valley Times* (Las Vegas)

*Wall Street Journal*

## Periodicals

*Casino Chip and Token News,* Fall 2006.

*Fabulous Las Vegas,* Aug. 18, 1951, and Dec. 8, 1951.

*GQ,* December 1999.

*Grantland,* May 1, 2012.

*Legacies,* Spring 2006.

*Sports Illustrated,* Jan. 25, 1971.

*Texas Monthly,* Oct. 1991, Nov. 1999, and Feb. 2001.

*Winning Gamer,* Pi Yee Press, La Jolla, CA, Jan. 1986.

## Government Documents

City of Dallas: *Report of Dallas Police Department Survey, City of Dallas, Texas.* Written by August Vollmer, 1944.

Dallas Police Department: Internal investigative files of Lieutenant George Butler. Archived at the Texas Ranger Museum.

Federal Bureau of Investigation: Investigative files for L. B. Binion, Ted Binion, Harry Claiborne, R. D. Matthews, Paul Roland Jones, William Coulthard, Bill Decker, Henry Wade, and others. Also, a comprehensive 1964 report titled *Nevada Gambling Industry.* Parts of these files were released after requests to the bureau under the federal Freedom of Information Act. Others are among the documents collected by the U.S. House Select Committee on Assassinations and later assembled by the Mary Ferrell Foundation.

Texas Rangers: Papers of Captain R. A. (Bob) Crowder. Archived at the Texas Ranger Museum.

U.S. Bureau of Prisons: Binion's inmate file, released after a request under the Freedom of Information Act.

U.S. Department of Energy: Nevada National Security Site History, January 2011. www.nv.doe.gov/library/factsheets/DOENV_1024.pdf.

U.S. Department of Justice, Office of Pardon Attorney: After a Freedom of Information Act request, the pardon attorney's office released Binion's files from 1975 forward. Those previous to that were apparently destroyed as a matter of office routine.

U.S. Federal Census, 1910.

U.S. Senate Special Committee to Investigate Crime in Interstate Commerce: Kefauver committee transcripts. Many of these are available at www.nevadaobserver.com/ReadingRoom.htm.

U.S. Supreme Court, Case No. 623, October Term, 1952, *L. B. Binion v. United States of America.*

# Index